Towards a

Nationalist Narrative of India's Ancient Past

Including Recent Research on the Indus Civilization

The Book:

In 1966 the famous Indian parliamentarian Ram Manohar Lohia regretted in Parliament that the minds of our children were ingrained with the belief that "India had nothing of its own; everything was either imitated or influenced by outside factors". He called the Indian historiography 'diseased'. His opinion was echoed by M.C. Chagla, the education minister, who advocated the idea of re-writing Indian history.

Taking Dr. Lohia's opinion as the starting point, the present volume goes on to argue that post-Independence Indian archaeologists, despite making many new discoveries, have been most unashamedly neocolonial without the least awareness of the interrelationship between archaeological data and nationalism. The volume deals with multiple aspects of this interrelationship and undertakes a critical review of the recent research on the Indus civilization, showing that the very idea of the integrity and homogeneity of this civilization, which is the fountainhead of India's mainstream civilization, is being currently undermined by both Indian and foreign archaeologists who consider it only a veneer on top of the regional elements.

Finally, the volume argues that the geographical and chronological implications of some recent discoveries *conclusively* underline that India's protohistoric archaeological column and the literary column represented by the Vedic literature are inseparably linked, thus forming the first block of the seamless narrative of India's ancient past.

The Author:

Dilip K. Chakrabarti (1941) is emeritus professor of south Asian archaeology at Cambridge University. He was awarded *Padma Shri* in 2019. In 2021 he received a 'life-time achievement' award from the UK Bengali Convention (UKBC).

On the jacket:

Top: Impression of a seal depicting a seated figure surrounded by animals, believed to be Śiva in his aspect of Paśupati (Lord of animals), Mohenjo-daro, Mature Harappan.

Bottom: The 'signboard' found at Dholavira.

Towards a

Nationalist Narrative of India's Ancient Past

Including Recent Research on the Indus Civilization

Dilip K. Chakrabarti

Aryan Books International
New Delhi

TOWARDS A NATIONALIST NARRATIVE OF
INDIA'S ANCIENT PAST
Including Recent Research on the Indus Civilization

ISBN: 978-81-7305-666-6

First Published 2022

Disclaimer: The views and contents of the book are solely of the author. The publisher may not subscribe to them.

Published by
Aryan Books International
Pooja Apartments, 4B, Ansari Road, New Delhi-110 002 (India)
Tel.: 23287589, 23255799; Fax: 91-11-23270385
E-mail: aryanbooks@gmail.com
www.aryanbooks.com

Printed in India

In Memorium

Shri Samir Gupta

Preface

In my *Nationalism in the Study of Ancient Indian History*, I pointed out how the post-Independence Indian archaeologists turned out, in the name of science, to be almost totally indifferent to the nationalistic dimensions of the study of archaeology. In claiming, as late as 1973/74 that India was always a colony, meaning thereby that all technical and cultural innovations in Indian history were derived from developments in west Asia or elsewhere, the doyen of Indian archaeologists, H.D. Sankalia, set the seal of approval on what E.J. Rapson, a Cambridge Indologist and editor of the first volume of *Cambridge History of India* wrote many years ago. Academically, post-Independence Indian archaeology has also been a minor underling of the discipline as practised in United Kingdom and USA. The reference point of Indian archaeology in the first two decades of the twenty-first century has continued to be the Anglo-Saxon world. Almost as a natural corollary of this situation, what has also developed among the present Western specialists in Indian archaeology is a downright racist contempt for the Indian past and the Indian scholarship in the subject. This racism is more strident than what could be traced before 1947. Western archaeologists who operated in the Indian scene before 1947 had at least some grace which was the result of long years of interaction with Indians, whereas the modern 'anthropological' and 'scientist' archaeologists suffer from no inhibition of this kind. It may also be pointed out that many of the research themes advocated by the Western archaeologists in the Indian context are irrelevant from the Indian point of view.

The present volume looks closely at this admittedly murky academic scene. It does not, however, try to offer any explanation of why archaeology in India has been so spineless and neocolonial after Independence and why it continues to be so.

This volume, written during the period of the Covid lockdown in Kolkata and Cambridge, is dedicated to the well-loved memory of a friend of mine, Shri Samir Gupta, Deputy Comptroller and Auditor General of India (Commercial). He was a friend whom I had known and grown up with since 1958.

Contents

By the Same Author

AUTHORED BOOKS

1. *The Antiquities of Kangra* (with S.J. Hasan): Delhi 1984: Munshiram Manoharlal.
2. *A History of Indian Archaeology from the Beginning to 1947*. Delhi 1988: Munshiram Manoharlal.
3. *Theoretical Issues in Indian Archaeology*. Delhi 1988: Munshiram Manoharlal.
4. *The External Trade of the Indus Civilization*. Delhi 1990: Munshiram Manoharlal.
5. *Ancient Bangladesh, a Study of the Archaeological Sources*. Delhi 1992: OUP.
6. *The Early Use of Iron in India*. Delhi 1992: OUP.
7. *Archaeology of Eastern India: Chhotanagpur Plateau and West Bengal*. Delhi 1993: Munshiram Manoharlal.
8. *The Archaeology of Ancient Indian Cities*. Delhi 1995: OUP.
9. *Copper and Its Alloys in Ancient India* (with Nayanjot Lahiri). Delhi 1996: Munshiram Manoharlal.
10. *Colonial Indology: Sociopolitics of the Ancient Indian Past*. Delhi 1997: Munshiram Manoharlal.

11. *The Issues in East Indian Archaeology*. Delhi 1998: Munshiram Manoharlal.
12. *Bharatvarsher Pragitihas* (in Bengali). Kolkata 1999: Ananda Publishers.
13. *India—An Archaeological History*. Delhi 1999: OUP.
14. *Archaeological Geography of the Ganga Plain: The Lower and the Middle Ganga*. Delhi 2001: Permanent Black.
15. *Archaeology in the Third World: A History of Indian Archaeology since 1947*. Delhi 2003: Munshiram Manoharlal.
16. *The Archaeology of European Expansion in India, Gujarat, c. 16th-18th Centuries*. Delhi 2003: Aryan Books.
17. *The Archaeology of the Deccan Routes, the Routes which Linked the Ganga Plain with the Deccan*: Delhi 2005: Munshiram Manoharlal.
18. *The Oxford Companion to Indian Archaeology*. Delhi 2006: OUP.
19. *Archaeological Geography of the Ganga Plain: Upper Ganga (Oudh, Rohilkhand and the Doab)*. Delhi 2007: Munshiram Manoharlal.
20. *The Battle for Ancient India: An Essay in the Socio-Politics of Indian Archaeology*. Delhi 2008: Aryan Books.
21. *Globalization and Indian Archaeology, and Other Essays*. Banaras 2009: Banaras Hindu University.
22. *The Problem of the Sarasvati River and Notes on the Archaeological Geography of Haryana and Indian Panjab* (with Sukhdev Saini). Delhi 2009: Aryan Books.
23. *The Ancient Routes of the Deccan and the Southern Peninsula*. Delhi 2010: Aryan Books.
24. *The Geopolitical Orbits of Ancient India, the Geographical Frames of the Ancient Indian Dynasties*. Delhi 2010: OUP.
25. *Royal Messages by the Wayside: Historical Geography of the Asokan Edicts*. Delhi 2011: Aryan Books.
26. *Fifty Years of Indian Archaeology (1960-2010): Journey of a Foot Soldier*. Delhi 2012: Aryan Books.

27. *Nation First: Essays in the Politics of Ancient Indian Studies (including an analysis of the CAG report on the ASI)*. Delhi 2014: Aryan Books.
28. *The Borderlands and Boundaries of the Indian Subcontinent: Baluchistan to the Patkai Range and Arakan Yoma*. Delhi 2018: Aryan Books.
29. *Ancient Rajasthan: Research Developments, Epigraphic Evidence on Political Power Centres, and Historical Perspectives*. Delhi 2019: Aryan Books.
30. *Ei Desh: Janaika Puratattviker Smriti (This Land: Memories of an Archaeologist)* in Bengali (in press).
31. *Nationalism in the Study of Ancient Indian History*. Delhi 2021: Aryan Books.

EDITED BOOKS

1. *Essays in Indian Protohistory* (co-editor D.P. Agrawal). Delhi 1979: B.R. Publishing.
2. *A Source-Book of Indian Archaeology* (co-editor F.R. Allchin), 3 volumes (Delhi 1979, 1997, 2003): Munshiram Manoharlal.
3. *Indus Civilization Sites in India: New Discoveries*. Mumbai 2004: Marg Publications.
4. *History of Ancient India* (co-editor M. Lal), Vols. 1 to 5, Delhi 2014: Vivekananda International Foundation & Aryan Books International.
5. *History of Ancient India*, Vols. 6 to 7, Delhi 2018: Vivekananda International Foundation & Aryan Books International.
6. *History of Ancient India*, Vol. 8, Delhi 2020: Vivekananda International Foundation & Aryan Books International.

1

Introduction

I. NEED FOR A COHERENTLY INDIAN NARRATIVE FOR INDIA'S ARCHAEOLOGICAL PAST

In my *Nationalism in the Study of Ancient Indian History* (2021), I pointed out that for a long time after Independence it was held by professional archaeologists of India that there was no innovation except foreign intervention in technological and cultural fields in the course of the archaeological development of the country. The overall conclusion, as H.D. Sankalia put it as late as 1973 (in *World Archaeology*) and 1974 (in *Prehistory and Protohistory in India and Pakistan*), India was always a colony. In different forms the opinion persists even now, although some of its edges have become somewhat blunt because of an increasing number of early dates obtained for food-production and early copper and iron technology in the country. However, archaeological studies in India are still largely and disgustingly neocolonial in the sense that we have not yet been quite successful in offering a coherently Indian narrative for the archaeological past of our country. This does not mean that we have to glorify our past by taking recourse to outrageous claims regarding our chronology, as some people stubbornly resistant to logic or scholarship have long been trying to do. Basically, this implies a continuous and connected story of the economic and cultural developments in various parts of the land in terms of what we understand of this subcontinent as a whole and what we perceive to be intimately related to such developments. In two of my books, *India – An Archaeological History* (2009) and *The Oxford Companion to Indian Archaeology* (2006), I made such attempts but it is not for me to judge the extent to which they have been successful from this point of view.

There is another point. Have we ever tried to understand or define the basic scope or at least some of the basic nationalist dimensions of archaeology in India? The second chapter of the present volume is an attempt in this direction but in no way can this be said to be definitive. Nationalism in a country as diverse as India has to be multi-dimensional with some threads linking them together, and other archaeologists of the country, or at least those to whom nationalism as an archaeological issue matters, still have to spell out in the light of their own experience and expertise what do they mean by a frankly nationalist approach to the archaeology of the land they study.

Another issue is methodologically relevant in the present context. One of the positive features of archaeological research in modern India is the wide induction of scientific and technological expertise in the field. Scholars of different nationalities have also begun to participate in this development. However welcome such participations and the primary expansion of science-based and technology-based archaeological research are, we have to stress that all these scientific and technological data need interpretations in historical terms and it is precisely in this area that we have to be careful about how we reach these interpretations, especially when the scientists or technologists concerned have had no organized grounding in history and culture related to India or even possess any feeling of respect for the Indian past. In fact, this is an interesting situation. Anybody who can distinguish between grains of wheat and rice in the excavated record finds it almost obligatory to offer theories regarding agriculture without spending a day in the wheat or rice fields of India or having any credibility as a professional agricultural scientist. Or, somebody who can study human skeletons feels the related study incomplete unless this leads to the cause of decline of the culture, of which the studied skeletons were a part. There was a time when Bhola Nath of the Zoological Survey of India used to identify excavated animal bones in Indian archaeology but he did not consider it necessary to offer on that basis grand theoretical schemes of animal utilisation or animal domestication in ancient India. However, the academic scenario is much changed and all of us are expected to theorise to be respectable, and especially in a Third World context like India where in archaeology, or for that matter, in any branch of the humanities and social sciences, the opinion of anybody with the right skin colour and Western origin, will be the point of avid discussions.

The situation in a way is reminiscent of what took place in Indian archaeology after Mortimer Wheeler joined it. It is very true that he presided over the transition to modernity in India's archaeological research but at the same time it is also true that many of the theories he offered were generally based on a hastily contrived understanding of the ancient Indian historical situation. There is no reason to believe that the situation has changed for the better now, because these days people are not so much keen on arriving at conclusions which resonate with Indian historical reality as on offering theories, hidden behind an array of 'scientific' disciplines which most of the students of that historical reality would find difficult to follow and critically evaluate. Also, the focal points of scholarship based on skin-colour and/or group affiliations seem to be more marked in the field of Indian archaeology now than it was during the time of Wheeler.

II. RAM MANOHAR LOHIA'S THOUGHTS ON INDIAN HISTORY IN INDIAN PARLIAMENT IN 1966

The validity of the foregoing point was understood not by any professional Indian historian or archaeologist but by Ram Manohar Lohia, one of our great Parliamentarians and socialist thinkers. The occasion was the publication of the first volume of the UNESCO 'history of mankind series' and the matter is contained in *Lok Sabha Debates, Third Series, vol. LIV, no. 47, Tuesday, April 26, 1966*. The original speech of Dr. Lohia is in Hindi, and for the English version, we have to turn to *Collected Works of Dr. Rammanohar Lohia* edited by Mastram Kapoor, vol. 6, pp. 653-665. (I thank Dr. Anirban Gangopadhyay of Shyamaprasad Mukherji Foundation for drawing my attention to this.)

The subject matter of this parliamentary discussion was the UNESCO volume titled *Prehistory and the Beginnings of Civilization* which included, among others, a section on the Indus civilization. Dr. Lohia writes:

> The errors that I am going to point out in this book may not at the outset seem very important, but misunderstanding of Indian history by writers within and outside the country is so great that I shall try to explain its significance by a number of examples. Firstly, it is supposed that whatever occurs in India must be imitation of some other country or civilization. It is either from China, or Misr or Ur or Chaldea or some other place. It has been said in this book by Leonard Woolley that when one looked at the north gateway of the great stupa at Sanchi one could not help feeling that it was inspired by the wooden architecture of China. And the strange part of it is that this statement was challenged not by any Indian member on the commission nor by Dr. Radhakrishnan but by a Russian historian, Prof. Ilyn. And then Mr. Woolley writes in a small note, "it is an impression, and there is no

> proof, but the impression is worth recording." This is how history is being written. Mr. Woolley writes that the stupa at Sanchi had inspiration from China. He is challenged by a Soviet historian. Then the learned professor Woolley writes because that impression was on his mind that was to be recorded although there was no proof for it. Historians both Indian and foreign are such rotten headed people. It is ingrained into the minds of our children that India had nothing of its own; everything was either imitated or influenced by outside factors. These historians can go to absurd lengths. In the book there is mention about another book called 'Five Thousand Years of Pakistan'.

On this particular book Dr. Lohia's comment is that it was the intention of the western writers to "give Pakistan the impression of being very ancient and familiar" and also to "strengthen the roots of India's partition".

With regard to the Indus or Harappan civilization Dr. Lohia points out that at the back of the opinion accepted by the volume that the fortification walls of Harappa were intended to overcome the countryside, was the assumption that "the ruler and citizens were of an alien stock which had reduced their indigenous inhabitants to the states of serfs". Dr. Lohia goes on to comment,

> ... these historians rule out the possibility of new trends emerging from the core of Indian society. And they rule the mind of the Indian historians, the biggest of them, in such an overwhelming manner that even the historians of India suppose that any renewal of the Indian culture was impossible without contact with the foreigner. The latter could be either the Afghan or the Mughal or the English and so on.

At this point Dr. Lohia expresses very clearly his dissatisfaction with the prevalent idea that India has always assimilated her aggressors.

> We must cry a halt to this kind of thinking. Assimilation is always of two kinds. It is either of the slave or of the master. The history of India of the last one thousand years can teach only the assimilation of the first type. It is no use blaming only the foreign historians. The Indian historians are wallowing in the same poison.

Dr. Lohia's comments in this parliamentary debate include some more valuable points, but from our point of view, I shall cite only one more of them.

> ... the problem of the Nagas, the Mizos, Kashmir, Adivasis and the like have behind them this poisonous error of interpreting our history in a wrong way, of dividing the people into Aryans, non-Aryans, Dravidians and Mongols. And this whole edifice has been erected on the slender evidence of linguistic variations.

Please note Dr. Lohia's emphasis on the whole edifice of these differences being based on 'the slender evidence of linguistic variations'. He was apparently not ready to give these variations the status of cast iron historical truth because, as we know, in no way can such variations lead to chronology-based positive historical conclusions.

Dr. Lohia's characterisation of Indian historiography as 'diseased' and his emphasis on the inability of Indian academic historians to come out of the rut of foreign influences and invasions may seem harsh but is nonetheless true. This, in fact, is glaringly true in the case of archaeology. We have already cited H.D. Sankalia's opinion expressed as late as 1974 that India was always a colony. This attitude persists in various forms till today, especially in the institute which Sankalia headed and also in the university department set up by Sankalia's student, B. Subbarao, at Vadodara. Around 1976 when I put forward the claim of India being an early and independent area of iron metallurgy (in *Antiquity 50*), there was a great reluctance on the part of such scholars to accept it (cf. *Recent Advances in Indian Archaeology, Proceedings of the*

Seminar Held in Poona in 1983, comments on the paper on the Iron age). It was only after Rakesh Tewari's discovery of early iron-bearing levels in the central Ganga plain (in *Antiquity 2003*) that the idea was eventually accepted. In 1968 I pointed out (in *Indian Studies: Past and Present*) the mutual contradictions and various inaccuracies in the attempts to identify Aryans in the Indian archaeological record but nobody was interested to discard the Aryan hypothesis at that point. Now, even after the nuances of vicious racism implicit in the Aryan theory and the unacceptability of the various assumptions behind this theory have been pointed out by an increasing number of people, there are not many scholars who are ready to see the Aryans as a mythical entity modelled on the triumph of the Europeans in the modern period. Scholars have also shut their mind to the improbability and illogicality of linguistic hypotheses to establish historical truth, although some of them have begun to come round to this view.

III. INDIFFERENCE OF INDIAN ARCHAEOLOGISTS TO THE NATIONALISTIC DIMENSIONS OF THE INDIAN ARCHAEOLOGICAL SCENARIO

Equally importantly, Indian archaeologists have been completely indifferent to the nationalistic dimensions of the Indian archaeological scenario. One may cite a few specific examples in this regard. The Californian Text Book Controversy several years ago was fought with some bitterness and the senior author of the concerned book was J.M. Kenoyer who refused to retract anything he wrote regarding Hinduism in that book. Kenoyer is an archaeologist and what I find amazing is his acceptability, despite his clearly anti-Hindu stance in the entire controversy, to a wide range of Indian archaeologists and archaeological organizations. For instance, in *Walking with the Unicorn. Social Organization and Material Culture in Ancient South Asia* (eds. D. Frenez et al., Oxford, 2018: Archaeopress), a felicitation volume dedicated to him, there is a large number of Indian contributors, many of whom are senior scholars and influential in the Indian scheme: G.S. Abhayan, P.P. Joglekar, P. Ajithprasad, K. Krishnan, K.K. Bhan, S.V. Rajesh, I. Mahadevan, M.V. Bhaskar, A. Patel, V.N. Prabhakar, V.C. Gadekar, Manmohan Kumar, V. Dangi and Rajesh Rao. Distinctly visible among them are scholars from Deccan College (Pune), M.S. University (Vadodara) and Indian Institute of Technology, Gandhinagar, with sprinklings from the Archaeological Survey of India and miscellaneous areas of Haryana. It is absolutely apparent that nationalism or the implication of the California Textbook Controversy is not a matter of concern to the above-mentioned Indian scholars. On p. 18 of this volume it has been asserted that Kenoyer is commonly called *Sikander* at Harappa 'and in different parts of Pakistan and India'. He may be known by this name in Pakistan but it is unlikely to be true in the case of India where it is doubtful if anybody, possibly not even the Indian scholars mentioned earlier, would think of Kenoyer as *Sikandar* or 'world-conqueror/Alexander'.

Now that the Govt. of India pursues an open door policy regarding foreign participation in archaeology, all that the foreign archaeologists have to do is to contact a suitably pliable Indian university archaeologist and get him or her to work on the project. The Indian university people are only too eager to jump into this bandwagon because this brings them some 'international' reputation and some publications without even being aware of the implications of what the concerned projects have been doing. Their role in these projects is essentially that of the native underlings in the days of the East India Company. They would explore the native situation and turn it to the advantage of their foreign masters in return for considerable personal gains for themselves. Thirdly, although the concept of the socio-politics of the past has been current in global archaeological literature since 1986 and although I have published several works related to this concept in the Indian context, this has fallen on deaf ears in Indian archaeology. By 'socio-politics of the past' many Indian and foreign archaeologists mean only what they call 'Hindutva archaeology' and some of them have even gone to the extent of criticizing the legal aspect of the Supreme Court judgement on Ayodhya. The link between the Indian left-liberal group and the foreign anti-India groups is crystal clear, as it will be emphasized in the next chapter.

Nationalism covers innumerable details of our national life, culture and landscape. It cannot be a uniform set of ideas, and individual archaeologists have to find their own feet in this multi-spectral national world. What I have perceived on the basis of my own investigations is that the ancient landscape of India has not significantly changed since the protohistoric and the historic periods, keeping the basic pattern of its site-distribution, route network, and metallurgical and craft practices intact or basically unchanged. My idea is that there are various elements of continuity since the formation of the Indus civilization landscape as well.

The third chapter of the volume critically reviews the research which has been conducted on the Indus Civilization in the last couple of decades. It is important that we do so because to us the Indus civilization is the fountainhead of the mainstream Indian culture and religious tradition, and it is wholly natural that a nationalist archaeology person like the present author would look carefully into the attempt, if any, to de-link this civilization from the Indian mainstream. It is worth recalling that the idea that there was a foreign ruling class in the citadels of the Harappan cities was argued first by Mortimer Wheeler and it is this hypothesis which was considered as an example of the prevalent historical attitude to the Indian past by Ram Manohar Lohia. That the Indus civilization was the fountainhead of the Indian mainstream was something that was understood by the early excavators of Mohenjodaro on the basis of the demonstrable continuity of craft, art and religious traditions which they observed in the excavated archaeological assemblage. It is singularly unfortunate that some Indian archaeologists of the post-Independence period consciously tried to deny this continuity and follow Wheeler blindfold. H.D. Sankalia's attempted denial in *Indian Science Congress* of 1969 (in *Proceedings of the Indian Science Congress* of that year, Presidential address of the Anthropology and Archaeology section) to explain the phallic stones found at Mohenjodaro in terms of the later-day Siva-*lingas* is a major example of this kind, and more recently some Indian historians like Upinder Singh have tried to deny palpable echoes of later-day Hinduism in the Indus assemblage.

From the Indian point of view it is important to people like the present author that this civilization is interpreted and understood from an essentially Indian point of view, i.e. how this civilization has been the main spring of the culture and civilization that we call the Indian culture and civilization. *This is major area where a nationalistic approach to Indian archaeology should come to the fore without any possibility of compromise and this is the reason why in a volume concerned with an examination of nationalist issues in Indian archaeology, there has to be an essay on how the research on the Indus civilization is proceeding currently.*

The next chapter of the volume also relates to the Indus civilization and shows how the location of a site as important as Harappa can be contextualised in terms of what we know of the geographical location and economic importance of this place as late as the 19th century and even later. This will hopefully demonstrate that the site of Harappa is rooted in a landscape which with its own route network continued till the pre-modern period. That the essential pattern of the Harappan or Indus Civilization's route network continued till the pre-modern period was pointed out by Nayanjot Lahiri in her Ph.D. work – *The Archaeology of Indian Trade Routes* (1992). The same type of continuity in the route network between the early and pre-modern periods was emphasized by the present author in his fieldwork-based *The Archaeology of the Deccan Routes* (2005). In the two volumes reporting his Ganga plain survey – *The Archaeological Geography of the Ganga Plain – the Lower and the Middle Ganga* (2001) and *The Archaeological Geography of the Ganga Plain – the Upper Ganga* (2007) – the present author explained the locational importance of major sites in the Ganga plain in terms of the economic and other roles these sites were likely to have fulfilled in their own landscapes in the light of the various pre-modern sources available on them. The hypothesis in the background is that of an essential continuity of the general features of Indian landscape through at least the protohistoric and historic periods. An essay of this volume brings this out clearly in the case of the precise location of Harappa and may in this case be cited as an example of working out a nationalist approach to Indian archaeology. This may also emphasize that remote-sensing need not be the only guide to a site-location and the associated interpretative tool in the Indian landscape.

An important section of the Indian Parliamentary reports that we have cited dwells on the education minister M.C. Chagla's comment on Wheeler's *Five Thousand Years of Pakistan*:

> Pakistan came into existence only nineteen years ago. As I said in the Security Council, before nineteen years, the only culture was Indian culture; the only history was Indian history and the only background was Indian background. No Pakistani can look to his country beyond nineteen years. If he tries to look back, he can only look back to Indian culture, to Indian history, and may I add, to Indian forefathers. Therefore, it is ridiculous for any historian to talk of five thousand years of Pakistan.

Historically, the following comment by the education minister of the time, Mr. Chagla, is very significant and possibly very apt in the present context when any talk of rewriting Indian history raises hackles on various sides, especially among the communist and left-liberal lobby.

I have always felt that one of the misfortunes of our country is that most of our history books have been written by foreigners who have injected poison into our country, and have given a totally false reading of what happened.

Now I shall tell you what we are doing. That is more to the point. We have set up a board of distinguished people who are re-writing Indian History from the point of view of India, from the point of view of our national integration, from the point of view of our culture. These books are not ready yet, but some of them will be ready by the end of this year. My view is that these books will be sent to the various states and will be translated into our different Indian languages and will be brought to the students. There is nothing more important in education than to give to the young boy and young girl in school a correct view of his or her own country, of his or her own history, and of his or her own past. Therefore, I agree with the view that we should attach much more importance to history.

Then, take the other thing that we are doing. We have set up recently the Nehru Library and Museum where we are collecting all the books possible for the period which starts from Raja Rammohun Roy till the modern age. The idea is to get Indian scholars there and try to write the history of modern times. Raja Rammohun Roy played a very big part in our Indian history, but there is hardly any history about him. From that period down to Independence or beyond, we had a galaxy of men who have contributed to India's Independence and India's struggle for freedom. So, there again, we are doing what we can to help young people to think about the past of India and to write about India. We do not want a history which is biased in our favour, and I do not think that we need that bias, because our history is great enough, and even an honest and fair interpretation would be sufficient to prove to ourselves and to prove to the world what a great past we have had.

What is striking about the education minister's comment is his allusion to the fact that as early as the early 1960s the

Government of India had set up a committee or at least had assembled a number of scholars to re-write history from the Indian point of view. It would be interesting to know what happened to it. As the information came from the education minister himself, and that too from a person of the personal stature of M.C. Chagla, there is no reason to doubt it, and only a careful search among the files of the education ministry of the period can throw light on it. Interestingly, any proposal to re-write Indian history sends jitters these days through a vast mass of people and it is rather refreshing to note that there was indeed such a proposal from no less a person than M.C. Chagla whom not even a communist or left-liberal lunatic would associate with 'Hindutva'. The name of Mohammadali Currim Chagla adds lustre to the history of India's legal luminaries.

The postscript, apparently added by Dr. Lohia, is also interesting, sharply raising some valid questions in this connection.

1. The real question is, to what extent is India's history really rotten and how far has historical writing aggravated this rottenness. What are the possibilities? It is possible that the Indian people have been specially prone to the voice of foreign subjugation.
2. It is possible that historiography in this country has turned this vice into a virtue and has caught successive generations to confuse enslavement with synthesis, surface changes with renaissance, disintegration with diversity.
3. It is possible that Indian history-writing has further sinned in looking for synthesis where it does not exist, for foreign inspiration and even influx all over the place.

There is not a shadow of doubt that the post-Independence Indian archaeological literature fits the foregoing analysis by Dr. Lohia in every way. The problem has also been recently highlighted by the fact that there has been some attempt on the part of a Deccan College archaeologist to deny the extent of significance of the Indus civilization in Indian history.

IV. ATTEMPT TO CREATE A NORTH-SOUTH DIVIDE IN INDIAN ARCHAEOLOGY

K. Paddayya, a former Director of Deccan College, Pune, has recently complained in print (Mr. Vikas Arya kindly pointed this out to me) that far more space was devoted to the Indus Civilization in the volume *Protohistoric Foundations* edited by me and Makkhan Lal than what was earmarked for other topics of Indian protohistory, as for example, the Neolithic cattle-keepers of the south, a topic on which Paddayya himself had worked. I quote Paddayya:

> One could for instance cite the thoughtless and fragmented way the topic of the Southern Neolithic culture and ashmounds inseparably associated with it have been dealt with in the recently published volume *Protohistoric Foundations,* jointly edited by Chakrabarti and Lal (2014). This volume devotes a staggering space of 371 pages grouped under 16 sections to the Indus civilization (2014: 87-458). As we now know for certain, more or less contemporaneously the other parts of India supported a number of flourishing village farming cultures which are allotted altogether a mere 105 pages. Within this diminutive space the Southern Neolithic is given a miserly 25 pages and also intriguingly treated under the modern political divisions of Karnataka, Andhra Pradesh and Tamil Nadu (2014: 498-522). This unequal treatment, I am constrained to remark, may be a reflection simultaneously of the longstanding bias of Indian archaeology in favour of Indo-Gangetic plains and of the lackadaisical attitude towards the archaeological record of Peninsular India. (Paddayya in *Neolithic Ashmounds of the Deccan*, Delhi 2019: Aryan Books)

We firmly declare that there was no 'academic politics of north India versus south India' in this regard, as Paddayya alleges. To my knowledge, this statement by Paddayya is a somewhat strange and presumably the first statement invoking, quite unjustifiably, a divide between the archaeologists of the north and the south. The reason why we decided to devote a large part of the volume *Protohistoric Foundations* to the Indus Civilization was that it played a singularly important role in shaping the later and regional forms of Indian culture and that in any publication on protohistoric India as a whole, this role must be suitably made clear and properly highlighted.

V. THE ISSUE OF RE-WRITING INDIAN HISTORY

We have pointed out earlier in this chapter that persons like Ram Manohar Lohia and M.C. Chagla thought seriously of rewriting Indian history as early as 1966 and Mr. Chagla reported that a committee for this purpose was already appointed. The question which is important in the present context is: how is it that any talk of re-writing Indian history on the government level is considered a kind of political conspiracy by a section of the media. Two such examples can easily be submitted. The first one is dated 6 March, 2018 – https://www.reuters.com/investigates/special-report/India-modi-culture. This is written by Rupam Jain and Tom Lasseter.

> Interviews with members of the 14-person committee and ministers in Modi's government suggest the ambitions of Hindu nationalists extend beyond holding political power in this nation of 1.3 billion people – a kaleidoscope of religions. They want ultimately to shape the national identity to match their religious views, that India is a nation of and for Hindus. In doing so, they are challenging a more multicultural narrative that has dominated since the time of British rule, that modern-day India is a tapestry born of migrations, invasions and conversions. That view is rooted in demographic fact. While the majority of Indians are Hindus, Muslims and people of other faiths account for some 240 million, or a fifth, of the populace.

The second piece is dated 29 September 2020 and written by Gautam Mehta: codastory.com/disinformation/India-reframing-history and captioned 'Hindu nationalists rewrite history in India's classrooms'.

> For Vinay Sitapati, a political scientist at Ashoka University and the author of a forthcoming book on the history of the BJP, reshaping perceptions of India's past in the classroom is a logical strategy for Modi's party. "Since learning lessons from history is a key component of Hindu nationalism, influencing how it's taught is a key component of their ideology," he said. Following Modi's election in 2014, the BJP's drive to reshape education gathered momentum once again. That year, the Rashtriya Swayamsevak Sangh—a nationalist paramilitary group closely affiliated with the BJP—set up a committee to draft suggestions to "Indianize" the education system. Since then, Modi's administration has amended syllabuses at both national and state levels .... Changes have included rewriting the outcome of a historical battle to claim that a Hindu king defeated the Mughal emperor in 1576, and downplaying the importance of independence movement leaders such as Gandhi and Nehru.

The question which inevitably comes up is: if rewriting history in Chagla's time did not evoke any shadow of Hindu nationalism, how is it that in the 2020s and a little earlier, any talk of rewriting history should usher in an atmosphere of bigotry and Hindu religious fundamentalism? Interestingly, this contrasts with what is expressed by F. Gautier in his book *An Entirely New History of India*. According to a report published in *The Hindu* of 6 March, 2021 he expressed disappointment with the BJP government's performance in this area.

> Even within the government, there is no attempt to change the curriculum although it is supposed to be a right-wing pro-Hindu government. We expected so much, but it has not happened in the last seven years.

On the whole, this is an interesting situation. Basically, the importance of re-writing Indian history or offering an Indian narrative of Indian history is currently realized as it was realized by the government in 1966.

VI. HISTORY-WRITING IN INDIA IN THE GRIP OF THE INDIAN LEFT: A RECENT EXAMPLE

At the same time, nothing much has been done towards achieving this objective. Whatever the media may say, the spine of history-writing in India, especially in the field of ancient India, was generally shattered by the communists and the left-liberals, a process which began in the middle of the 1960s and is still in some sense operative. No amount of Hindu-baiting by the left-liberal and communist media will change this academic picture. Under the rubric "the death of a 'progressive and 'secular' ancient historian" the present author analysed this picture in some detail with reference to the report of the death of a communist historian in the Indian media. This was published in the articles and commentaries section of the Vivekananda International Foundation publications, dated March 9, 2021 and is incorporated in the following paragraphs of the present volume. The situation is very much reminiscent of what Ram Manohar Lohia expressed as 'diseased historiography' in 1966.

The death of a retired professor of ancient Indian history of Delhi University and a card-carrying member of the Communist Party of India, D.N. Jha, generated a lot of interest in the media. The reason of this media attention, which reflects very well the current status of ancient Indian historical studies and also what exactly is wrong with it. The publications which the present author has seen in this context are *Scroll.in, The Wire, The News Minute, Frontline, The Indian Express* and *The National Herald*, all dated 5 or 6 February, 2021. The tone is the same in all these publications, and here we cite only *Indian Express, National Herald* and *Frontline*. According to *Indian*

Express "he was fearless in his evocation of pluralism, dissent and rationality" whereas according to *Frontline*, "until his death, he was a staunch warrior against rampant majoritarianism". He was "a historian extraordinaire", according to *National Herald*. These three and the others that have been cited only by name allowed no scope for doubt that the main thing about him was that he was a progressive and secular historian of ancient India. The present author's professional view of him as a historian is contained in an assessment on beef-eating in ancient India in his book *Nationalism in the Study of Ancient Indian History* (Delhi 2021). This professional assessment, however, is irrelevant to the present context but what is relevant is the question why should a historian of ancient India be judged primarily for his politically 'progressive' and 'secular' views and not for the range of his professional publications? Why should the study of ancient India be tinged primarily with political connotations in modern India? This does not reflect well on the way this study has proceeded or is proceeding in the country. One can, of course, point out how this has come about and how the current official leadership of historical research in the country, i.e. the Indian Council of Historical Research (ICHR), or the government behind it, has yet shown no indication of being aware of the issue.

Although a minor subject in the fringes of the Indian academia and the Indian employment world, the subject, ancient Indian history and archaeology, still plays a major role in shaping the nation's idea of its own ancient past. Professionally speaking, the subject came of age by the closing decades of the 19th century. In about 1911 Calcutta University introduced the study of ancient India as a separate MA subject, laying down the foundation of its academic development. There was no shadow of politics over this development during this period.

Things began to change in the 1960s and the full impact of this politically was felt in 1972, with the establishment of the Indian Council of Historical Research as a wing of the central education ministry in Delhi. This was the time when the Indian political world was full of such slogans as 'secularists versus communalists' and 'progressives versus reactionaries', 'Garibi Hatao' (remove poverty), etc. – slogans which in retrospect were nothing but catch phrases to delude the Indian voters in favour of the ruling clique of the time, Mrs. Indira Gandhi's Congress and its 'progressive' Parliamentary allies in the form of Communists of various hues. As far as Indian education is concerned, it is the communists who made most of this god-sent opportunity, establishing, among other things, the ICHR in 1972 to centralise the funding and general control of historical research in the country. It has also been alleged that the establishment of a new university in Delhi after the name of Jawaharlal Nehru, in whose development the Indian communists would play a major role, was part of the deal between Mrs. Gandhi and the communists. Unless the relevant documents are released it is impossible to assess this allegation. In view of the fact that the new university soon became a rallying point of the left-liberals of all kinds in its faculty appointments, there is perhaps a lot of truth in this allegation.

As far as the ICHR was concerned, care was taken to ensure that the ICHR remained entirely or largely under the Communist control in 1972-1999 and in 2004-2014. What was also spectacular was the way the Communists were put in control of various university departments of History, creating ripple effects all over the country.

This was the general historical situation of the period which is more or less well-known to the public by now and has also been dealt with by the present author in the book mentioned above. What, however, is not appreciated in detail is the extent of the damage this had caused historical research, especially ancient Indian historical research in India. First, the primary source-related ancient historical research was not encouraged during this period, the Communists in control being themselves unable to handle primary data in original and this would include epigraphs and coins, literary texts, sculpture, architecture, iconography, and the innumerable related divisions of knowledge that more than 200 years of research in the field since the mid-18th century has built up. There were two groups of people among those in power during the period of Communist ascendancy: card-carrying Communist party members whose sole quest was to study ancient India in the light of the ideas regarding ancient societies that one finds in the Communist literature; and the left-liberal sophisticates familiar with Western social science theories and keen on relating them to ancient India without a moment's pause to consider the quantity, range and limitations of the concerned data. Further, both these groups joined together to keep the Communist dominance alive and castigate the ancient historians before their period as 'nationalists' and 'revivalists', keeping cleverly the term Hindu silent before such epithets.

What was a more dangerous ploy was the fact that the historical beliefs of the fringe groups of the Hindus were considered as mainstream historical ideas of the earlier generations. The whole thing was done to strengthen their progressive image vis-à-vis the Hindu backwoodsmen and thus acquire power to manipulate money and positions allotted for ancient historical research in the country. As far as the communist deviousness goes, it may be difficult to better this example. The communists and their fellow-travellers apparently modelled their plan on the model of Mrs. Gandhi who raised the slogan of 'Garibi Hatao' to wrest power from the old Congress stalwarts. That this ploy could be used widely in the history-related academia to the advantage of Communist anti-national agenda is indeed remarkable showing the deep roots of the Communists in this arena of learning. What lends further piquancy to the situation is that the Indian archaeologists of institutions like the Archaeological Survey of India, Deccan College, etc. were eager to declare India's archaeological past as a colonial past where no originality was possible. The Indus civilization, in the context of which Dr. Ram Manohar Lohia drew attention to certain Western writings and the Indian silence in the matter in Indian Parliament, was tacitly recognized as an extension of the contemporary Mesopotamian power in India.

One has to confess that this archaeological scenario was not the result of any communist conspiracy. This is Indian archaeologists' own contribution. However, if one looks into the background, one notes the following features. First, the archaeologists in power in the Archaeological Survey of India, Deccan College, M.S. University and similar institutions did not have any critical attitude to what the Western scholars wrote on the archaeology of the country in the 1950s, 1960s and in some cases even later. For instance, the ease with which the scholars of Deccan College and M.S. University divided India into areas of attraction, relative isolation and isolation, following the writings of Cyril Fox who wrote in the context of Britain and certainly not in the context of India, was amazing. They apparently were quite oblivious of the implication and impact of grading different parts of the country in terms of development and progress. That the idea does not fit in the reality has been shown by the present author in a number of his publications, notably, *The Geographical Orbits of Ancient India, the Geographical Frames of the Ancient Indian Dynasties* (2010). Secondly, there is no hard evidence that the post-Independence Indian archaeologists truly appreciated the key role of the Indus civilization in the development of the sub-continent's civilizational tradition. In recent times, B.B. Lal has made ample amends for it (cf. *The Sarasvati Flows On, the Continuity of Indian Culture*, 2002), and before him, one may cite the publications by S.R. Rao who put this civilization firmly and squarely in the context of the Indian mainstream (cf. *Lothal and the Indus Civilization*, 1973). Thirdly, it may be noted that although from the 1950s and 1960s onward American scholars like W. Fairservis (cf. 'The origin, character and decline of an early civilization', *American Museum Novitates*, 1967) and G.F. Dales (cf. 'A suggested chronology for Afghanistan, Baluchistan and the Indus valley', in R.W. Ehrich ed. *Chronologies in Old World Archaeology*, 1965) began to devise developmental schemes in the light of which scholars tried to visualise the Indus development, it is difficult to prove that Indian archaeologists had become properly aware of the dimensions of such schemes. Fourthly, a generally uncritical acceptance of the Western ideas and theories seems to be a distinguishing feature of the current Indian archaeological literature. In fact, to the discerning readers, many Indian archaeologists, notably of Pune, Vadodara and other Indian centres seem to have grouped themselves around the writings of some Western scholars, especially those of the American anthropological school. Many of these 'anthropological' writings are difficult to read and understand and very often one cannot be sure that their authors know the Indian situation well or where their originality lies. What may seem to many really amazing is that even under the direct British rule there were many Indian scholars who could boldly put across their ideas and specific points in academic discussions with British scholars. By and large, this bold and free spirit is completely missing from the current Indian archaeological literature. What is also amazing is the short shrift given by a large section of the Western archaeological literature to the Indian side of the story. *This has been going on for ages in Western Indological literature; in fact, the present author cannot recall if, with only a handful of honourable exceptions, he has come across any Indologist or what is known these days as a south Asian archaeologist with genuine interest in the Indian side of the narrative or with any kind of serious respect for the native scholarship in the matter. This indifference to, and racist contempt for the native appears to be a general feature of the current First World archaeology, especially in the section dealing with India, and with the disappearance of persons like Peter Ucko or Bruce Trigger from the scene and the apparent general weakening of the 'one world' archaeology movement, this tendency is certainly more visible than what it was, say, 30 years ago. Equally noticeable is the increasing number of Indian camp-followers of even minor Western characters in Indian archaeology. Western Indology was, of course, thoroughly racist, almost right from its inception, and one regrets that one has to add Western archaeology in relation to India to it.*

An excellent channel of collaboration between archaeology in India and archaeology in Britain should have been the non-departmental 'archaeology units' of various British universities or at least organizations like English Heritage. The CAG report on the functioning of the Archaeological Survey of India (for an analysis of this report, the present author's *Nation First: Essays in the Politics of Ancient Indian Studies*, 2014) has illuminated some dark depths of archaeology as it is practised in India, and one of the ways to get out of it is a new organizational structure modelled on various British university 'archaeology units'. I have had the privilege of having an idea of the work of the Cambridge Archaeology Unit and I would certainly recommend this model for the pursuit of archaeology in India. Finally, one of the reasons of the general indifference of the modern Indian archaeologists to the nationalist implications of Indian archaeological data is the academic level of the people recruited. In normal circumstances, they would not have been in the academia but as the academic roles have been thrust upon them, they are frequently at a loss what to do with these responsibilities. In a widely circulated video of Sinoli or Sanauli excavations, one of the experts from the Archaeological Survey of India argues that the basic question was to determine who these people were and from where they had arrived. Considering that unmistakable Harappan stuff has been found at this site along with what is known as the OCP culture, a complex associated with at least 'late

Harappan', one would have thought that there would have been no doubt in the excavating archaeologists' mind about the character and provenance of the concerned people, i.e. the people whose remains were found buried there. However, this simple approach is unlikely to satisfy the historical imagination of an Indian archaeologist; he or she will look for some mystery associated with these people and in the case of Sinoli (or Sanauli), he or she will possibly imagine that they have been lucky enough to grab the axle of the chariot of that famous charioteer of ancient India, Sri Krishna himself!

There was a time when B.B. Lal (cf. *Ancient India, 10-11,* 1955) associated many Doab sites mentioned in the epic Mahabharata with their Painted Grey Ware. Subsequent field-research has sharply and widely brought out the spread of Harappan settlements in this region, dating in some cases from the mature Harappan stage itself. I find no reason to doubt that the epic association of the archaeological context of the Doab should be clearly rooted in the Harappan context.

The Government of India's current archaeological policy allows foreign personnel and their Indian collaborators without the slightest scrutiny or appraisal of the theories these researchers are pursuing, and as we have shown in the case of D.N. Jha's demise, the communist propaganda is still alive and well in the field of ancient historical studies. It is important in the national interest that these issues are adequately highlighted and some ways of neutralising communists and their historical ideas are found. The same may be said about the current Indian archaeological scenario. It is time it was drummed into the heads of Indian archaeologists that the nation matters and that the archaeologists of the country cannot disassociate themselves from the nationalistic implications of how they research, present and interpret their data.

2

Towards a Nationalist Archaeology of India

I. ABSTRACT

First, we offer a general picture of the problem of nationalism and its correlation with archaeology in some representative Western literature. This literature views the issue in a pejorative sense, equating it to 'ethnically inspired' archaeology which often likes to glorify this tradition even at the expense of the veracity of archaeological data. Of far more significance to the Indian context, is the great historical and cultural driving force of nationalism which does not necessarily detract from the yardsticks of an objective archaeological assessment and is related to various related cultural issues like the romantic movement and the concept of ethnicity as found embedded in multi-ethnic states like Turkey and Egypt. In the frame of European Union too the need of a new historical-archaeological narrative covering its different geographical components is gradually becoming important. In place of the old problem of ethno-genesis which is centred around Celts, Anglo-Saxons, etc., New Europe calls for a re-orientation of the old questions and a new narrative to go with them.

With this theoretical preamble we come down to the Indian context and draw attention to the generally non-nationalist tone of post-Independence Indian archaeology which was happy by ascribing all technological and archaeological developments to impulses from west, central, east and southeast Asia. This was the dominant narrative during the colonial period and this was the narrative followed by Indian archaeologists of the post-Independence period. We also point out in this context how certain monuments and sites of the country, such as Ayodhya, Pattinam and Keezadi in recent times and Bodh Gaya and Sanchi in earlier times had got embroiled in essentially political issues and controversies. We also have a look at what had happened to certain Muslim monuments of Delhi and Alwar during the Partition of 1947. We take exception to some of the anti-India outbursts regarding these sites and related incidents in some of the current archaeological literature. In this context we point out that the anti-India outpourings of many Indian and Western scholars are related and apparently grow out of the same intellectual roots. We emphasize that the difference we notice between many modern-day Western archaeologists in relation to the Indus Civilization and other archaeological aspects of India and the general nationalist and objective approach of some Indian scholars to the same issues is based essentially on colour. The white-skinned scholars have regrettably formed in the context of Indian archaeology their own group vis-à-vis the brown-skinned ones. Most of the Indian scholars show yet no sign of realizing this. This dichotomy has come about rather prominently in recent years and is applicable to fields like Indology and Indian archaeology.

After elaborating this background context, we turn to examine the salient features of the socio-political frame of the ancient Indian past, which essentially meant an interrelationship between race, language and culture. We examine, although briefly, how this relationship has been built up right from the beginning of racial, linguistic and cultural studies, the last based on generalizations regarding the suggested contribution of the different language groups to the general cauldron of Indian culture. We also point out that the whole frame emerged in the colonial period and this was accepted by the Indian professionals and still continues to be accepted by a large section of the Indian professional class in these fields. The need for a different frame of the Indian past was emphasized by certain prominent thinkers of the 20th century including Rabindranath Tagore. Regrettably, this questioning spirit remained neglected for a long time among India's historical and archaeological community.

The questioning of the Aryan hypothesis in all its forms was done earlier by several Indians including the present author. This paper discusses the implications of the recently expressed anti-Aryan arguments offered by Alan Davies and Christopher Hutton.

This paper tries to focus next on the marginal position of archaeology in the Indian nationalist tradition, taking Bengal and Bengali literature as a case study. The theme is still waiting to be picked up in different regional literary traditions of the country.

Finally, the paper focuses on some ingredients of a nationalist Indian archaeology, highlighting mainly the interrelationship between history and geography in the ancient Indian context. The initial issue highlighted in this context is a detailed examination of the borderlands and boundaries, offering fresh insights into the much-publicised foreign invasions of the Indian land. The second issue relates to the traditional historical linkages and the issues of mutually interacting orbits, tying up the entire subcontinent in a strongly secure frame of interrelationships and rejecting the applicability of core-periphery concept in Indian archaeology. All parts of the subcontinent were strongly intertwined. Finally, what is important is the long and continuous archaeological sequence running through the land, with its richness, variety and depth of pre- and protohistoric development. Among other things, the richness and diversity of its agriculture, metallurgy and many other facets of technology call for primary attention. These nationalist components of Indian archaeology have been essentially in the line of this author's archaeological interest in the land. This will vary according to the archaeologists' individual interests but one certainly hopes that we shall be interested in working out a suitable archaeological perspective of the Indian land in all its broad phases – ancient, mediaeval and modern – showing the diversity and richness of the many divergent historical landscapes, but at the same time we shall possibly discover the extent to which the settlements and the landscapes of all these phases had some unifying threads running through them.

II. INTRODUCTION: COMMENTS ON THE THEME OF 'NATIONALISM AND ARCHAEOLOGY' IN ARCHAEOLOGICAL LITERATURE

The relationship between archaeology and politics is now a well-worn theme of theoretical studies of archaeology, and the category, which has come in for close scrutiny in recent years for its supposedly baleful influence on the practice of archaeology and the interpretation of archaeological data, is nationalism. Apart from the much-cited case of Nazi Germany, convenient examples have always been easy to come by in the less developed parts of Europe, despotic Middle East, Hindu India, Communist and post-Communist Russia, Communist China, and rigidly homogeneous Japan and Korea. With the exception of Hindu India which seriously figured in this context in the wake of the demolition of a sixteenth century mosque by a Hindu mob in Ayodhya in December 1992, case-studies from the other areas form the staple of the volumes edited by Philip Kohl and Clare Fawcett (1995) and Lynn Meskell (1998). The literature on this theme is ever increasing but we prefer to focus on these publications primarily because of their clarity. Kohl and Fawcett (1995: 5) write that, although "one can admire the positive role of an ethnically inspired archaeology that helps build justifiable pride in a specific cultural tradition and stimulates research into the past development of that tradition", the essays they have compiled and edited in their volume "are principally concerned with the *abuses* (their italics) of the relationship between nationalist politics and archaeology" and the related problems of racial superiority/inferiority and questionable political agendas.

There are some problems with this approach. The fact which has not been adequately emphasized in these two volumes is that nationalism can also act as a great cultural force persuading people to undertake the study of not merely archaeology but also history, literature, folk-lore, language and innumerable other expressions of their national culture. Those who have time to think of nationalism as a great historical and cultural driving force will not shudder every time archaeological data are viewed through the lens of national pride and self-respect, especially when this lens does not detract from the parameters of an objective assessment of the archaeological data. Further, when the role of nationalism in the development of archaeological researches in a given area is considered, it may not be done in isolation but in the general context of development in these other fields. The link with the romantic movement is important too, at least in Europe where this movement led to a shift of interest from the Classical Mediterranean lands to the features of their own countryside. Bruce Trigger (1995: 268-269) writes:

> Romantically inclined western European intellectuals called on all to take pride in their nation state and regard the historical, cultural and biological heritage that its citizens shared as being more important than the class antagonisms that were threatening the social order.

One is not sure that the romantic movement, as it manifested itself in literature and even in archaeology, was only an intellectual method to stem the tide of class antagonism which was a social consequence of the Industrial Revolution in Britain (1760-1820) and later elsewhere in Europe.

Trigger (1995: 269) further writes:

> Under the impetus of nationalism, archaeology abandoned a primary focus on evolution and concentrated on interpreting the archaeological record as the history of specific peoples.

It is doubtful if this is universally true. The texture and fabric of nationalism depended on the history of the nation state in which it flourished and the political circumstances in which this particular nation-state was born. If the catalytic factor behind its genesis was an overriding feeling of ethnic identity within its territorial limits, it is quite natural that there would be a lot of emphasis on the so-called historicity of this ethnicity. Ethnicity, however, is only a historical reconstruct based on the exigencies of specific historical situations in which this identity is formulated. There is nothing absolute or sacrosanct about ethnic identities. If one has to cite a convenient example, I would cite the case of Bangladeshi ethnic identity which is accepted as a case of separate ethnic identity in modern Britain. As a nation state Bangladesh emerged in 1971, mainly as a consequence of the dissatisfaction of the Bengali-speaking people who lived mostly in the province of East Pakistan of the state of Pakistan which was born on the basis of religion in 1947. The way this nation state was born in 1971 depended specifically on the way in which the dissatisfaction of the Bengali-speaking populace of East Pakistan was handled by the central state structure of Pakistan. The rallying force of the clamour for a separate nationhood by this populace was the Bengali language which emerged in its modern form only within the last two hundred years. One would also say that the Bengali language has had its own story of development in the former East Pakistan and modern Bangladesh, which is not quite the same with its development in the neighbouring Indian state of West Bengal since 1947. Ethnicity is not an immutable thing and hardly susceptible to close historical and archaeological enquiries. This does not mean that a nation-state whose main pillar is a perceived feeling of commonness of language, religion, or whatever, cannot take pride in the antiquity and glory of archaeological finds within its limits. As an example, the interest which the simple find of prehistoric fossil wood tools in Bangladesh in 1989 generated among its journalists comes readily to mind. The antiquity and richness of historical finds within the territorial limits of modern Bangladesh have also been matters of pride to the general run of its intelligentsia. There is no reason why such cases of simple pride should be run down in the name of an unwarranted political dimension of archaeology.

On the other hand, as we all know, there are many multi-ethnic states. Again, the concept of the past these multi-ethnic states may follow cannot be pinned down merely to the question of the dominance of a particular ethnic group over the other ethnic components of their population. The case of Turkey, as propounded by Mehemet Ozdogan (1998) is a pointer in this direction.

> In creating a nation out of the ruins of the Ottoman Empire, it was essential to formulate an ideology that would assure national pride, give moral direction and identity. Most of the elite of the time were utterly desperate and had lost confidence as a result of the events that led to the collapse of the Ottoman system. They took a more retrospective view by looking back to the glorious days of history and to their Turkic origins in Central Asia. Thus, they promoted the Pan-Turkist ideology.
>
> Ataturk was one of the few, if not the only person, who rejected Pan-Turkism and still had confidence in Anatolia.

> He developed an antithesis to the prevailing anti-Turkist ideology and insisted upon Anatolia being the homeland. To substantiate this totally new concept, an ethnohistorical theory was formulated, relating Sumerians and Hittites to the Turks, and integrated into the ideological framework of the new state. This approach considered Anatolia and the present population as an ethnic amalgamation of thousands of years. Pan-Turkists, who later became the ideologists of the racist movements of the present times, were rather pleased with the idea of affiliating Sumerians and Hittites to Turkish origins, but they never accepted a pre-Turkish history of Anatolia as a part of their heritage. In some respects, conflict between "Anatolianism" and Pan-Turkism continues to the present day – although there was some consensus, at least in history books, by stressing both the Anatolian heritage and over-stressing Central Asian origins. The latter, particularly in books written in the 1930s under the impact of prevailing nationalistic trends of its time, posited a Turkish exodus from Asian steppes. Ataturk's view, summoning all the pasts of Anatolia – regardless of ethnic origin – as national, was incorporated into the ideology of the modern state. (Ozdogan 1998: 116-117)

As we shall see later, the Turkish situation has a similarity with the Indian case. Both are multi-ethnic states with deep roots in history, and a past acceptable to all sections of populace is important to both of them.

The complexity in building up a nationally acceptable sense of the past in modern Egypt has been analysed by Fekri Hassan (1998). In the late 19th and early 20th centuries the first Egyptian nationalists looked toward Pharaonic Egypt for inspiration. Hassan points out how, after the revolution of 1919, the sense of national solidarity "was legitimized by an appeal to 'eternal Egypt', 'young Egypt' and, above all, 'Pharaonic Egypt'" and how pyramids were invoked in a genre of nationalistic poetry and historical plays. The concept of 'Arab nationalism' propounded by Gamal Abdel-Nasser in the 1950s undermined this emphasis, and under Anwar Al-Sadat in the 1970s there was a reawakening of an *Egyptian* identity. According to Hassan (1998: 212)

> A stable political future of Egypt depends upon an ability to integrate its pasts and recognise its Pharaonic, Hellenistic, and Islamic heritage, and to place that variegated heritage within the course of a global civilization.

Hassan does not suggest the base on which this integration can be achieved. What is important is that neither Ozdogan nor Hassan mentions any specific misuse of archaeology in the service of Turkish and Egyptian multi-ethnic nationalism. The way a nation views its past – the significance it attaches to its heritage – is a yardstick of its self-respect and identity, but the fact that a nation takes pride in its past does not necessarily mean that this serves as the base of its territorial aggrandisement or means the domination of one of its ethnic groups over others.

China seems to be more than concerned than Turkey and Egypt about maintaining a single 'ethnicity' with the label of 'Chinese'.

> Within the on-going scholarly and political discourse, the unity and homogeneity of the Chinese nation is axiomatic, and formulations that might conjure up questions of ethnic identity in the present era are strictly taboo. Historians and archaeologists concur that all the nationalities mentioned in the ancient texts were long ago fused into the Han nationality. When concentrating their efforts on enhancing an ancient nationality such as Jin, then archaeologists are not claiming that present-day inhabitants of Shanxi are in any way ethnically distinct from other Chinese. Neither should, for example, one scholar's attempt to derive the origins of the Shang dynasty from the far-away north-eastern provinces of China ... be misread as questioning the "Chinese" ethnicity of the Shang royal house. At issue is, instead, the historical importance of a particular region in

> the formation of Chinese civilization, which, symbolically reified in archaeological cultures, is conceived as a metonym of the present-day power and prestige of the political unit that happens to contain that region, and of its ruling authorities. (Falkenhausen 1995: 210-211)

Even in this case, where the ethnic label remains single and uniform over a vast geographical area and more than a billion of people, one fails to see how archaeology is being put to misuse. It may serve as an ideological underpinning of the nation-state of China's necessity to retain a homogeneous Chinese identity but wilful distortion of archaeological facts does not seem to be on its agenda. Similarly, in the case of Japan,

> "the notion of the Japanese people as a cohesive and homogeneous 'ethnic' group" has been claimed to be the central theme of archaeology from the late 1960s, aimed at creating "a sense of cohesion and homogeneity among the Japanese people and to deny internal social conflict" (Fawcett 1995: 245). Does this national objective have to be viewed in a pejorative sense? In a different area, democracy might not have flourished in Portugal in 1932-1968 when Antonio de Oliveira Salazar was the prime minister, but can he be accused because he "strove to restore the confidence and nationalistic pride of the Portugese by reminding them of their historic 'golden ages'". (Lillios 1995: 67)

One of the reasons why ethnicity figures so frequently in the current discussions on the relationship between archaeology and nationalism is the fact much of the European past or much of the past of different European countries was conjured in terms of such groups – Celts, Anglo-Saxons, Slavs, and so on. This has been succinctly expressed by Ian Banks (1996: 6):

> Historically, the appeal to ethnic origins has featured strongly in European nationalist projects. The ethnic groups with which many modern nations declare their ancestral

links are commonly those which can be identified as distinctive peoples in the periods when early historical records first appear.

But even in Europe the situation varies from country to country. In France, for instance, the significance of archaeology was realized rather late, the discipline being considered for a long time a mere 'servant of history' (Schnapp 1996). In Spain modern archaeology has to contend with the regional aspirations of the Andalusians, Basques and Catalans (Diaz-Andreu 1996). M.L.S. Sorensen (1996) emphasizes that the link between the past and the present in Denmark was to legitimatise and naturalise the territorial form that Denmark took in the wake of the Napoleonic war and the loss of her colonies.

Since the 1990s there has been a clear, and perhaps increasing, emphasis on finding links between archaeology and nationalism. A good part of this emphasis is to enquire into the socio-politics of archaeological writings within their national contexts, but by and large, as we have pointed out before, there is a strong undercurrent of negative attitude against any kind of equation between the nation and the archaeological data. On the other hand, this is also the phase when common elements are being consciously sought among the pasts of the nation-states within European Union.

Attempts to establish an European identity as opposed to the developments in west Asia, for instance, go clearly back to Gordon Childe's *The Prehistory of European Society* (Childe 1958) where the freedom of the itinerant smiths in the European Bronze Age were contrasted with their subordinate role in the context of the Oriental Bronze Age society. In 1994, in the now-powerful context of European Union, Colin Renfrew (1994) took up the theme again. He points out that

> The real problem in the archaeology of Europe today is that to a considerable extent we are still answering yesterday's problems, and in some cases continuing to fight battles

> whose outcome should long ago have been determined. It is difficult to underestimate the extent to which the broad beliefs of earlier decades about the European past – the myths of archaeology if you like – continue to dominate our thinking. (Renfrew 1994: 164)

He identifies three 'myths': the myth of ethnic predetermination based on the notion that "ethnicity may be assumed from early times, and certainly for the Mesolithic and subsequent periods"; the myth of economic predetermination based on the belief that the European Bronze Age was the result of a dissemination from the west Asian Bronze Age; and finally, the myth of spiritual predetermination associated with the bearers of "Indo-European speech, mythology, religion, and social structure, whose male-oriented, militaristic values supposedly came to dominate, and whose tripartite social and religious structures (according to Dumezil) came widely to prevail".

Renfrew acknowledges that it is difficult to root out these myths because they have so long provided the framework of the understanding of the prehistory of Europe. However, "rather than assailing these myths further" – and, according to him, "that task is indeed a useful one" – he decides to indicate what he feels "are some of the more important questions".

"It is out of these new and intriguing issues that we should, I believe, be formulating *our new narratives, the new myths (if you prefer), which we should be using to provide a fresh framework for the prehistory and early history of Europe over the next few decades*" (italics added, Renfrew 1994: 165-166).

The details of the new issues formulated by Renfrew – paths to urbanisation and the foundations of barbarian Europe with its own complement of sub-issues such as 'value and metallurgy', 'the gods of war' and 'the different roles of men and women in the emerging societies of barbarian Europe' – do not concern us, but what is important and relevant to our point of view is *that there can be a reorientation of questions asked of the past of an area and that there should be a new narrative to go with it.*

It may also be important to emphasize that there is a clear line of distinction between such new narratives and the use and/or manipulation of archaeological data for specific political agendas of territorial claims, aggrandisement and the suppression of dissenting political groups. The distinction has to some extent got blurred in modern archaeological literature. We further believe that 'misuses of archaeology' have been most frequent where ethnogenesis – the so-called formation of somewhat immutable ethnic identities – has been taken to be a primary goal of archaeological research. This is one of the major end-products of a very old and not-so-worn-out paradigm of race-language-culture correlation. This paradigm is not dead yet; it is easily possible to cite archaeological literature emanating from the liberal Euro-American contexts, which is a distinct throw-back to the essentially nineteenth-century notions of this kind. Why we should be so worried at present about establishing correlates between biology, modern language groups and archaeological cultures is a question I leave to those archaeologists who are far more familiar with the complexities of the global socio-political realities than me. Can there be any proof that the first two factors shape in any way the form of archaeological cultures? If there is no such proof, nor is there any possibility of such proof, why are we concerned with establishing links between 'archaeo-genetics', 'archaeo-language' and archaeological cultures?

The highly volatile relationship between nationalism, politics and the practice of archaeology in the Caucasian region, which Kohl (1993) demonstrates with precision, is mostly due to the preoccupation of this region's archaeological tradition with questions of ethnogenesis. One fully agrees with him when he writes:

> Ethnic identifications extending back over millennia, which are a favourite form of nationalist interpretation, are problematic and hazardous .... The professional responsibility of the archaeologist confronted with such interpretations is straightforward: Emphasize that the identification is uncertain and tenuous and stress the real epistemological limits that circumscribe our ability to people the remote prehistoric past. (Kohl 1998: 241)

There can also be no disagreement with the following opinion:

> Ethical standards for accepting or rejecting nationalist uses of archaeology may vary in specific cases, but they should ideally satisfy the following three criteria: (a) the construction of one group's national past should not be made at the expense of others'; (b) all cultural traditions should be recognized as worthy of study and respect; and (c) the construction of a national past should not be made at the expense of abandoning the universal anthropological perspective of our common humanity and shared past and future .... (Kohl 1998: 243)

Three more points may be emphasized by us in this section. First, there is absolutely no reason why nationalist archaeology should be preoccupied primarily with ethnogenesis. This may be true in some cases, as in the case of the Caucasian region and the Balkan states of Europe, but that certainly is not the concern of nationalist archaeology everywhere. Secondly, the fact that national symbols have been borrowed from the monuments or archaeological objects in the nation-state's territory does not necessarily mean that archaeology is used for political reasons there and that archaeology occupies an important part of the nation's historical consciousness or historical education. This is a point which, in their enthusiasm to list traces of sins in this direction, the writers on this theme have consistently ignored. One of its primary reasons is that the archaeological writers on this theme do not originate in the areas whose politics of the past they write about and thus do not possess any kind of link with the concerned area. Thirdly, a lot of the harking back to the past is fairly innocuous. By staging his coronation ceremony in the ruins of Persepolis the last Shah of Iran was no doubt suggesting that his dynasty was an inheritor of the Achaemenid tradition of Iran. Whether this was true or not is a different matter, but as far as the harking back to old traditions goes, it is far more innocuous and less threatening than such terms as 'traditional Western viewpoint', 'dominant Western view' etc. which are increasingly becoming common in the Euro-American writings on Indian archaeology.

It is within this framework of archaeological literature and its general postulates on the theme of nationalist archaeology that we discuss the complexities of the Indian archaeological tradition in this regard and *argue that we need a new 'nationalist' archaeological agenda and narrative*. The need is felt all the more strongly in view of the interpretative context that archaeology faced in post-Independence India. I have concisely summed up this context in my *Nationalism in the Study of Ancient Indian History*, 2021. There is no reason why certain archaeologists of Euro-American descent should be given the status of cult-gurus in modern India. Mortimer Wheeler was one such figure in Indian archaeology till the 1970s and currently he has been replaced by several others. It is not a desirable situation from the point of view of India's national interest, but to be honest, it will be difficult to argue that Indian archaeologists – or at least most of them – have ever considered the factor of nationalism or national interest at all important in the post-Independence years. There may have been some exceptions but they establish only the general validity of the essentially anti-national tone of post-Independence Indian archaeology.

III. POLITICAL UNREST AND MONUMENTS

The area where this tone has been most strident is the literature built around the demolition of a 16th century Mughal-built mosque in the city of Ayodhya on 6 December 1992. Among other things, this incident was the main cause of mayhem at the World Archaeology Conference in Delhi in 1994, the tension between the two Indian opposing groups running high during the conference. One group clearly represented the opinion of the Indian left, according to which this virtually meant the end of secularism in the country and the incident of demolition itself was a conspiracy hatched by the Indian right which in turn was fostered by Hindu fundamentalism. The people in the opposing group stressed the fact that the place occupied by the destroyed 16th century mosque was believed by a vast number of Hindus to have been the birth-place of the Hindu god Rama, an incarnation of a supreme deity, Vishnu. Besides, the history of the site has been, since records on this are available, marred by disputes between the Hindu and Muslim communities. This implied that the Hindus could never accept the fact of the forcibly constructed mosque at one of the most holy spots of Hinduism, the spot which is overwhelmingly believed to have been the birth-place of Rama.

III.1. Some Recent Literature on the Babri Mosque Issue, Ayodhya

The literature on the site has been steadily increasing since the destruction of the mosque in 1992 and this has gained a new lease of life since the Indian Supreme Court in November 2019 handed over the management of the site to the Hindus, accepting the basic argument of the Archaeological Survey of India which, under an order of the judiciary, conducted excavations at the disputed site and reached, on the basis of the evidence obtained, that there were multiple structural phases of a Hindu temple below the destroyed mosque at the site.

III.1.1. Bishnupriya Basak

The bitterness in certain quarters as an aftermath of the Supreme Court decision is clear from the following comments made by Bishnupriya Basak in her editorial in *Public Archaeology* 17, May-August 2018. As the Supreme Court judgement was delivered in 2019 and as Basak in her editorial refers to this judgement, the May-August issue of the journal must have been delayed till at least November 2019.

> Any editorial on public archaeology in India cannot escape one of the most contentious issues of current times that compels us to probe deep into the mesh of social power relations, namely the destruction of the Babri Masjid mosque in Ayodhya, Uttar Pradesh, a 500-year-old structure that was razed to the ground on 6 December 1992. The date of 7 November 2019 may go down in the history of the nation as a watershed moment. The Supreme Court of India delivered their verdict on the long-running Ayodhya legal case, which has been hailed as 'sealing' the long-drawn-out conflict of the disputed land of the demolished Babri Masjid. In the title suit the claims of the Hindus – that the mosque had been built on a demolished Hindu temple – were recognized; those of the Muslims were not, and their inability to establish their claims to the 2.77-acre land (where the Babri Masjid once stood) was stated as a key reason. The claim is conjured from allusions to the disputed site being the Hindu god Rama's birthplace, which were found scattered in Hindu and Sikh texts and colonial gazetteers. Absolute reliance had been sought in excavation findings of the Archaeological Survey of India that mention 'non-Islamic structures' below the destroyed mosque in their 2003 report, which were heavily mediated by judicial interventions, as Rachel Varghese has shown so succinctly in this volume. The Supreme Court ruling ultimately proclaimed the *faith* of the majoritarian community as the basis for authorizing the construction of a Hindu temple at the site .... A Hindu temple is therefore due to be constructed on ruins that never existed.

> The judgment is beset with contradictions. On the one hand it rebukes the demolition of the 500-year-old Babri Masjid in 1992 as 'an egregious violation of law', and admits that this mosque, where *namaz* was offered regularly at least from 1857, was desecrated on 22/23 December 1949 when an idol of Rama was installed under the central dome, creating a de facto Hindu temple. On the other hand, the Court refrains from recognizing the fundamental right of the minority Muslim community to defend its freedom of religion, which is sanctified by the Indian Constitution. When the Constitution came into existence, *namaz* was being offered at the site. If a place where *namaz* is offered is considered as a *masjid*, then the minority community has a fundamental right to defend its freedom of religion. In its act of refraining to recognize this right, the Court fails to protect the Constitution. By affirming their belief that there was once a temple prior to the building of the mosque, it has tried to settle an ownership issue traced to a 500-year-old past, or more. The judgment is paradoxical to the core. If the minority right to defend their religion is denied by the Court, how can it be used as a justification to direct the government to give the Muslin community five acres of land to build a mosque elsewhere in Ayodhya? (Basak, editorial, *Public Archaeology*, vol. 17, issue 2-3)

The author's questioning of the Supreme Court judgement is clear in her opinion which has been cited above. The questioning of the Supreme Court judgement possibly required a proper knowledge of what constitutes legality, but the author in this case has no such compunction. What, to the present author is more surprising is that she declares, in the following citation of her opinion, that there is no evidence of a temple at the excavated site of the mosque.

> In this case, the validity of 'faith' is juxtaposed with 'historical evidence'. Rightly so, when no evidence of ruins of a Hindu temple actually exists below the demolished mosque. Even the much-orchestrated excavations of the

Archaeological Survey referred only to the presence of 'non-Islamic structures'.

The whole tenor of Basak's argument leads us away even from considering the possibility that there could be the destroyed material heaps of a Hindu temple beneath the now-destroyed mosque.

III.1.2. Rachael Varghese

The same attitude is displayed in the article by Rachel Varghese in the same issue of *Public Archaeology*. The tone of this second article is set by the opening sentences where the destruction of the mosque by an irate Hindu mob in 1992 has been described as a "watershed moment in the history of Indian democracy, bringing into question ideals like secularism and plurality that has been claimed as unique features defining the nation's existence as democracy." She does not discuss the result of excavations conducted at the site at the behest of the judiciary, but her attitude is clear from her reference only to the opinions of scholars who appeared on behalf of the Sunni Waqf Board, one of the main parties in the judicial case, i.e. S. Ratnagar, D. Mandal, S. Verma and J. Menon. They all argued that the evidence adduced by the Archaeological Survey of India was all wrong and explanations offered by the Survey were not necessarily correct and acceptable. The above-mentioned scholars are all well-known members of the Indian left.

III.1.3. Observations

On the whole, both these articles published in *Public Archaeology* adopt a clear anti-Archaeological Survey of India position. As far as I have been able to understand it, the Survey's position in this dispute – whether there was a pre-existing temple before the mosque was built at the site or not – was non-political and objective throughout. There are innumerable sites in India and the working archaeologists of the country do not always have to excavate a particular site to make a rational guess about its character. Further, they seldom have enough money to arrange for scientific aids. In most cases they have to make do with what they have got – a pair of eyes and what they have previously learnt in the field. Even with such a simple and elementary approach, the basic observation is likely to be correct in most field situations.

The starting point is that the Babri mosque was located on a fairly high mound. In the medium to high rainfall zone of the Gangetic plain the normal occupational debris of a habitation do not automatically lead to the formation of deposits in the form of a mound as they do in comparatively dry climates. Even a moderately high mound of the central Gangetic plain where Ayodhya is located will have to be a structural deposit, i.e. on excavations it will be found to contain burnt bricks which will not be carried away by the next year's monsoon. The archaeologist concerned will then go around the mound and study whatever can be studied on the surface and in the peripheries. If the archaeologist feels that there is indeed a deposit of mainly burnt brick structures below the surface, he shall look carefully for any sign which can be the base for making a further surmise. This is what B.B. Lal did in his first tentative search at the relevant mound in Ayodhya. He scraped around the lower sides of the mound to make a guess of what could lie inside. He found a few architectural fragments which were normally associated with the ruins of temples.

As far as a working hypothesis goes, there is absolutely nothing wrong with this hypothesis which is based purely on field-observation and experience. Other burnt brick constructions, not necessarily temples, could also be contained in this mound. The issue of Buddhist and Jaina brick stupas comes readily to mind but those who have an idea of the site of Ayodhya as a whole know that the locations of Buddhist and/or Jaina remains do not seem to be anywhere near the Babri mosque mound or the *Ramjanambhumi* site. The Nageswarnath Siva temple in Ayodhya contains one of the most finished examples of an Asokan lion capital, and my personal impression is that the adjacent mound is likely to contain the pillar which showed this capital on its top. There should be some other Buddhist ruins too in this sector. The uncertainty persists with the remains of Jaina affiliation. One is not even sure if Ayodhya contained a major Jaina structure or a large range of Jaina *Tirthankara* images. This uncertainty apart, Ayodhya was a major fortified early historic city of the Ganga plain. It is regrettable that the entire interest of the site has now been focussed on a particular mound at the expense of acquiring a detailed idea of the ancient city as a whole. The route from ancient Sravasti to Pratisthana or Paithan in the upper Godavari valley in the Deccan passes through Ayodhya and gives the site an added economic importance. Ayodhya is the first major city site on this route from the Sravasti side, Manhej (ancient name unknown) near Jaunpur being the second but a much smaller city site before the route crosses the Ganga at modern Mirzapur and travels further west. Ayodhya also figures prominently on the route which ran diagonally across the Ganga valley from the east to the west, from Pataliputra and Rajagriha to Takshasila. It is unfortunate that the importance of Ayodhya as a major fortified early historical city site has been completely bypassed in the discussion on heritage issues regarding this site.

I shall offer some comments on the analysis made by Basak and Varghese. Both of them are very pessimistic about the position of secularism and democracy in India after 1992 when the Babri mosque was destroyed, and both of them view the Ayodhya incident in isolation from the history of the country both during and after Partition. The holocaust which accompanied Partition and accounted for more than two million people dead ('butchered') has left behind an indelible scar in the minds of people who were affected by it in various ways, and to argue that religion was no longer a social and political factor is absurd and only tries to avoid the unpleasant social reality. One can offer many examples from the archaeological scene itself. The exquisitely crafted mosques of the Gujarat Sultans in Ahmedabad are all centrally protected monuments but in reality they are in the apparently illegal grip of a particular group of Muslims who do not mind using these monuments as their living space. The monuments of Sarkej, once famous for its indigo, near Ahmedabad are frequently overcrowded mostly by Muslims who consider these monuments as 'their' monuments. Ahmedabad or the area in the vicinity of Ahmedabad alone does not offer such examples; such examples can be seen all over the country, regardless of the religious affiliations of particular monuments. In post-Partition India you cannot take religion out of any social and political equation and the sooner we cease to lament about the death of secularism in the country the better. Secularism is a matter of personal faith or a way of life and cannot be imposed by any government injunction. Similarly, casting aspersion on the future of democracy in India on the part of these two Indian ladies, apparently of 'left-liberal' inclinations, was neither logical nor commensurate with global reality. Democracy flourishes only in limited segments of the globe – and as Indians we are proud of our democratic tradition which has survived for no less than 75 years, and if it ever comes to the choice between democracy and dictatorship, the vast sections of the Indian populace, regardless of their religious affiliations, will make a stand for democracy. The democratic tradition is deeply embedded in the Indian political life, and all that one has to do is to read K.P. Jayaswal's *Hindu Polity* or the Uttaramerur inscription of the Chola period, the last exemplifying the working of democracy at the grassroots. The Basak-Varghese lament about the end of the Indian democratic tradition because of the destruction of a 16th century mosque in Ayodhya is not merely farfetched but also an exaggerated and politically motivated emotion. This destruction cannot be viewed in isolation; it is an inseparable part of the hatred and sense of separation between the Hindu and Muslim communities, which came to a crux during Partition and also in 1971 when among the vast number of Bangladeshis killed by Pakistan army, an overwhelmingly large proportion was that of the Hindus. As long as we face it squarely and try to overcome it, the bitterness will die down; attempts to portray a doomsday scenario are most unlikely to be helpful.

The long-winded argument to deny the absence of a temple below the level of the destroyed mosque, which Basak and Varghese offer on the basis of the people they have cited – Ratnagar, Bhan, Mandal, Verma and Menon – is unacceptable. The architectural fragments and pillar bases found in the excavations certainly denote the presence of a temple at this level, and no amount of sophistry is likely to be fruitful in this case. The thread which binds these scholars together is their communist and/or left-liberal affiliation and one wonders why they are so keen not to see the obvious. Their general silence about the existence of ancient inscriptions testifying to the existence of a temple of Vishnu, whose incarnation is Rama, is inexplicable, especially when one of them was found engraved on a stone slab which came to light when the walls of the mosque were pulled down by the Hindu mob. This inscription was subsequently edited by A.M. Shastri, an epigrapher with credibility, in the Indian Archaeology Society journal *Puratattva*. The inscription is clear about the former existence of a Vishnu temple at the site. Rama was an incarnation of Vishnu. The fact that the Hindu emotion was allowed to be carried to such a pitch that would lead to the destruction of a 500 year old mosque as a result of mob frenzy was certainly unfortunate and possibly avoidable, but the details of proposals of solution from the Hindu side and the corresponding response from the Muslim side, as parts of the protracted negotiations over the site are all available. The point is that the negotiators on the Muslim side failed to appreciate the enormity of Hindu feeling regarding the sacredness of the site. If I remember correctly, quite early on, there was a proposal from the Hindu side to transfer the same mosque, brick by brick and stone by stone, to an adjacent place. I would say that the boiling situation could have been avoided if the negotiators on the Muslim side were less obdurate and more willing to compromise. Archaeology entered the picture only when the judiciary was virtually compelled to look for some evidence throwing tangible historical light on the disputed spot. Perhaps the most sordid part of the whole episode, apart from the communal riot which took place after the mosque was pulled down, was the way in which the archaeologists deputed by the Indian left to argue on the Muslim side were indulging in sophistry to deny the obvious, i.e. there were temple ruins below the mosque. The heritage issues in a multi-ethnic nation like India are invariably complex and the journal *Public Archaeology* has not set a good academic example by publishing the type of articles and editorial comments which have been published in their India issue.

III.1.4. Link-up between the Indian Left and Western Scholarship on India: Ann-Julie Etter

Perhaps more strident and directly political and combative in tone is the paper written by a French scholar – Ann-Julie Etter, 'Creating suitable evidence of the past? Archaeology, politics and Hindu nationalism in India from the end of the twentieth century to the present', *South Asia Multidisciplinary Academic Journal* (online), 24/25, 2020.

> This paper explores how archaeology has accompanied the rise of Hindu ideology and politics, showing—if proof were still needed—that Indian past(s) have become a vigorous and harsh battle arena. I first give an overview of the Indian

archaeological stage as it has developed since the nineteenth century, insisting on features that shed light on Hindutva's successful appropriation of this field. I then describe the archaeological politics of the BJP through the lens of a project launched in 2020, before detailing two examples: the Ayodhya dispute and the controversies on origins and identity. Both cases are in the forefront of archaeological and political stages and illustrate two related uses of archaeology. At Ayodhya, archaeology has been yoked to the project of erasing, both symbolically and physically, Islamic heritage and the place of Islam in India's culture and landscape, while nurturing the politics of exclusion through the character of the Other—the invading Muslim. In parallel, archaeological knowledge has played an instrumental role in the Hindutva project to endow Indians with what is supposed to be a brilliant and indigenous ancestry.

The foregoing preamble shocks one by its sheer audacity. To assert so glibly about the visible and invisible connections between archaeology and politics of such a vast area and complexity as India, visibly without any firm control over the primary sources or even the general range of problems of Indian history on the author's side, represents a type of writing which was possible generally when the Europeans and Indians were in a master-servant relationship. These days, even in archaeology, Indians expect some politeness and a better professional acquaintance with Indian archaeological situation on the part of those Westerns who are apparently keen to apprise the Indians of the archaeological contexts of their own country. It is seldom that we are treated to such an arrogant assertion as to suggest that at Ayodhya archaeology has been linked to the project of symbolically and physically erasing the Islamic heritage and the place of Islam in India's culture and landscape. From a single point at Ayodhya the author does not hesitate to pass judgement on the country as a whole. Similarly, it is wide off the mark to assert the following:

> A nation-serving archaeology developed in Independent India. It was meant to substantiate its politics of secularism and depict India's cultural unity, as illustrated by the works of H.D. Sankalia. Archaeology has remained embedded in national and political concerns since then. The will to demonstrate the triumph of the nation and shape a narrative of its historical achievements and cultural cohesiveness continues to skew archaeological practice and theory. A similar position has been endorsed by historians of Indian archaeology. This nation-serving archaeology and its historiography share similarities with British archaeology in colonial India, in terms of methods and aims. Both rely on a positivist approach to material remains, tending to view them as valid and unquestionable evidence, disregarding the fact that archaeological data and knowledge do not exist in nature but are artefacts of history.

As the name of the Deccan College archaeologist Sankalia has been specifically mentioned above, I would point out, as I have pointed out in my *Nationalism in the Study of Ancient Indian History,* that to him India was always a colony and in this he did not differ from the Cambridge Sanskrit professor E.J. Rapson whose contempt for India's ancient past is still shocking. In the same book I cited enough evidence to suggest that nationalism or the implications of different interpretations of archaeological data was never an issue with some of the important Deccan College archaeologists, and one suspects that most of the people who have passed through the archaeological wing of its portals never bothered to specifically consider India as a nation or the implications of various interpretations of her archaeological past on a proper historical understanding of the country. There was seldom any will to demonstrate the triumph of the nation and shape a narrative of its historical achievement in the post-Independence period. I am not sure if the situation has changed significantly for the better even now.

There is no point in pursuing the contents of Etter's paper further. This has been cited to demonstrate the similarity of approach between Indians like Basak and Varghese and Westerns like Etter. All of them share a common platform to run down the state of affairs in India and express a basically anti-India tone. The link-up between the Indian left and the anti-India lobby among the Westerns is very clear.

What also remains an inescapable truth is that many Indian archaeologists are not even aware of the national or anti-national dimensions of archaeological interpretations of the Indian past. Nationalism of any kind does not cut any ice with a vast number of Indian archaeologists. As I have argued in my *Nationalism in the Study of Ancient Indian History*, it was true of many principal archaeologists of the Deccan College, M.S. University of Vadodara and the Archaeological Survey of India for many years after Independence. There is no reason to believe that the situation has changed in any way in the archaeological wings of the Indian universities or in other Indian institutions concerned with archaeology. If my personal assessment of the situation since 1963 is of any value, I would argue that Western archaeology concerning India and traditional Western Indology have been consolidated in recent years as a unified group which is ready to ride roughshod over the Indian opinions in these matters. The basis of this consolidation is essentially the colour of the involved scholarly skins – nothing more and nothing less. As there is hardly any self-respecting Indian group in these fields, the Western group marches virtually unopposed, at least in the concerned Western literature on Indian archaeology.

III.2. Pattinam and Keezadi

Ayodhya is not the only Indian site where archaeology has been taken to assume serious political overtones. Two sites in south India are relevant to this context: Pattinam northeast of Kochi in Kerala, and Keezadi near Madurai in Tamilnadu. The following is stated about the site of Pattinam in E.H. Seland's general review of 'archaeology and trade in the western Indian ocean, 300 BC – AD 700' in *Journal of Archaeological Research* 22(4), 2014, pp. 367-402:

Arguably the most important Indian site excavated after Arikamedu is Pattanam, generally identified with the port of Muziris, mentioned in Roman as well as Tamil literary sources. The Kerala Council for Historical Research has excavated at Pattanam since 2007. Along with locally produced pottery and beads, finds include building structures, a wharf, a log boat, imported Mediterranean glass, Roman Terra Sigillata pottery, and a range of amphorae (Mediterranean transport jars), all dating to the first century BC through the second century AD. Specimens of Sassanian-period (AD 224–651) torpedo jars from Mesopotamia, late Roman (fifth to seventh centuries) Aila/Aqaba amphorae, glazed Partho-Sassanian pottery, and sherds of probable South Arabian origin also are reported. While the link to textual sources and the massive evidence of trade in bulk commodities and luxury items have brought well-deserved attention to Pattanam, the site is only one of many along the coasts of Pakistan, India, and Sri Lanka.

It seems that the site got itself embroiled in unsavoury controversies soon after excavations began there under a NGO named Kerala Council of Historical Research. This NGO was accused of having received foreign donations which were not in accordance with the Government of India rules for the NGOs to receive foreign money. At some point the Archaeological Survey of India cancelled the license by which it sanctioned the excavations at the site by this NGO. The situation where this excavation project stands at present is unclear to the present writer, but the following is written on the basis of what has been published in *India Facts Staff Identity (Distortion and Appropriation), January 23, 2015.* In this publication B.S. Harishankar throws light on different controversies related to this site and excavations by what is called Kerala

Council of Historical Research. First, at a meeting of the Joint Annual Conference of Indian Archaeological Society, Indian Society for Prehistoric and Quaternary Studies, and Indian History and Culture Society in Thiruvananthapuram, the state capital of Kerala in November 2011, a number of historians and archaeologists who were all familiar with the site and the area where it is located, strongly criticised the standard of work conducted there. The names of A.S. Sundara, M.G.S. Narayanan, R. Nagaswamy and T. Satyamurti, all renowned scholars and archaeologists of south India, figure in B.S. Harishankar's report in the above-mentioned publication as strong critics of the way excavations had so far been conducted at the site and the haste with which the site had been identified as Muziris. Perhaps more seriously, in an article in *Mathru-bhumi* in 2014, "Professor P.M. Rajan Gurukkal, historian ... admitted that the site was unfit for any archaeological excavation as the soil has been virtually tampered for various construction purposes". The digging of wells at the site "left no space for stratigraphical analysis of the cultural remains".

The present author could make a hurried visit to the site in the summer of 2006 before excavations began, in the company of Dr. Selvakumar who was kindly requested by Professor K. Rajan to take him there. It was a fairly watery landscape with at least one major channel representing the Periyar river. The traces of occupation marked by well-spaced scatters of sherds and reddish colour of surface soil (indicative in this case of the presence of burnt bricks below the surface) were clearly there in the midst of large coconut groves. The precise identification of the site with what has been called Muziris in the relevant text fragment made of papyrus and in the document named *Periplus* will ultimately depend on some clear written evidence from the site. Such a document has not yet appeared at the site and perhaps it is premature to firmly identify the area with that of Muziris at present. I also have no reason to dispute the identifications of 'foreign' pottery at the site but the list seems to be too diverse to be real after some short digs. For instance, pottery of Byzantine period has been said to exist at the site. Perhaps more specific details were called for. However, such details can easily be sorted out among scholars themselves as long as it is a straightforward archaeological matter.

The political dimension of the Kerala Council of Historical Research excavations at the proposed site of Muziris lies elsewhere and for that we have to depend on what Harishankar has reported in the above-mentioned number of *India Facts*:

> In the KCHR brochure published in February 2008 on MHP (Muziris Heritage Project) and Pattanam excavations, Chairman of KCHR, Professor K.N. Panikkar stated in his editorial note that archaeological and historical research are not solely meant for experts and professionals in the field. Everyone with thinking power should handle it. Later elaborating further, in an interview given to *Frontline* dated April 2010, Panikkar made his stand much clearer. He suggested public participation in archaeological excavations at Pattanam – which he termed "Democratic Archaeology" – in which the local people would be part of the excavation. In other words, *archaeologists and ASI need not interfere in excavations since guidelines and diggings shall be by 'People's Democracy'* (italics added).

What is more ominously political in view of what Rajiv Malhotra and Aravindan Neelakandan have made clear in their book *Breaking India: Western Interventions in Dravidian and Dalit Faultlines (2011)* is the entrance of the Christian church in the scene. As Harishankar writes,

> What has now snowballed into a major controversy is the open declaration by KCHR Director, Dr. Cherian in the official bulletin of the Assyrian Church of the East on March 2011, that Pattanam has been identified as ancient Muziris,

where Apostle Thomas landed in India 2000 years back for propagating Christianity, which he claims has been vindicated by the excavations. In 2011 July, he presented a paper on Pattanam archaeology at a seminar organised by Syro-Malabar Church in Mumbai.

Equally, if not more deadly in its implications for Indian security, is the site of Keezadi in the general area of Sivaganga near Madurai, far to the southeast from Pattinam. Some people see in the vigorously driven Dravidian angle of the site a reflection of the urge on the part of some people to find a separate Dravidian land. What is available to the present author (in April 2021) is a series of newspaper reports published in the second half of 2019. The general public interest in the site is evident from the fact that 1.16 lakh people visited the site between September 20 and October 10 in 2019. The political angle is made amply clear from the following two reports: 'Keezhadi excavation opens a Pandora's box in Tamil Nadu politics', report filed by K. Karthikeyan in *DT Next*, October 4, 2019; and 'Keezadi excavations open age-old debate of Aryans vs. Dravidians', report filed by Vinodh Arulappan in *The New Indian Express*, 27 October 2019

According to the political parties operating in Tamil Nadu, the following cultural labels were ascribed to the excavated material at Keezadi. DMK president M.K. Stalin visited the site and apparently labelled it as Dravidian. Naam Tamilar Katchi (NTK) labelled it as Tamil Civilization. Whereas the 'Dravidian' would encompass the whole of the Dravidian language belt of the south, 'Tamilian' would reserve it only for the modern Tamils. The Bharatiya Janata Party of Tamil Nadu called it 'Tamil' whereas AIADMK had the sagacity to call it 'Bharat civilization', looking at India as a whole inclusive of non-Tamil and non-Dravidian areas.

III.2.1. Observations

In all honesty, we do not have to get unduly agitated about Keezadi. It is a site where occupation goes back to c. 580 BC and this general chronological range was earlier available from Kodumanal and Porunthal. In my book on the ancient routes of the Deccan and the southern Peninsula I argued that even without the help of radiocarbon dates it was possible to take the beginning of history in the south to about the 6th century BC. After the occurrence of inscribed sherds of Tamil-Brahmi around the middle of the 5th century BC at Anuradhapura in Sri Lanka, it ought to have been crystal clear that the similar inscriptions found in different parts of Tamil Nadu and the other southern areas should be equally early. For reasons best known to them, some important Tamil scholars refused to accept this early date for these inscriptions till radiocarbon dates were obtained from Kodumanal and Porunthal. By 500 BC, Brahmi script was in use in the southern region and the use was extensive enough to incise Brahmi letters and even inscriptions on potsherds in an extensive area of southern India. One would suggest that this marks the onset of what is called the Sangam period in south Indian history, whatever the literary scholars may say about the date of the Sangam literature. The prosperous state of affairs in the Sangam period has been clearly highlighted by the rich finds of burnt brick structures and terracotta ring-wells at Keezadi. What is left generally unsaid in this context is that there was well-demonstrated contact with north India during this period, and possibly the most important sign of contact, apart from the Brahmi script itself, is the occurrence of NBP, the typical black-polished, golden-hued pottery from the earliest historical sites of north India, at some southern sites including Alagankulam near Madurai. Even conservatively, this pottery dates from about 800 BC in the central Ganga plain. There is absolutely no reason why this should not date from at least 600 BC or even earlier (cf. an early but generally ignored date from Korkai) at Alagankulam. Our ideas about the early history in the southern peninsula are revised and the issues like Dravidian, Tamilian, etc. are not archaeological and possibly even historical problems. It is unnecessary that the study of south Indian archaeology should be affected by bigotry of any kind. Regrettably, there is already a heavy baggage of bigotry in the popular understanding of south Indian archaeology in south India. The hypothesis that the Indus civilization people were likely to belong to the Dravidian language family was offered in 1928 and has been acting like wild fire in the imagination of the Tamil-speaking population. There is no straightforward proof of any kind, nor are the concerned people interested in appreciating that a civilization whose script is undeciphered and whose language is unknown cannot be linked to a language by popular choice, so to speak. However, this is precisely what has happened in Tamil Nadu as far as the Indus civilization is concerned – a prolonged bout of popular madness which has been abetted and aided by scholars who should have known better. This is a well-understood case to demonstrate that beliefs closely bordering on fundamentalism do not have to do all the time with fundamentalistic religious beliefs. Cultural fundamentalism also can be a factor to reckon with in a land as culturally diverse as India.

III.3. Bodh Gaya and Sanchi

Some religious fundamentalism was also at work before a principal Buddhist site in India, the Mahabodhi Temple of Bodh Gaya, could be got rid of its control by the Hindu religious sect of the Giris, which had been in control of the sacred area around Bodh Gaya since the 17th/18th century by virtue of the grant they obtained from the Mughal court. It is a complex story, beginning visibly with the efforts of a Sri Lankan Buddhist monk, Anagarika Dharmapala (1864-1933) who established Mahabodhi Society in Colombo on 31 May, 1891. As David Geary writes in his book *The Rebirth of Bodh Gaya, Buddhism and the Making of a World Heritage Site* (Seattle 2017: University of Washington Press, pp. 28-29):

> The main objective was to revive Buddhism as a pan-Asian force and to internationalise the campaign to make known to all nations the sublime teachings of the Arya Dharma of Buddha Sakya Muni, and to rescue, restore and re-establish as the religious centre of this movement, the holy place of Buddha Gaya, where our Lord attained supreme wisdom.

From the very outset Anagarika Dharmapala made obvious his intention to bring the place under Buddhist control. The *Mahant* or the chief of the Hindu group which was in possession of the site since at least the 17th century refused to budge, despite all the direct and indirect pressures he was subjected to. A solution in sight had to wait till 1949 when by an act named the Bodhgaya Temple Act, the Bihar state government "assumed responsibility for the protection, management, and monitoring of the temple and its properties on June 19, 1949 under the Bodhgaya Temple Act (Bihar XVII, 1949)" (Geary, 2017). The Hindu *Mahant* petitioned the Supreme Court declaring the Act a violation of the Indian constitution. The matter dragged on till the end of 1952 and it needed impatience from somebody as important as Pandit Nehru before a new government moved in to take control of the temple.

The foregoing is only a basic note on the recent history of Bodhgaya. K.T.S. Sarao in his *The History of Mahabodhi Temple at Bodhgaya* (2020) sets out illuminating details about the phase of Mahabodhi Temple's history under the Saivite monks since about 1590. The first such monk was a wandering Saivite *sannyasi* named Gosain Ghamandi Giri, an heir to the tradition of Sankaracharya, who visited the site on a pilgrimage. Impressed by the religious importance and beauty of the site he built a hermitage opposite the temple. Sarao (2020: 96-97) writes:

> Appropriation of a derelict temple by a sannyasin such as this one, located near a small village, was an act that no one questioned. The practice of derelict Indic sites with a sacred background being reused by other Indic faiths was not

> uncommon at all during the ancient and mediaeval period. Multiple-affiliation was quite normal rather than exceptional among the various Indic faiths. Consequent upon the occupation of the Temple by the Saivite Giri mahants, Buddhist symbols, rituals, or images were left undisturbed. Remarkably, the Saiva worshippers embraced all that was there and nothing was destroyed. Even today, in addition to adaptation as well as adaptation of images of the Buddha and Bodhisattvas, the Hindus propitiate their deceased ancestors at the Mahabodhi. The Giri mahants of Bodh Gaya always adopted an inclusive approach in which Buddhist pilgrims were readily and unquestionably accommodated as worshippers.

Sarao goes on to emphasize that under the Mahant control Buddhist pilgrims 'were able not only to pay their respects but also to take on the task of repairs'.

Sarao's comment (p. 99) on the beginning of the modern phase of the Mahbodhi temple is clear and forthright:

> The tranquillity and peace of Bodh Gaya was for the first time disturbed in modern India by semi-religieux Anagarika Dharmapala who was partly carrying with him a baggage of Sinhala intolerance and who was partly instigated by the British Indologists. In this regard, it may be pointed out that by about the first quarter of the nineteenth century the colonial masters of India, through textual studies, began to see Buddhism and Hinduism as two irreconcilably different religions, whereby Buddhism was portrayed as a protest movement against Brahmanism. Here in the 'heavy handedness' of the brahmins, efforts were made to see 'the other' in the context of Buddhism vis-à-vis Hinduism.

The historical background of the general interaction between Buddhism, Saivism and Vaishnavism at Bodh Gaya has been worked out by Abhishek Singh Amar in a book titled *Cross-disciplinary Perspectives* (2012)

> This is illustrated by the documentation of several Hindu sculptures from the precincts of the Mahabodhi temple

> complex between the sixth and twelfth centuries. The Hindu orders of Saivism and Vaishnavism, which emerged in the early centuries of the Common Era, appeared and grew in the surrounding region of Bodhgaya from the fifth century onwards .... The growth of these orders forced the Buddhist sangha to take notice of their growth and subsequently compete with them in the region. In order to maintain its dominant position, the Sangha attempted to appropriate these orders by installing images of Hindu gods within its own sacred precincts. The documentation of three Vishnu etc. sculptures along with an inscribed four-faced Mahadeva from the Mahabodhi complex reflects this approach of the Sangha. The appropriation of Hindu gods through the installation and active worship of these images within a Buddhist shrine suggests a conscious attempt by the Sangha to speak to its local socio-religious context, which ultimately resulted in the acceptance of these Hindu gods as minor deities within the Buddhist order. This practice by the Sangha transformed the Buddhist order and resulted in the development of an inclusive Buddhaksetra.

This inclusive character of Buddhism was, however, ignored by people like Anagarika Dharmapala.

Sanchi was another major Buddhist place where the Mahabodhi Society applied pressure to take control of the monument going to the length of raising even the issue of Muslim chowkidars at the site.

The entire issue of the religious fundamentalism at work has been outlined by Lahiri, and considering the importance of these two monuments in forming the background of the current conservation and preservation policy of the government, I shall cite her observations in these cases in full.

> More serious were those cases where this exclusive religious frame of reference, by definition and in reality, attempted to exclude and evacuate several shrines of their varied patronage. One example of such exclusion was at the Mahabodhi complex at Bodh Gaya where Siddhartha

Gautama, the historical founder of Buddhism had attained enlightenment in the 6th c. BC. While this shrine was sacred to the Buddhists, it was also an object of reverence for Hindu pilgrims. This was because by the 14th c. AD, the Bodhi tree, under which the Buddha had meditated, was incorporated into the circumambulation of holy places that Hindu pilgrims to Gaya (a religious town, 8 km from Bodh Gaya) were to visit, a circuit that was steeped in Vaishnava tradition and which continues well into the present century.

Moreover, from 1727 onwards, the village of Taradih where the temple stood had been granted by a Mughal firman to a Saiva Mahant. Incidentally, different types of pilgrims continued worship without rancour until the creation of a pan-Buddhist axis towards the end of the 19th century which saw the beginning of a contentious politics that has since surrounded the temple complex. This politics was, in fact, tragically exacerbated because Curzon actively supported the Maha Bodhi Society in its aim to 'reclaim' the Mahabodhi temple from a Hindu proprietor and Hindu forms of worship. In Curzon's scheme, the multiple lineages of that shrine, involving patrons, proprietors and pilgrims of several faiths were of little consequence. Bodh Gaya was only "a Buddhist shrine, built by Buddhists in commemoration of one of the most sacred incidents of the life of their master" over which no "Hindu Priest" could exercise proprietary rights. So, centuries of composite patronage were sought to be written off because religious complexes were either to be considered as "protected monuments" or "restored to founders".

The case of Bodh Gaya, however, also demonstrates that such classifications could be effectively resisted. The Hindu priest, Krishna Dayal Giri, chose to remind the Viceroy that the "Bodh-Gaya shrine is not a singular one where men of different faiths come and worship ... the celebrated Hindu shrine of Hinglaj in Baluchistan beyond the Indus is owned by the Muhammadans (the present proprietress being a Muhammadan lady) where numbers of Hindu pilgrims from all parts of India visit every day without any dispute with the Muhammadans". Subsequently, in 1904, Curzon was forced to abandon his agenda of making the main temple an exclusive Buddhist shrine, partly because of the stout resistance offered by the Mahant. Regarding Sanchi, Lahiri points out the following:

> Similarly, with regard to the Sanchi monuments, John Marshall believed that the protection of the Buddhist stupa there was only possible through the appointment of Buddhist chowkidars (guards). Without consulting Sultan Jahan Begum, the local ruler of the princely state of Bhopal, who had all along had borne the cost of maintaining Sanchi, he had even arranged with the Mahabodhi Society for such a caretaker. The Begum, however, was horrified at the idea, and very effectively withstood all pressure for making such an appointment. Over time, she successfully showed how the religion of the guardians of Sanchi, be it that of the humble chowkidars or the ruling house, was irrelevant to the issue of providing support and effective protection to these monuments.

The situation which prevailed at Hinglaj – and possibly prevails even today – could have served as a model for Ayodha unless there had been less obduracy on the part of the Sunni Waqf Board and the radical scholars who apparently tried to strengthen its position by indulging in archaeological sophistry of all kinds.

Regarding the primacy of the Buddhist voice at Bodh Gaya I shall add an interesting footnote. One of the most treasured antiquities at the site is the Bodhi Throne which was donated by Asoka to the site. Under the Buddhist care and under the supposedly watchful eyes of the Archaeological Survey of India, this stone 'throne' which bears on its top a surface embellished by intersecting circle motif, and on the sides a row of geese in Mauryan art style, has been given a coat of gold in complete violation of all principles of preserving an ancient art object, and that too an object of such importance in the history of Indian art as the *Vajrasana* donated by Asoka. Barring a notice written in *Marg* by the present author, this ghastly act of sacrilege has gone unnoticed by all heritage-enthusiasts of the country, suggesting once more that concern for heritage among the Indian educated class is at present nothing much more than a fashion.

Not being somebody with an idea of the different branches of Indian law, I cannot comment on the utility and otherwise of the formation of National Monuments Authority of India in 2010. The only good thing that I find in it is the rigorous way in which a centrally preserved monument under the care of the Archaeological Survey of India is, under the provisions of the act which led to the formation of this authority, supposed to be inventoried and recorded with its drawings, land and the perimeters of the land on which it stands. I was informally shown a copy of such a well-prepared record of a south Indian temple by Professor Rajan. Such records and details are always welcome and necessary but one suspects that all these things could have been done even within the provisions of the Ancient Monuments and Preservation Act of 1904 when the monument concerned was put under the government care and one wonders if a new organization with its function overlapping with that of the Archaeological Survey of India was really necessary. Meanwhile, by injecting a strong dose of bureaucratic procedures in any building activity in the vicinity of a centrally protected monument, even if the proposed building activity is outside the perimeter of the monument and is in privately owned and legally acquired land, the Act under which this new Authority is set up has undoubtedly opened a new scope of putting pressure on the public with all that it regrettably means in India. I find it difficult to believe that National Monument Authority and the act under which it was established were based on careful considerations and with only public interest in mind.

III.3.1. Observations

An issue which is generally forgotten in the case of monuments like Bodh Gaya is that as sacred spots they drew respect not merely from the Buddhists but also from the Hindus and Jainas, two other religious groups of the pre-Muslim period. The presence of such non-Buddhist traces of worship, mostly in the form of images, varied from one Buddhist site to another, but they were present, whatever the number. If one remembers correctly, there were more than a hundred images of Hindu and Jaina deities in the compound of the *Mahant* palace at Bodhgaya. All these images were recovered from the site itself, clearly testifying to the worship of the concerned deities in this otherwise Buddhist complex. Bodhgaya, like many other pre-Muslim religious sites of India, were multi-religious places.

The furore caused by the destruction of the Babri mosque should also be seen in proper historical perspective, rather than as a catastrophic event in the religious history of India, spelling the doom of religious tolerance in the country, as scholars like Basak, Varghese and many others have argued. In India the number of major Hindu, Buddhist and Jaina monuments which were destroyed in the Islamic period may be mind-boggling. They were also done in the most brazen fashion. There is no point in trying to brush the easily visible cases of Qutub Minar, Delhi, and Adhai-din-ka-Jhopra, Ajmer under the carpet. That the Christians converted old Greek and Roman temples into churches is well-known. It has been claimed that even the Parthenon of Athens served for a very long period as a church, and even housed a small mosque. The conversion of Hagia Sophia in modern Istanbul into a mosque in recent times is another convenient example of this type. Built as a church in the 6th century by the empire Justinian, it was converted into a mosque in 1453 after the fall of Constantinople or modern Istanbul and continued to remain so till the period after the First World War when Kamal

Ataturk, the Turkish leader changed it to a museum. Now it has been converted again into a mosque.

III.4. Indian Monuments during Partition: Nayanjot Lahiri

The purveyors of doomsday scenario after Babri mosque demolition could also look back, somewhat gleefully, at what happened to Indian monuments during Partition. Nayanjot Lahiri in her *Monuments Matter* (published by the Marg Foundation) details what happened to monuments in Delhi and Alwar.

> Pressures on monuments came from looters, from refugee camps, as also from the callous acts of omission and commission of various government departments. Delhi is an example of this. It was in September 1947 that the capital became the site of a particularly vicious campaign in which Muslims were butchered by the thousands, and in its wake, symbols of Muslim culture such as tombs and mosques were attacked. The scale of the damage is vividly documented in the ASI files: the manner in which Mehrauli's Moti Masjid had its marble minars torn off; the demolishing of four tombs in the crypt of Sultan Ghari and the unsuccessful attempt to convert it into a temple; the same intention at the Chauburji Masjid on the Delhi Ridge where, in fact, a cement Hanuman came to be set up (to be eventually removed with police help); the destruction of the grave of Shah Alam at Wazirabad, and of red sandstone jalis surrounding it; and a great deal else.
>
> If in Delhi, looters targeted mosques and tombs, in some states, it was the administration that oversaw more organised campaigns of destruction. In the princely states of Alwar and Bharatpur, in 1947, mosques and tombs were targeted under the orders of the government with specific contracts being given for demolition. The profit to be made by grabbing the land on which these stood was the primary motive of demolition.

One also reads in Lahiri about the enquiries the Pakistan government was making about the fate of Islamic monuments in India, although scholars of Lahiri's delicate historical sensibility should also have tried to find out what happened to Hindu and Buddhist monuments of Panjab, Sind and the Northwest after the Muslim refugees from India reached there. Before we pour out our sorrow regarding the damage done to some Muslim monuments of Delhi and Alwar, as Lahiri has done, we might possibly pause for a moment to consider the fact that more than two million people were slaughtered, for no fault of theirs, during Partition which reputedly was brought about by non-violent means and many more millions (the present author is one of them) were displaced and reduced to the level of sub-human beings seeking only food and shelter. The *Sahibs* and *Memsahibs* involved in modern India's heritage industry must learn to view monuments not as isolated entities but very much as objects subject to all kinds of socio-political tensions of the day. The aftermath of the rebellion of 1857 on at least the monuments of Delhi including Lal Qila was, as is well-known, horrendous. As one goes through Lahiri's catalogue of damage in Delhi and Alwar, all that I can say is that in view of the holocaust in the background, the amount of this damage done to the monuments of these places, as detailed by Lahiri, has to be considered only marginal.

Before we leave this topic we have to point out that many Hindu temples were destroyed and/or converted into mosques in Pakistan and Bangladesh after the Babri mosque was destroyed. People writing on the demolition of the mosque in Ayodhya somehow forget to mention this fact. The present author, for one, also does not understand why the area of the old mosque containing a new Rama temple and a new mosque built in place of the old one could not stand side by side.

IV. SOME ASPECTS OF THE SOCIOPOLITICS OF THE INDIAN PAST

The Indian identity, as built within the colonial Indological framework of race, language and culture and its Aryan–non-Aryan dichotomy, is unacceptable to modern India and Indians. It is unacceptable because its emphasis on the notion of Aryan invasion, and the subjugation of, and interaction with, the native population as the key elements of ancient Indian history, culture and archaeology keeps a vast segment of Indian population away from a sense of positive participation in the country's past. Further, the key ingredient of this notion is the Indian Vedic literature, which thus makes it primarily a textual notion, and as long as this notion persists, the Indian upper castes who *ipso facto* are given a place in the Aryan ruling order, have no special reason to seek a primarily archaeology-based past for themselves. However, before we examine these twin formulations in some detail, it might be useful to look at how the question of identity is emerging as a major phenomenon in India in current years.

There are many 'tribal', originally hunting-gathering groups in India, but as there has been a continuous process of their absorption in the fold of Hindu caste society, such indigenous groups never felt quite cut off from the social and economic forces operating around them. For instance, they figure in various ways in the Indian epics and mythology, often with virtuous roles being attributed to them. In many of the relevant areas there was also a process of secondary state formations (cf. Sinha 1962), which continued down to the Mughal period in the sixteenth to eighteenth centuries. The rulers of these states invariably claimed a descent from the great legendary dynasties of India, and there was no difficulty at all in their being parts of the general 'princely' society of the country. Thus, whilst there is no shortage of groups who have a 'tribal' identity, none have as yet used it to question the archaeological interpretation of treatment of its past.

However, India has her problems, and these have been aggravated in recent years by the inability of the economic growth to keep pace with the growth in population. Clamours for an increased share in the national cake are the most persistent and strident noise in modern India, and such clamours are strengthened by appeals to caste, regional and religious identities. In some cases, especially along the borders where separate political niches can be carved out reasonably easily, much is made of ethnic differences. Group identities, as we know, are multi-dimensional and multi-level, and on the whole there is a great play about them in modern India.

There is much scope of investigating the emergence of different kinds of secondary identities, as apart from the basic historical identity of the nation, in the modern socio-economic and political contexts of India, especially with reference to the notions of the past which these identities claim for themselves. For instance, with the consolidation of the untouchables as a strong political power group (Bahujan Samaj Party or BSP) in the state of Uttar Pradesh under the leadership of Kanshi Ram and Mayawati, there has been a strong interest on the part of the untouchables or *Dalits* to discover powerful historical figures among their own communities. Their current identity, and the political language of the BSP which goes with it, are being built around such figures as Maharaja Bijli Paasee and Jhalkari Bai. The first one fought against the Muslim invaders while the second one fought against the British in the rebellion of 1857 (Narayan 1998).

However, movements such as these should not detract our attention from the ways in which the ancient Indian past has been viewed in post-Independence India by different sections of the Indian elite. How, for example, do historians and archaeologists of different socio-economic, educational and institutional backgrounds view the Indian past? In the course of a long teaching career in two Indian metropolitan universities – Calcutta and Delhi – I have myself witnessed the expansion and consolidation of a group of students and teachers who feel more at home in English than in their native languages and literature and consequently are isolated from their own literary and other related streams of cultural heritage. It is this group which is increasingly forming the bulk of India's dominant educational and bureaucratic elite vis-à-vis the 'native' students who pursue their education in their mother-tongues and find themselves disadvantaged while trying to seek whatever riches the 'system' has to offer.

The sense of the past of these two groups – or even the way they approach the study of the past – is not the same. For instance, "Hinduism: one or many" is not an issue with India's ordinary populace; we are quite happy to follow the traditional way of life of a 'Hindu' within the over-arching framework of Brahmanism. However, the 'elite' class we have referred to finds no difficulty in arguing that Hinduism existed primarily as an amalgam of different sects before the Western Indologists invented it, so to speak, as a unified religion (Thapar 1989). The fact that very early in India's religious history emphasis was put on monism despite a plurality of gods and goddesses and the fact that most of the devout Hindus worship gods and goddesses of all these 'sects' in the course of their journey through life mean hardly anything to this class. Apart from such instances of 'Hindu-baiting', one may also point out that most of the historical research in modern India is focussed either on the contemporary issues or on the history of the last 200-odd years. In both cases the sources written in English constitute the basic historical documentation. The point is that the different ways in which the sense of India's past has affected different socio-economic and other groups of Indians and the implications they have for the future of this is something which provides a singular field of research.

IV.1. The Present Argument

The present argument is rooted in this context. It seeks to outline the kind of past which has so long been offered to Indians and define why this past is unsuitable for providing a common historical platform to all Indians. My focus is on a notion of India which has been built up by about two centuries of Indological research since the late eighteenth century.

The history of this research can be undertaken both in terms of different subjects and different themes. However, there is also an underlying conceptual framework which, in the course of its long history, has no doubt seen some modifications and undergone some variations in emphasis, but is still in place. In a study undertaken in 1994-95 I defined this framework as being based essentially on racism and the premise of race-language-culture correlation (Chakrabarti 1997). This was preceded by a chapter on this in *Theoretical Issues in Indian Archaeology* in 1989. Edward Said (1978: 322) pointed out that racism was a scarcely concealed part of Orientalism. He himself did not elaborate on the issue, nor has there been any detailed examination of this premise in Indology. One can dispense with 'racism' in the present context, although I must say that the boundless arrogance and the claims to superiority which the Western Indological writings have frequently arrogated to itself have already led to a situation where the Western Indologists – and not infrequently Western archaeologists specialising in India too – write essentially for other Western Indologists and archaeologists. There should be a very clear awareness of this in India. However, the thrust of my present paper is not to elaborate this argument which I have done in some detail in my *Colonial Indology: Sociopolitics of the Ancient Indian Past* (Chakrabarti 1997). The emphasis here is only to show how the theoretical framework of race-language-culture correlation emerged in the context of India and how the Indian historians accepted it.

IV.1.1. The Race-Language-Culture Framework in Colonial India

By the beginning of the nineteenth century, scholars in Europe had already infused a language element into the concept of race. The idea of a masterful race of people coming down from the heights of Caucasus or other highlands of central Asia and marching towards Europe gained currency during that period (Poliakov 1974: 187-91). Perhaps nobody did more to take this group of people to India than F. Max Muller around the middle of that century. According to him, there were at least two races of men in India, "distinct in mind as well as in body" (Max Muller 1854: 342) – the Aryan settlers and the aboriginals. In fact, the idea that the "immigrant Brahmanical races" drove the earlier inhabitants of India into the jungles can be traced much earlier in a book by the French missionary, J.A. Dubois. The book was published around 1820 by the British Indian government but its manuscript was ready by 1806 (Pope 1879). In 1849 Brian Hodgson (1849) preferred to put all non-Aryans under the category of a "Tamulian race" and he argued that the unity of this race was demonstrable through linguistic means, just as it had been the case with the Aryans. In 1856 Robert Caldwell (1875) speculated about the "Dravidian physical type". Ethnological studies began in right earnest with people like George Campbell (1866) who in his classification of Indian population considered physical appearance, language, laws, manners and moral characteristics. He wrote of three main physical types: Caucasian, Mongolian and Negrito. He was not enthusiastic about introducing a separate 'Dravidian' group to the scene; he attributed Caldwell's Dravidian premise to "his amiable enthusiasm for his beloved Dravidians", this being an allusion to the fact that Caldwell was a missionary in Madras.

Craniological studies based on the cephalic and nasal indices and supplemented by the studies of the type of hair and the colour of the skin came into sharp focus by the 1880s. Throughout the 1880s, 1890s and later, H.H. Risley published extensively on the Indian situation (cf. Risley 1903; for a detailed discussion on Risley and the roots of his ideology, Chakrabarti 1997: 116-129). He established seven main Indian physical types, all with some linguistic implications; Mongoloid, Mongolo-Dravidian, Aryo-Dravidian, Indo-Aryan, Scytho-Dravidian, Turco-Iranian and Dravidian.

As far as the notions of Indian racial types, their history and the issues of racial links with different aspects of Indian culture are concerned, Risley's publications consolidate the earlier hypotheses, offer a forceful image of India's racial components and history on the basis of anthropometric measurements, and formulate, in fact, an authoritative version of India's past (Chakrabarti 1997: 122).

The Risley framework remained for long the essential framework of Indian racial studies. The most important attempt to modify and elaborate Risley's scheme was by B.S. Guha and J.H. Hutton in 1933 (Hutton 1933). It is also important to mention that the first detailed linguistic survey of India by G.A. Grierson (for a summary, Grierson 1909) was undertaken at the time when Risley was conducting his ethnological survey. Incidentally, Grierson repeatedly uses such terms as "Dravidian ethnic characteristics".

IV.1.2. The Acceptance of the Race-Language-Culture Framework by Indian Historians and Archaeologists

It is only in the 1880s that one can detect the first major *Indian* statements about the ancient Indian past. This fact has to be viewed in the context of the nascent nationalism among the Indian upper class of that period. The Indian National Congress, a political party requesting more self-rule, was founded in 1885. The first major publication in this regard was a three-volume study of *A History of Civilization in Ancient India Based on Sanskrit Literature* by R.C. Dutt (1889), a member of the Indian Civil Service. There is a considerable emphasis on "wonder that was India" in these volumes, but this was accompanied by a constant refrain that all the 'wonder' lay only in the 'intellectual and religious life of the Hindus' and there was a sad 'absence of genius in the people at large in the ordinary pursuits and trades – in mechanical inventions and maritime discoveries, in sculpture, architecture and arts, in manifestations of popular life and the assertion of popular power" (Dutt 1889, vol. I: 5). This is a complete and mindless acceptance of the attitude of Max Muller and other Western Indologists of the time to India. Secondly, it was assumed to be the story of "a gifted Aryan people".

The Aryan hypothesis bound the ruling Englishmen and the upper castes or the ruling elite of the Hindus together. Attention has been drawn to the report of an Indian exclaiming in a Calcutta newspaper in 1874: "we were niggers at one time. We now become brethren". On the English side, the Aryan heritage made them appear as the inheritors of an ancient tradition to regenerate or re-educate the now-degenerated brothers or cousins just as the early group of Aryans introduced civilization in the land.

Colonial Indology led to the formation of this Indian identity. All subsequent protohistoric discoveries, including the discovery of the Indus civilization, were fitted into the Aryan–non-Aryan framework. The tradition continues (cf. Singh 1995). The proselytisation of the Aryan idea by Max Muller was, in fact, a watershed in the formation of Indian upper class identity. It is this identity which has since then been resplendent in Indian mind. We may cite three well-spaced post-Independence examples:

(1) The history of India is mainly that of the Aryans of India (Mookerji 1956: 48)

(2) The foundation of the civilization of India was truly laid in the glorious epoch when the people who called themselves 'Aryas' colonized one district after another of this country (Bhargava 1971: 1)

(3) The horse is an animal which is not native to India and was brought in by the Aryans from Iran and Central Asia .... The Aryans, when they settled in various parts of north India, were hostile to the indigenous people whom they referred to as 'Dasas' and 'Dasyus' (Thapar 1997: 41).

Archaeologists have not fared any better. The Aryan-Dravidian scheme provided the most significant theoretical focus of post-Independence Indian archaeology till the late 1960s and early 1970s and is still very much on the mind of sundry practitioners of the subject. Colonial Indology is still far from being dead in the portals of south Asian archaeology.

V. THE NEED FOR A DIFFERENT PAST IN MODERN INDIA

It has to be made clear that the Aryan identity held no charm for the depressed among the Indian castes. Many great Indian nationalist leaders had no appetite for racial theories because of their divisive character; usually we find no reference to such ideas in the writings of, say, a person like Mahatma Gandhi. Opposition came from the leader of the depressed castes, B.R. Ambedkar (1946, 1970 reprint: 73-74) who criticized this theory on two grounds. First, he found the theory based on 'nothing but pleasing assumptions and the inferences based on such assumptions'. Secondly, according to him, it is 'preconceived and facts are selected to prove it'. He also underlined the role of Indian upper castes in the perpetuation of this theory in India.

> The Brahmin believes in the two-nation theory. He claims to be the representative of the Aryan race and he regards the rest of the Hindus as descendants of the non-Aryans. The theory helps him to establish his kinship with the European races and share their arrogance and superiority. He likes particularly that part of the theory which makes the Aryan an invader and a conqueror of the non-Aryan native races.

For it helps him to maintain and justify his overlordship over the non-Brahmins.

B.R. Ambedkar was the law member in the Viceroy's Executive Council, chaired the drafting committee of the Constitution of modern India, and led the neo-Buddhist movement of the 1950s.

It is, however, not enough to dismantle the old colonial Indological identity of India. It is imperative to put in its place a sense of identity which can be shared by all categories of Indians. The knowledge, on which this new sense of identity should be based, can only be archaeological knowledge, because, whatever may be the religious and philosophical significance of our ancient textual corpus, it cannot yield in necessary detail any time-bound and area-bound perspective of the history of the Indian people. However, it is precisely this sense of over-riding importance of archaeological data in the reconstruction of ancient India which had been by and large ignored in our nationalist tradition. This point will need a brief but pointed analysis.

India also needs a new past because the entire Aryan premise is a racist premise based on nothing more than a series of suppositions from the beginning to the end. It was easy for this racist premise to model itself on that of the Europeans moving out and taking possession of the globe just as the ancient Aryans moved out of their 'homeland' and took possession of much of the ancient world.

VI. A RECENT QUESTIONING OF THE BASIS OF ARYAN HYPOTHESIS: ALAN DAVIES AND CHRISTOPHER HUTTON

I cited Alan Davies' opinion on the Aryan issue in my book *Nationalism in the Study of Ancient Indian History*, and considering the importance of his analysis of how the Aryan idea was shaped by various historical forces in modern Europe, I prefer to draw attention to his opinion again.

Alan Davies' article is titled 'the Aryan myth: its religious significance' (*Studies in Religion*, 1981) regarding the context of its ideological origins. Davies writes the following:

> Thus the Aryan myth, the great myth of the European racists, a myth that cast a halo of racial supremacy around the head of white humanity, arose spontaneously on the intellectual, scientific, and spiritual soil of modern Europe. It could not have arisen in its classic form in any other place at any other time. Not merely the findings of Darwinian biology and physical anthropology, but the study of language and history as well, seemed to confirm its claims. Even art lent its existence, for the glorification of Greek aesthetic ideals that had begun during the Renaissance produced a model of the perfect human shape, the most beautiful type of man, against which it was easy for Europeans to measure other inferior, that is, aesthetically less pleasing types. Ancient canons of bodily proportion informed the nineteenth-century white European's idealization of himself – the so-called Aryan image. Literature also made its contribution, for a romantic preoccupation with the literary and folklorist past of the European nations with their newly stirred sense of national consciousness stimulated the creation of myths of national origin with racial connotations (e.g., the Frankish myth in France, the Anglo-Saxon myth in England, the Teutonic myth in Germany) and these prepared the way for an overarching race-myth that would embrace itself.
>
> The rise of racism, moreover, coincided with the age of imperialism and the consolidation of the huge colonial empires of the major Western states, although the only great European state destined to adopt racism as an official ideology was the state that felt cheated of empire by its rivals. Hence, the social Darwinians could infer white supremacy from the white man's conquest of the world, and in the same breath, vindicate this conquest on the basis of an innate white supremacy; such inference was, for obvious reasons, a peculiarly British temptation. All of these factors merged in the fashioning of the Aryan myth as the logical rationale of institutions widely shared.

The beauty of this analysis by Davies lies in the fact that he has clearly isolated the European soil composed of different angles and different ideas, in which the Aryan idea was but a natural growth. As I wrote,

> Davies' article provides insight into the various facets of European culture which all led to the formation of the Aryan myth, including the myth of an Aryan Jesus.

What is tragic in modern archaeological literature is the continued *a priori* acceptance of the notion of Aryans as a linguistic and biological entity under the guise of 'archaeo-linguistics' and 'archaeo-genetics'. The modern purveyors of this notion seem to be regrettably unaware of the different elements of the historical context in which the idea took shape as a way of looking at the historical changes and the historical world. Nor do they seem to be aware that by infusing an element of biology in the mixture in the form of DNA studies, they are departing from the long-accepted historical axiom that biology has no meaningful relationship with the course of human history. The same is true of the languages as well. Has there been any proof that the historical changes of a given area have been due to the language or languages spoken there? On the contrary, they seem to have forgotten that the infusion of biological element as a factor in human history had brought about genocide on a grand scale in the recent past in Europe and elsewhere in the world. As far as India is concerned, my opinion is clear (2021):

> As far as India is concerned, I cannot think of a single Aryan theory which can stand the scrutiny of logic for a moment. You have to accept a whole series of pre-suppositions before you can even think of an Aryan migration to India at a specific point of time or can consider the Aryans as a distinct human cultural and linguistic group in any context. The lobby, which accepts the Aryans as a human group with the volition to move about but considers India as their

> homeland, only tries to invoke a late 18th century notion that India sent out civilizing groups to the West in remote past. As one who has no appetite for bizarre theories based on only a chain of unverifiable subjective assumptions I shall claim that any theory invoking the mythical Aryans should have no place in an objective history of India which can be based only on verifiably dated sets of data. I am not sure if the Aryan idea has been associated in India with an ideological underpinning of the caste system and consequent social injustices where the Brahmins with imaginary Aryan descent were allotted the primary position, but the possibility of such an argument behind caste oppressions, especially in the south, exists.

Christopher Hutton takes the issue further, questioning the very basis of all the supposed fundamentals in this connection – whether the supposed language similarities are acceptable and posit a 'proto' or 'base' language and whether this in turn posits a homeland. Considering the importance of Hutton's argument, its summary may be given in detail:

> The question arises as to whether there is an objective linguistic fact of the matter determinable by an academic expert in relation to whether two language varieties are cognate or variants of the same underlying system and whether they can be traced back to a common ancestor and yield evidence about place of origin, migration patterns, etc. For academic Indology and historical linguistics, there is a real scholarly debate to be identified beneath the layers of ideological contestation in the Aryan debates, even in relation to the homeland question .... However the Aryan paradigm, with its assumptions about the evidentiary status of linguistic reconstruction, is itself open to sceptical objection, even from within the discipline. The Romance scholar Ernst Pulgram called any reconstructed language 'something of a fiction' .... Absent non-linguistic evidence that the proto-language actually existed, 'any *a priori* association of speakers with this fictitious tongue is absurd'. It was akin to 'solving an equation in which both members are unknown'.

My contention is that there never was an Aryan language, homeland, people, or race in any meaningful sense, and that the concept is a projection of late European assumptions about the relation between language and identity as they developed from the early modern period into the Romantic era. The massive scholarly and ideological edifice is built on a basic flaw in reasoning, namely that a set of correspondences between attested languages implies an original speech community (ethnic group, race ...) with an identifiable homeland. This reflects a more basic assumption that an identifiable language implies a well-defined community, group, ethnicity, or race (the terminology varies with academic fashion), either in the present or at some definitive point in the past. In this sense the basic principles and methods of Indo-European linguistics are fundamentally flawed, and, the erudition deployed there notwithstanding, its conclusions are in scholarly terms no more authoritative than the methods and typologies of racial theorists. The Indo-European paradigm depends on a search for earlier unities that can be reconstructed from perceived diversities. On those grounds alone, it can be categorized as a scholarly form of myth-making. No amount of evidence can settle a mythical question. There is a direct parallel with the search for the site of the lost city of Atlantis or the "lost land of Lemuria" .... The homeland question is a particularistic variant of the search for the Garden of Eden. Max Müller used the term the "Aryan paradise" ..., and his writings form part of a literature which evoked an Aryan "Romantic utopia" ....

From this it follows that I agree with the argument ... that Western linguistic theorizing created a rift or schism in the population of India. I arrive at this conclusion ... since I do not accept the validity of any "genetic" distinctions drawn between language families. I regard this as yet another ill-conceived quasi-biological metaphor within the discipline of linguistics, reflecting as it does a characteristic hedging

> about whether it is languages or peoples that are being classified. Linguistics has constantly shifted responsibility for toxic political ideologies onto race theory (as if according to a slogan, "language good, race bad"), yet it was study of language that provided the conceptual architecture of modern understandings of diversity, especially for the emergent discipline of racial anthropology .... The Aryan Invasion Theory and the linguistic-ethnic distinction drawn between Aryan and Dravidian has had, arguably, much more damaging and long-lasting consequences for post-colonial India than the colonial-era introduction of racial anthropology.
>
> .... The Aryan story is one with no evident beginning, given the contentious nature both of the history and the historiography. It is a hall of mirrors with no identifiable referent.

The Aryan story regrettably does not end here, despite Hutton's remarkably sharp questioning of its foundations which have been adduced in various forms since the formation of the hypothesis – whether the relationship between different languages can be established in the way it has been 'established' by comparative philologists; whether this relationship can lead to the postulate of a 'proto' language and whether this 'proto' language implies in turn an original homeland. The postulated theories of migrations which are supposed to have taken place in different directions from this 'homeland', often try to base themselves on archaeology but in all cases the archaeological chain of reasoning is non-existent and arbitrary including history and archaeology. They do not have any leg to stand on and like the hypothesis itself purely imaginary. To us, the basic historical question is not the validity of the Aryan hypothesis but the fact that this has affected a whole range of studies for such a long period and begun to influence even some premises of genome studies. Which dark recesses of our historical mind that this imaginary racist hypothesis appeals to?

It is certainly a case of having appeal to a dark recess of our historical mind. This must not be swept aside and hidden under the carpet. We forget that the waves of killing which human history has undergone in its different phases have got a lot to do with the feeling of separation between different human groups. Take the case of those who believe in the concepts of archaeo-linguistics and archaeo-genetics. In a multi-ethnic country like India with different language families and languages these concepts are disastrous and will only drive home the difference between vast masses of Indians. If all these human groups seek their own trajectories of civilizational development on the basis of languages and biological elements (cf. DNA), the result from the point of view of the unity of the nation will be totally disastrous. We Indians cannot go into the mindless language-based or DNA-based sophistries. The importance of Hutton's paper is that it clearly outlines and expresses the limitations and pitfalls of the various assumptions on which the theories like the Aryan hypothesis are based and with which the people like the present author have felt unhappy since the beginning of their career. We Indians also tend to forget that a new form of racism has already raised its ugly head in the country after various people have gone overboard with enthusiasm to seek various, often unverified, inferences regarding the DNA basis of Indian populations. The insults which the students from the northeastern parts of India are frequently reported to suffer in the Indian capital are singularly unfortunate and only show the danger of reaching conclusions regarding human history on the basis of languages or biological elements.

In the case of India this has determined for long how we look at the historical trajectory of the Indian universe and how we consider the entire corpus of Vedic literature, the earliest and singularly diverse corpus of Indian literature as something created by people with foreign origins and wide-reaching foreign links. Although there is not a scrap of acceptable material data to support its veracity, people still continue to believe in its basic premise and try to thwart all attempts to offer a verifiable and cohesive column of India's ancient past. That it is possible to do so on the strength of the archaeological data alone has been demonstrated by the present author (Chakrabarti 1999, 2006, 2009) but if the reading lists of the Indian university syllabi are concerned, this approach and thus the relevant publications by the present author cannot be claimed to have made much headway.

In his review of Asko Parpola's book *The Roots of Hinduism: The Early Aryans and the Indus Civilization* (2015), Varun Singh ('origin of Hindu religion and Sanskrit in Central Asia: a recent claim and its rebuttal', *Indian Historical Review* 2017, no.1) makes some comments with which the present author agrees wholly.

> Any possibility that Sanskrit as a language and the Vedic tradition could have evolved in India remains an anathema in the eyes of the Europeans and the cause of relentless attacks on India. Had the evidence used in support of placing India in a peripheral position been credible and secure and product of sound and unbiased scholarship, then, of course we Indians will have no grounds to contest or challenge the dominant European and Western mind set. But the facts ... speak otherwise. Assertions and claims, even though put forward with unshakeable conviction, when looked critically appear to be based on beliefs and assumptions, and not compelling or credible evidence.

In his notes to Varun Singh's paper, the present author commented that the origin of the Aryan linguistic theory, formulated by William Jones, was based on the Biblical theory of creation and thus irrelevant to the present context. Comparative philology, whatever claim it may make, should be kept out of historical studies because it does not have any independent basis of dating. The fact that the Aryan idea, essentially a racist idea, has still its hold over a large number of scholars throws more light on the personality of these scholars than on anything else. Further, the DNA study did not develop to verify or reject racial and linguistic ideas which originated mostly in the 19th century. There is no reason why the DNA view of human groups should be brought within the fold of archaeology or history. Nor should the modern human groups be unduly excited over the types of DNA they carry. The simplest fact is that they bear no relationship with the way their historical evolution has been unravelled. Our claim is that the very first step towards a nationalist archaeology of India should have nothing to do with the linguistic or physical elements of the country's population.

VII. MARGINAL POSITION OF ARCHAEOLOGY IN THE INDIAN NATIONALIST TRADITION: A CASE-STUDY OF BENGAL

Because of my personal limitations, I can discuss the theme only with reference to the nationalist tradition in Bengal and the related Bengali literature. Other regional literary traditions should also be analysed by archaeologists from this point of view. However, even in my limited context I can discuss the theme only in its outline. The importance of monuments and similar other remains was no doubt realised by people like Rajendra Lal Mitra by the late 19th century, –and Henry Vivian Derozio (1809-1831), a noted Anglo-Indian poet of Calcutta who wrote in English, composed a poem on the rock-cut monument of Jahangeera by the side of the Ganga at Sultanganj between Bhagalpur and Munger in Bihar – but it would be wrong to claim that archaeological data *per se* played a role in the contemporary national consciousness. In his attempt to trace 'the genealogy of modern historiography in Bengal' Partha Chatterjee (1994) has pointed out how by 1878 the emphasis on the idea of the Hindus as being of *Arya-Vamsa* (Aryan lineage) was fully in place in such Bengali writings as Tarinicharan Chattopadhyay's *Bharatvarsher Itihas* ('History of India').

> What distinguishes the giant from the dwarf or the mighty from the frail is nothing compared to the difference between the ancient and the modern Hindu. In earlier times, foreign travellers in India marvelled at the courage, truthfulness and modesty of the people of the Arya *Vamsa*; now they remark mainly on the absence of those qualities. (cited in Chatterjee 1994: 28)

Further,

> In ancient times, when virtually the whole world was shrouded in the darkness of ignorance, the pure light of learning shone brightly in India. The discoveries in philosophy which emanated from the keen intellects of ancient Hindus are arousing the enthusiasm of European scholars even today. (Chatterjee 1994: 29)

It is an interesting reflection of the spirit of the times that the nationalist Indian Tarinicharan decided to produce certificates from the colonial Indologists to claim that ancient Indian philosophy was glorious.

Chatterjee (1994: 29) writes:

> If the nineteenth-century Englishman could claim ancient Greece as his classical heritage, why should not the English-educated Bengali feel proud of the achievements of the so-called Vedic civilization.

The point of difference is that "the nineteenth-century Englishman" and his eighteenth-century ancestors contributed enormously to the building up of the notion of a pure 'classical heritage' through original studies including extensive antiquarian field-investigations, whereas Tarinicharan and his ilk were happy enough only to brandish testimonials from their colonial masters. The only offshoot of this Bengali interest was the translation of some Sanskrit texts including the *Rigveda* in Bengali. As far as archaeological field-investigations are concerned, one is not sure if these nationalists, with the exception of people like Rajendra Lal Mitra, were particularly aware of the significance of the work of Alexander Cunningham and others in this direction. There was also hardly any excavation conducted in India in the nineteenth century.

Towards the end of the nineteenth century, there was a shift of interest in the Bengali nationalist writings on history, language and culture from the 'Vedic civilization' to the far more mundane items of Bengali heritage – mainly literature and folklore. The establishment of *Bangiya Sahitya Parishad* as a continuation of the Bengal Academy of Literature (established on 23 July, 1893, at the house of *Maharajkumar* Binay Krishna Bahadur at 2/2 Raja Nabakrishna Street, Sobhabajar, Calcutta) was a milestone in this regard. The aim of the Bengal Academy of Literature, established mainly due to the initiative taken by L. Leotard and Kshetrapal Chakrabarti, was to improve, and attain the spread of, Bengali literature with the help of English and Sanskrit literatures. The proceedings of the Academy began to be published – mostly in English – in a monthly magazine of the same name. The emphasis on English to improve the lot of Bengali led to a debate, and the Bengali version of the Academy's name, *Bangiya Sahitya Parishad*, was proposed by U.C. Batabyal and generally accepted. For a time the monthly magazine of the Academy was published under both the English and Bengali titles – Bengal Academy of Literature in English and *Bangiya Sahitya Parishad* in Bengali. In April, 1894 the English name was dropped and the Academy began to meet under its Bengali name. This reconstitution owed much to the efforts of Sarat Chandra Das, Hirendranath Datta and *Maharajkumar* Binay Krishna Bahadur. The first chairman of the *Parishad* was Ramesh Chandra Datta (already cited by us as R.C. Dutt), with Nabin Chandra Sen and Rabindra Nath Thakur as Deputy Chairmen and Debendra Nath Mukhopadhyay and L. Leotard as Secretaries. According to the first clause of the rules of the *Parishad*, "*Bangiya Sahitya Parishad* will discuss Bengali books or Bengali language and literature", and according to the second clause anybody with an interest in Bengali literature could be a member.

The foregoing details are available in the first annual statement of the *Parishad*, which was published by its Executive Committee from 2/2 Raja Nabakrishna Street in B.S. 1302. Almost right from the beginning there was emphasis on introducing Bengali as a medium of examination in the lower levels and listing technical words of chemistry, botany and mathematics in Bengali.

In the first part of the *Parishad*'s journal in 1894 Ramesh Chandra Datta wrote the following:

> Fifty years ago we used to get educated in Western learning – even now we are educated in that and hope that this will continue for a long time. Fifty years ago we had no riches of our own; we used to move about like beggars. However, today we have a little wealth of our own. Madhusudan (Datta) and Bankim Chandra (Chattopadhyay) are its main collectors. Now we speak of Bengali literature with pride, care for it with affection and tend it filial devotion. With wealth we have gained a little strength; whatever we think of – politics, ancient history, literature, ancient religion –, we have learnt how to take pride in our own wealth in these matters. Today we are no mere panegyrists of foreigners; we are not averse to our own manners and way of life; we are not fools in the field of our history, and we do not neglect our religion. It is as if we have gained a little strength, developed a little courage, recognized our national wealth and learnt the spirit of our national religion. This is a sign of progress and also a sign of goodness. May we continue to move forward along this path.

Archaeology – *Pratnatattva* – is missing from this list. In consonance with the *Parishad*'s spirit, the betterment of the vernacular literature was the main cry, and whatever progress or modernity was achieved in this detection by 1894 was not more than 50 years old.

The need for learning in vernaculars was not realized only by people like R.C. Dutt but also by some contemporary British administrators of India. The annual convocation address of Calcutta University delivered by the vice-chancellor Alfred Croft on 3rd February, 1894 is one of the clear indications of this trend. In the course of his address he cites the following opinion of one of his predecessors and extends to it his own warm support.

> The Bengali language has now a rich literature that is well worthy of study ... I firmly believe that we cannot have any thorough and extensive culture as a nation, unless knowledge is disseminated through our own vernaculars. Consider the lesson that the past teaches. The darkness of the middle ages of Europe was not completely dispelled until the light of knowledge shone through the medium of numerous modern languages. So in India, notwithstanding the benign radiance of knowledge that has shone on the highest levels of our Society through one of the clearest media that exist, the dark depths of ignorance all around will never be illumined until the light of knowledge reaches the masses through the medium of their own vernaculars. (Croft 1894/1301 B.S.)

It is also in the same issue of the journal that Debendra Nath Mukhopadhyay wrote on the necessity of a 'national literature'. The only thing related to ancient history in this volume is an anonymous summary of what was already published in English on the Gupta period Susunia rock inscription of Bankura. Any mention of the importance of antiquarian investigations is missing in the early volumes of the *Parishad*'s journal, although there is a conscious emphasis on the collection of old Bengali manuscripts to discover the history of Bengali literature. This substantiates my claim that archaeology or the need to relate ancient Indian texts and history to the ground formed no part of the Indian nationalist thought.

From this point of view, Rabindranath's essay on *Bharatvarsher Itihas* (Bharatvarsha's History) in B.S. 1309 (1902) is a remarkable and inexplicable exception which does not fit in with anything written by his contemporaries about the Indian past and foreshadows much of what is being perceived by nationalists about a hundred years later. He wrote that in the history of India that he read there was no place for Indians and that it brought about a sense of separation between Indians and India. 'A complete history of India' – that was what he hoped for.

The literary specialists in Rabindranath's writings should systematically analyse and contextualise his thoughts on Indian history. As I look around, I find that the period which occupies most of the Indian historians' attention is only the history of the country under the British rule, and that too, on the basis of sources written in English. The historical research related to the earlier periods has become virtually moribund in modern India. If one goes beyond various sectarian views and does a stock-taking of historical research on the pre-British period throughout the country, one realizes that there is not much current work based on a well-developed expertise to handle primary sources in original.

It is not wholly true that the spirit reflected in the establishment of *Bangiya Sahitya Parishad* did not find any expression in the antiquarian field-research. To some extent, the district-subdivision-village level enquiries which have been undertaken by ordinary Bengalis since the late 19th century and published in Bengali is related to this spirit. Tarapada Santra (B.S. 1407) has provided a thorough list of such writings, and it may be useful to research the extent to which they are based on original field-investigations and the extent to which they owed their structures and contents to the various relevant District Gazetteers brought out by the Government. However, it was primarily in the literary field that there were major achievements and perhaps it is not a matter of surprise that the most important multifaceted volume on Bengal's past – *Brihat Banga* (1935) – was published by Dines Chandra Sen whose scholarly reputation is based on his contributions to the study of the history of Bengali literature. This tradition of historical research has continued till today among the students of Bengali literature, some examples (cf. *Rabi-Jibani* by Prasanta Kumar Pal; the writings of Sudhir Chakrabarti on various obscure religious sects still surviving in the countryside) being based on grassroots investigation and of outstanding merit. In the historical field I remember the volumes of *Kausiki* which was founded by Tarapada Santra and now continued under the editorship of Indrajit Chaudhuri. I am not familiar with the journal *Itihas* published by *Paschim Banga Itihas Sanshad* but have been told by Jayanta Sengupta that it has developed a tradition of publishing articles based on knowledge of the local Bengali sources. In the same vein I recall the excellent web-site put up by Ambarish Goswami on Chandraketugarh, the first site-focussed web-site of its kind in India. What is important to note is that this tradition has flourished completely away from the mainstream historical research tradition of the country. I would even say that the study of Indian history is unlikely to move out its neo-colonial ruts till there is a much wider awareness among the general educated public, especially the scientists, that historical research is a part of the general curiosity about the land and should not be considered the exclusive preserve of different coteries of our professional historians.

In her outstanding scholarly analysis of historical writings in Bengali, *Indology, Historiography and the Nation, Bengal 1847-1947*, Krishna Bhattacharya Samaddar (2015) points out that the Bengali scholars, when they wrote professionally on the region's history, they did so in English but most of them wrote in Bengali as well, and when they wrote in Bengali, they dwelt on various social and political problems of the day. Some of them, even the eminent ones like Rakhaldas Bandopadhyay and Haraprasad Sastri, took recourse to writing historical novels in Bengali, giving expression to their feelings about Bengal's and the nation's past. An important aspect of these novels, as I recollect, is their sonorous prose evoking the landscape of different parts of the country. Partha Chatterjee in his 'foreword' to this book cites Niharranjan Ray's opinion that the picture of the nation which emerges from these writings is likely to be a federal image. It may be important to note that history of different parts of India has its special points and the regional historians are likely to put extra emphasis on those special points. It is not at all unlikely that the native historians of Maharashtra will be concerned primarily with the Satavahanas in the ancient context and with Sivaji in the pre-modern context. That does not mean that the image of the nation in Maharashtra is in any way different from that in, say, Bengal. Bengal in her turn has been more concerned with the regional dynasties of the Palas and Senas. On close examination, there is absolutely no reason to argue that the Maharashtrian notion of nationhood and the Bengali notion of the same are different. Further, we need not take the section on *Kulaji* in Das Samaddar's book seriously; *Kulajis* do not necessarily signify collective memory. More likely, they only mean artificial bolstering of the image of certain families or groups of people. Such myth-making always goes on but that does not really fall under the purview of serious historical analysis. An important offshoot of Bengal's concern with regional histories is the set of books which came to be written on the history of various Bengal districts from Mymensingh to Jessore-Khulna. These volumes are to some extent based on the district gazetteers compiled by Englishmen, but as general handbooks of the history of various Bengal districts they still retain their value. If one has to comment further on the general trend of Bengal's historiography, we have to point out that it was subject much to the premises of the hypothetical and uncorroborated ideas of the contemporary ethnography, folk-culture and comparative philology. Calcutta University had, in fact, set up a chair of comparative philology long back.

Coming to Bengal, we must give up the notion that Bengal had set up an objective tradition of historical research. I would say that it was no better than the contemporary tradition in other parts of India, i.e. an unholy mix of race, language and culture. To give an example of how it has continued to the present day, I would cite a piece published in *Anandabazar Patrika* of 16 April, 2021, which speaks of the element of Bengaliness flowing through the veins of a population – *rakte bangaliyana*. It is precisely such notions that give rise to xenophobia of various kinds in modern populations and has to be discarded on this ground alone.

VIII. SOME INGREDIENTS OF A NATIONALIST INDIAN ARCHAEOLOGY

The themes will vary from person to person and are also likely to be multi-layered. The fundamental thing, as far as I can understand it, is to view the archaeology and history of the land mass of *Bharatavarsha* in its own terms. From this point of view, the interaction of Indian history and archaeology with her geography plays a crucially important role, and in any nationalist endeavour geography should come in a big way.

(1) The first major theme should aim at a better understanding of the nuances of the interrelationship between geography and history in understanding south Asia's 'foreign' contacts. This land mass must have constantly interacted with her neighbouring regions, but there has to be a clearly defined geographical framework of this interaction. A clear distinction may be made between the direct 'foreign impacts' such as those created by the British rule and those of the earlier centuries when both the origins and the nature of such 'impacts' were mediated by some geographical parameters. In other words, a distinction has to be made between

'foreignness' and what emanates from the neighbouring, historically linked areas with decided geopolitical ties to the subcontinent. According to this argument, the Arab invasion of Sind was a foreign invasion but the whole series of the so-called 'foreign' inroads from the Indo-Greeks to the Mughals reflected only the significance of the close geopolitical ties of the subcontinent with the region stretching up to eastern Iran and the southern part of central Asia. On geopolitical considerations, this region cannot be considered 'foreign' in Indian history. The same thing may be said about the Ahom invasion of the Brahmaputra valley because the area from which the Ahoms moved to the Brahmaputra valley lay virtually at the doorstep of this riverine plain with which it had close traditional links. What we are trying to say is that there has to be a clear understanding of the difference between the 'frontiers' and 'boundaries' in the understanding of Indian history. 'Boundaries' are political constructs, subject to the vicissitudes of historical events. 'Frontiers' are more abiding historical realities and cannot always be considered 'foreign' to the core area.

This simple geographical premise seems to impart a different perspective to our understanding of many so-called foreign invasions of the country. In 1977 (Chakrabarti 1977), I argued that, in view of the constant political and economic interconnections between its component areas, the Indus valley, the eastern rim of Iran, the southern part of central Asia, Afghanistan and the Kashmir-Ladakh region constituted a distinct geopolitical orbit in the archaeology and history of the subcontinent. It was also argued that this premise had a number of historical implications. First, no component of this broad zone was 'foreign' to India. It was perfectly natural for any ambitious political power of the southern part of central Asia to think of the greener pastures of the Indus valley and beyond. However, to realize his ambition, he would have to consolidate his base first in the south of the Hindukush. The interesting point is that the southern side of the Hindukush is the natural frontier of *Bharatavarsha* in this sector, the Durand Line, the current boundary between Pakistan and Afghanistan, being a political product of only 1893. So, once a power has consolidated itself on the southern flanks of the Hindukush, it can hardly be called a 'foreign' power in the subcontinental context, whatever might have been its original roots. Heliodorus was the emissary of an 'Indo-Greek' king based in Taxila; the content of his inscription shows that he was as much Indian as Greek – in all likelihood more Indian than Greek. Secondly, the extent to which the thrust of power from the Indus-Oxus geopolitical orbit would be successful in moving out to the inner orbit of the Gangetic and Peninsular India would depend on the strength of the political powers based in those regions. On many occasions the Gangetic power stretched itself right up to the southern side of the Hindukush. Further back in time, the mature Indus civilization which extended up to the upper Doab and Gujarat up to the Tapti was the most important factor to reckon with in a vast zone of southern central Asia. Without trying to amplify the theme further in the present context, I would claim that the course of Indian history is in a sense the story of interaction between the two geopolitical orbits of the Indus-Oxus and Gangetic and Peninsular India. The idea is rooted in T.H. Holdich's *The Gates of India* (1910); I elaborated the concept in 1977 and showed its implications on assessing some diffusionary postulates in Indian archaeology. The details will certainly need more careful and detailed research, and among other things, this has the merit of showing that many of the 'foreign' invasions of India cannot be considered 'foreign' at all.

In 2001, on the basis of L.W. Shakespear's *History of Upper Assam, Upper Burmah and North-Eastern Frontier* (1914) I woke up to the significance of the Patkoi route to the Brahmaputra from the Hukong valley watered by the upper Chindwyn in northern Myanmar. It is from this region that the Ahoms migrated to the Brahmaputra valley in the thirteenth century AD and later. Geopolitically the Hukong valley lies at the mouth of the Patkoi route and constitutes a part of India's 'frontier' zone on the east. To this extent, the Ahoms were not 'foreign' either.

About the vast northern Himalayan zone our inference is simple: there are always links between the two saddles of a mountain, as there are traditional links between the Tibetan plateau on the north and the Nepal-India-Bhutan slopes on the south in the case of the Himalayas. The evidence of such links need not be construed as events of subcontinental significance, although the significance of Tibet in the artistic and religious history of Nepal, Bhutan and eastern India and a similar impact of eastern India, Nepal and Bhutan on Tibet need not be denied.

The point we have been trying to make *is that in any nationalist scheme of Indian archaeology the different nuances of the subcontinent's interaction with the frontier zones on the northwest, north and east cannot be ignored. These nuances have to be understood in detail, area by area and period by period.*

(2) Our second point is also geographical, but this time within the strict limits the subcontinent. *Each area has its traditional historical linkages and interacts within the orbit thus created. In its turn, an individual orbit interacts with other orbits, leading thus to an image of many historically interacting orbits within the limits of the subcontinent.* To some extent, such orbits are geopolitical; in 1999 I

pointed out the similarities between the patterns of Satavahana and Maratha expansions, separated by about 2000 years but both with base in the upper Godavari valley (Chakrabarti 1999: 29-30). However, this is more than a geopolitical issue. The linkages, both on the local and subcontinental levels, need close scrutiny. A study of these linkages will demonstrate two things. First, the pan-Indian interaction has been far more rapid than has been thought. In 1996 Nayanjot Lahiri and I (1996) argued that the 'Copper Hoard' implements of the upper Ganga plain were technologically rooted in the northeastern Rajasthan and the related parts of Haryana, that they reflected a 'late Harappan' tradition and that were disseminated along properly defined routes to Gujarat on the one hand and central India, the Deccan and the southern peninsula up to Ramanathapuram district of Tamil Nadu and Kerala on the other. This is not an isolated example. It is now possible to argue for an urban growth in the Kaveri delta and its adjacent region as early as c. 500 BC and K. Rajan, on the basis of whose excavations (Rajan 1997: 75-90) it is now possible to make this claim, argues that there was clear evidence of contact between the Kaveri delta and north India during this period. How many of us have thought that the diagnostic types of early historic pottery are singularly uniform all over the Gangetic valley right up to the Himalayas. The early historic pottery that I found at Ror in Kangra one season was identical with the pottery that I found next season in the cliff of the Damodar at Pokharna in Bankura, West Bengal. Such spreads – such signs of pan-Indian dissemination of cultural traits and other forces – still remain to be studied in detail and their implications emphasised.

(3) Our third point is geographical too. *Within the limits of Bharatavarsha there is hardly any major geographical*

impediment to the movements of people and goods. This point was driven home to me while following the routes between the Ganga plain and the Deccan (cf. Chakrabarti et al. 1999-2000). The lines of movement are still clearly traceable, and although at certain points the terrain is difficult, there is no evidence on the ground to suggest that these occasional difficulties ever stood in the way of human movements along them. The so-called north-south divide in terms of the Vindhya range and the *Agastya Muni* tradition cannot be considered as anything but a myth. The link between the Konkan coast and the hinterland was not easy, but everywhere the geographical lines of linkages are clearly defined. Such lines of linkages all over the subcontinent can be understood at the grassroots level and this understanding will certainly lead to an easier appreciation of its archaeology in its own terms. We do not accept the proposition that some sections of the subcontinent did not fulfil any major role in the mainstream development of its archaeology and history. While working on a sketchy but coherent survey of the Chhotanagpur plateau as a whole (Chakrabarti 1993), I realized that as the most important source of different types of raw materials to the west and south of the lower and middle Ganga plain, this has to be given a major role in the archaeological development of this vast section of the plain. We have found Black-and-Red ware of pre-1000 BC in Singhbhum, which possibly denotes the penetration of the chalcolithic settlers of the plain in this section in search of metals including tin. More extensive evidence of Black-and-Red ware settlements in the plateau has recently been found by R.K. Chattopadhyay, especially in Giridih and Santal Parganas. The so-called 'Asur' sites of Sarat Chandra Roy denote perhaps an organized political unit in the Ranchi plateau and its adjacent territories in the late centuries BC and early centuries AD – a political unit which, if the finds of semiprecious stone beads, Kushan coins, etc. are any indication, was well-linked with the developments in the alluvium below. The plain-plateau interaction was mostly in the form of exchange/trade of raw materials, and the hill valleys precluded large-scale settlements there, but by no stretch of imagination can our jungle tracts be called isolated areas. This is a geographical dimension well worth bearing in mind. Rakesh Tewari's work at Malhar in the upper Karmanasa valley and at Raja Nal-Ka-Tila in the upper Belan valley (cf. Tewari et al. 1999-2000) has highlighted the significance of this 'isolated' zone near Banaras as a major supplier of iron to the Banaras area of the Ganga plain as early as the first half of the second millennium BC. The mid-fifth century BC date for the NBP at Wari Bateshwar in the Meghna delta to the east and northeast of Dhaka (personal information from S.S.M. Rahman of Jahangirnagar University) amplifies that it is very unwise to judge the archaeological significance of an area on the basis of our perception of its geographical position vis-à-vis mainstream development. There must be innumerable examples of this kind from different areas of the subcontinent, and one of the specific angles of nationalist Indian archaeology may be devoted to this theme. *According to my perception the core-periphery concept is not particularly relevant to Indian archaeology, each area having contributed significantly to the make-up of the core.*

(4) I shall make a final point in the context of geography. The interaction between the different sections of the country – the interdependence between them for raw materials – is far more ancient than we realize. If one follows Nayanjot Lahiri's work (Lahiri 1996) – and follows the spread of objects made of different raw

materials at various archaeological sites and then turns to the possible webs of links between the areas where these sites are located and the areas from where it was possible to get the relevant raw materials – one realizes that the country was far more closely intertwined than we are willing to admit and that *the history of this intertwining is very deeply rooted in Indian protohistory.* In the same connection, I would point out that the location of individual sites throws in many cases insight into its geographical linkages or possibilities, such as I have argued for Mahasthangarh (Chakrabarti 2001: chapter 2), among others. This is a trend which can be followed in depth all over the land and may just demonstrate the truth of what Nirmal Kumar Basu wrote on the basis of his close familiarity with the way people actually live in our villages: "There is more unity in India's variety than one is likely to admit in moments of forgetfulness" (Bose 1961).

(5) One of the basic things which need highlighting in nationalist archaeology of the country is that there is a firm and continuous archaeological sequence running through the land and that this process began perhaps as early as the lower Palaeolithic. This does not mean that India was never exposed to interactions with outside areas. *This simply means that there is a demonstrable thread of continuity in India's cultural development right from the very beginning.* Anybody who has looked at our Palaeolithic stratigraphy in the field knows that there is a steady stratigraphic and typological continuity through them. The early hominid movements must have affected India; all that we are saying is that India may have her own story to tell even in this context. The date of 2 million years ago (mya) for the stone tools from Riwat in the Potwar plateau, the date of 1.8 mya for the tools from the Pabbi hills to the east of the Indus, the date of 1+

mya for the extensive Acheulian spread at Isampur and a few other dates going back to three-four hundred thousand years ago have gone a long way to establish the significance and antiquity of the Indian lower Palaeolithic. Above all, some of its features now categorically show the evidence of cognition: R.G. Bednarik's claim that the cup-marks and the narrow, meandering groove associated with them in a rock shelter at Bhimbetka near Ubaidullaganj in Madhya Pradesh belong to the middle Palaeolithic or the upper part of the lower Palaeolithic level of the site and that this may be the earliest example of such cup-marks in the world is worth thinking about. The proof that the Acheulian stage hominids as early as 1 mya (personal information from Michael Petraglia) were quarrying for the raw material used for making their tools at Isampur demonstrates once again that the story of the Indian lower Palaeolithic is in all likelihood far more interesting than we are willing to concede. Dates are more easily available for the middle and upper Palaeolithic, and everywhere there is a great variety, evolution and spread of artefacts, although in cultural terms the evidence is still sketchy, mostly because of the lack of suitable excavations of many of these spreads. However, the insight, which has been obtained into the possible ways of using the resources of their landscape by the upper Palaeolithic people by carefully studying the available 'wild' food-sources of these areas and the ways in which the modern-day hunting and gathering activities in the same area still use them, has in fact been invaluable in appreciating the significance of this phase – something which has also been highlighted by the discovery of an upper Palaeolithic shrine at Baghor in Sidhi in Madhya Pradesh and the finds the Lohanda Nala (Belan valley) bone harpoon, designs on the excavated ostrich egg shells at Patne (Maharashtra), etc. The cultural and economic image of hunting-gathering is sharper with the Mesolithic phase, of which there is a great deal of evidence, including a wide range of rock-art, of different chronologies in many parts of the subcontinent. Similarly, the beginning of food-production in different areas of the country is now a far more complex issue than was previously realized; things have moved much beyond such simplistic beliefs as the diffusion of wheat-barley cultivation from west Asia, of millets from Africa and of rice from China/southeast Asia. *The primary point in all these prehistoric cases is the fact of richness, depth, variety and continuity of India's prehistory. This is something which our nationalist archaeology should consciously strive to highlight and focus on, because now we have advanced far enough in our research to know that many aspects of the grassroots of modern India are rooted in prehistory.* Further, there is no break whatsoever in the Indian prehistoric development; the basic story is that of adaptation of prehistoric people to different areas. *A conscious aim of nationalist research should be to understand this adaptation in all its regional varieties.* Mercifully, this aim can remain uncluttered by the ambiguities of our literary tradition.

The field of protohistoric discoveries in the subcontinent is far-reaching, ranging from the first wheat-barley-based settlements dated c. 7500 BC in Baluchistan to the beginning of the historic period in the Ganga plain and elsewhere around 700 BC and later. The Indus civilization is basically the Bronze Age culmination of the wheat-barley-based Neolithic tradition in India, although this civilization could have significantly incorporated other agricultural traditions too, such as those based on rice and millets. Further, there could be earlier pockets of incipient cultivation, possibly in the form of slash-and-burn and digging sticks tradition, in the zone not directly within the distribution area of the Indus/Harappan civilization. However, the growth of wheat-barley based cultivation, which was certainly aided by ploughs in the first half of the third millennium BC, in the Harappan area, must have had impact on its adjacent territories or the general range of territories with which the mature form of this civilization had contacts for the procurement of raw materials. From this point of view the Harappan tradition contributed to the development of plough-based agricultural tradition of the non-Harappan India. This contribution must have become more direct as the civilization declined and eventually moved on a large scale towards Gujarat, south of the Tapti and the Doab. Throughout the second millennium BC we see a large-scale growth of village settlements in all the major agricultural areas of the subcontinent, and we believe that this derived strength from the dissemination of the Harappan plough-based agricultural tradition in inner India. *Viewed from this angle, there is a strong, connecting thread of continuity between the different geographical orbits and phases of India's protohistoric development, linking up the Harappan tradition and the tradition before that, with the tradition of the Neolithic-Chalcolithic communities of inner India, which culminated in the growth of the early historic period. This point of view makes it possible to view the Indus civilization as the fountainhead of civilization in India.* Archaeologically this is an eminently justifiable view, and both in my *The Archaeology of Ancient Indian Cities* (1995) and *India – an Archaeological History: Palaeolithic Beginnings to Early Historic Foundations* (1999) I have shown that this does no injustice to the current archaeological data. On the other hand, this makes it possible for us modern subcontinentals to view ourselves as the lineal descendants of the Harappan civilization, although with a lot of input from the various regional archaeological streams.

In an earlier section I have summed up my arguments why the notion of an Aryan invasion towards the end of the Indus civilization is a myth with singularly unpleasant implications for us. In fact, the invocation of archaeological data in favour of this invasion – and there have been many invocations of this kind – has been the worst abuse of archaeological data in the Indian context. An increasing number of archaeologists and other scholars are coming round to this view.

The world of Indo-European and Indo-Aryan linguistic scholarship is a bewildering mass of often contradictory, ambiguous and subjective arguments –a will-o'-the-wisp obligingly eager to mislead the archaeologist into linguistic quicksand –, and if Edwin's Bryant's lucid review of the Indo-Aryan migration debate (Bryant 2001) has told us anything, it is that there can be no acceptable rapport between archaeology and comparative philology in this area and that any suggested rapport can only be an article of faith and not the product of any clear and coherent archaeological reasoning. *Our nationalist archaeological position does not have any place for any superior group of people known as the Aryans.* This is something which can be clearly asserted without bending the archaeological evidence in any way, and I am happy that an increasing number of scholars are coming round to this opinion. My first questioning of the Aryan premise is dated 1968 (Chakrabarti 1968), and if anything, my understanding of the racism behind it and the damage it has done for a grassroots understanding of Indian history has become increasingly sharper over the years.

(6) A related theme is about the beginning of various technological innovations in India. Not enough attention has yet been paid to assessing India's part in the story

of the major technological developments in the country's archaeological sequence. Far too often the origin of every development of this kind has been equated to the real or imaginary cultural impulses and/or movements of people from west Asia and beyond. On the other hand, recent archaeological research has categorically shown that in the two most important areas of such innovations, i.e. agriculture and metallurgy, India's own role has been crucial. As far as agriculture is concerned, Harappan agriculture can no longer be considered a mere offshoot of the dissemination of wheat-barley agriculture from Iran, central Asia or elsewhere. The significance of the early Baluchistan development as an independent subcontinental development in this regard is well understood, although we do not for a moment deny the possible significance of the interactions of the contemporary Baluchistan with the other components of such early agricultural development in Iran, central Asia and Afghanistan. What does need detailed attention is the way in which the entire gamut of protohistoric agriculture in the subcontinent took shape and developed. *The richness and diversity of preindustrial Indian agriculture – the richness and diversity of its crops, animal-uses and husbandry practices – remain to be explained in detail, especially with reference to their history. This can be one of the most useful arenas of nationalist archaeological research in the subcontinent.* Similarly, the richness and antiquity of early Indian metallurgy form another significant arena of research of this kind. Whatever little has been done in this field suggests the importance of this research, although in this case the focus should be, not on the rummaging of mostly puerile and stereotyped textual data but on the actual laboratory work on the excavated specimens and different ore bodies. The laboratory work should, of course, be accompanied by excavations of metallurgical sites and in-depth field investigations of preindustrial mining remains. In short, *the story of India's technological achievement is a vast field of nationalist archaeological enquiry.*

It has been far from my intention to try to isolate all the areas and approaches of such a nationalist enquiry. I have only tried to highlight some themes, in the enunciation of which I may be said to have been personally involved. What I have tried to do, however, is to argue that the pursuit of a nationalist goal in archaeology is entirely justified as long as this does not bend archaeological data and is not used as an intellectual support for chauvinism. Further, in such multi-ethnic nation-states as India the notion of the ancient past should not be based on the perceived and historically evolving and changing ethnic, linguistic and other differences but on the story of their interactions and common achievements. A positive archaeological attitude to these achievements is both necessary and justified.

After I prepared this paper I read Nathali Richard's article on "archaeological arguments in national debates in late 19th-century France: Gabriel de Mortillet's *La Formation de la nation francaise* (1897)" in *Antiquity*, March 2002. There are some similarities between what I have argued in this paper and what de Mortillet, who is better known as the person who offered a detailed classificatory scheme of the French Palaeolithic, wrote in his book on the formation of the French nation in 1897.

First, according to him, "the nation is exclusively a geopolitical entity ... in which the diversity of ethnic and linguistic origins is overcome by the unifying power of shared sentiments". Secondly, only prehistory (in our case, archaeology) "can appreciate and make evident" that the roots of the nation's past (the French nation in the de Mortillet and the Indian nation in my case) are "incredibly deep". I now quote from Richard's analysis of de Mortillet's idea in this regard.

> The depth of prehistoric time appears then as the warranty of national unity, a unity that transcends the original diversity of the populations inhabiting the national territory .... With these arguments, the prehistorian added another theme to the classic definitions of the nation – that of the continuity of the past as a guarantee of national unity ... de Mortillet stressed the overwhelming continuity of development across the Palaeolithic. From the first arrival of a human race on the national territory to the end of the Neolithic, all the physical transformations and development in stone tool industries were strictly autochthonous and totally continuous.

Finally, de Mortillet was very critical of the soundness of arguments derived from history and linguistics. Archaeological knowledge had to be given the first priority in the scheme of reconstruction of the nation's history. This is also something which I have argued.

The precise character of interrelation between nationalism and archaeology will vary from country to country and even from region to region of a single country. This has become remarkably clear in the various articles on this theme in *Nationalism and Archaeology in Europe* (2nd print, 2015) edited by M. Diaz-Andreu and T. Champion. We have earlier pointed out the element of tension, possibly the element of racial tension, between the approach of some Western scholars and their Indian followers to Indian archaeology. We believe that this tension is likely to increase considerably in future and reflects in a way in which the colonial period archaeology was followed in India after Independence. Most of the colonial period archaeologists, which included both Britons and Indians, had no problem with the originality and antiquity of the ancient Indian civilization. The most famous and perhaps the most influential archaeologist of the time, V. Gordon Childe, had no problem, along with John Marshall of the Archaeological Survey of India, to put forward the notion that the Indus civilization was deeply rooted in the Indian soil. When Independent India became a part of the Third World, the Western archaeological attitude to the Indian past rapidly changed and the earlier belief that the Indian civilization like the Indus civilization was a development strongly rooted in the Indian soil had changed into a belief in a strongly Mesopotamian contribution to it, and the fact that the dominant Indian archaeologists of the time fell in line with it speaks of the strong grip Western archaeology had still enjoyed in India. The Indian archaeologists of the time had no idea at all of the possible nationalist dimensions of archaeology in the country. If the situation is broadly unchanged even now, as we have shown with some specific examples from the Indus context, that is because of the generally inferior position of India in the eyes of many Western and Indian scholars. The Indus studies, for instance, have long been divided into a dominant Euro-American group and its Indian followers and a still marginally effective nationalist Indian group, of which the present author is a part. To anybody closely familiar with the ideas current in the Indus studies, any piece of interpretative writing on this civilization will clearly show the political affiliation of the writer to one of these two groups. How plain racism affected or affects ancient Indian studies or Indology was shown by the present author in his *Colonial Indology—the Sociopolitics of the Ancient Indian Past* (1997). The racist streak in Indian archaeology has become reasonably prominent in recent years, especially after the induction of a number of anthropological archaeologists of a comparatively younger generation from across the Atlantic to the field. They have been joined by people of the same inclination from Europe and 'Down Under' and also by enthusiasts for 'linguistic archaeology' from the east of Asia. What is somewhat unacceptable in this scenario is that to these people the only reasonably good work in the field is done by the members of their own skin colour and the few Indian camp-followers they have. To some extent this has something to do with the composition of the newly inducted Western students of Indian archaeology. About fifty or more years ago, they were very few in number and all of them were academically nurtured on issues related to India. Their grip of the Indian situation was impressive because of the varied details they knew and understood about the land. Also, the academic world was not as competitive as it is now, and one did not have to be unduly aggressive to make a reputation for oneself. As it is in 2021, the number of people specializing in Indian or south Asian archaeology has considerably increased, all of them keen on displaying their scientific expertise in one way or another. It does not matter to them if all this display of 'science' has brought us any close to the truth related to ancient India; each scientific fact, however, has been forced into a new theoretical frame to explain the ancient Indian universe. For instance, it does not matter that there is not a single recorded instance of the Buddhists or any other types of monk being involved in constructing great irrigation systems anywhere in the ancient context in India but that does not prevent the modern irrigation specialists and their archaeology/ancient history associates from working out a picture combining possible irrigation lakes, Buddhist monks and new agricultural crops. The presented scenario may not bear any relationship with the reality but it is supposed to be great science and what is important is the offered bold and neat historical picture, regardless of the possibility of its having any relationship with the reality. The Wikipedia article on 'post-truth' expresses the picture beautifully.

> Philosophers including Michel Foucault, Jacques Derrida, and Bruno Latour are skeptical of the division between facts and values. They argue that scientific facts are socially produced through relations of power. In 2018, the *New York Times* ran a profile on Bruno Latour and post-truth politics. According to the article, in a series of controversial books in the 1970s and 1980s, [Latour] argued that scientific facts should instead be seen as a *product* of scientific inquiry. Facts, Latour said, were "networked"; *they stood or fell not on the strength of their inherent veracity but on the strength of the institutions and practices that produced them and made them intelligible.* (italics added)

The truth of the last sentence of the preceding quotation is so obvious to people like the present author that the situation can frequently be utterly disgusting.

If we turn our gaze from the Buddhist monks to the Indus civilization, we find a similar situation gradually developing and becoming powerful under the guise of 'science'. When the civilization was first reported in 1924 and when the first details regarding it were published in 1931, it was regarded as a Bronze Age manifestation of what later developed into Hindu civilization. The archaeologists concerned had no problem with that. They explained its religion, for instance, in terms of what they saw before themselves as different varieties of Hindu ritual behaviour. Researches since then have demonstrated that what is termed the Indus civilization or the Harappan civilization was the fountainhead of the great Indian tradition which has persisted till today. This, of course, is the perception of the nationalist scholars like the present author. However, to a large number of scholars who comprise the modern Euro-American students of this civilization and their underlings in India and elsewhere, this issue of continuity does not seem to matter. In fact, most of them would be happy to see a clear break between this civilization and what transpired later. They are not at all reluctant to accept what the Western Indologists had always been trying to say in relation to Hinduism as a later development brought about by the Aryan migration. In a comparatively recent you-tube presentation on the Indus civilization in Karachi, Mark Kenoyer was found to repeat all the earlier Indological assertions regarding this civilization. As the next essay of this volume will show in detail, all the 'science' and remote science imageries which have been pumped into its study in recent years have not necessarily amplified our perception of this civilization in terms of what we know about historical India, the India which persisted in some essential form till at least the dawn of the 20th century. Remote sensing seems to have thrown up new sites, both large and small, all over, but those of us who do not forget that till about the beginning of the 19th century, the total population of the subcontinent as a whole was only 140 or 150 million in place of many millions over a billion that we find today, cannot but wonder if in the Indus context the concerned area was as heavily populated as what is indicated by the dots representing sites found by remote-sensing. Similar examples can be given from other scientific areas of Indus civilizational studies. Although the scientists have endeavoured to add a large variety of crops and other plant products to the agricultural repertoire of this civilization, they seem to have forgotten to emphasize that all that the people of this civilization cultivated were parts of the Indian agricultural landscape through the ages, and if these crops required any great scientific explanation, these explanations had better be in terms of the agricultural practices current in India. Nor do these 'agricultural scientists' lay enough emphasis on the fact that this landscape has been historically very stable; we do not know enough of it to claim that the different agricultural areas of the country have frequently changed the basic character of their crops in different historical eras. What we are trying to emphasize here is the division which is getting increasingly sharp between the Euro-Americans and their Indian camp-followers in Indian archaeology and the traditional Indian students of the subject who try to assess the situation in terms of the land they know.

The scenario may not be specific only to Indian archaeology. The editorial of 19 May, 2021 in *Nature*, the famous science magazine, writes the following

> Racism in science is endemic because the systems that produce and teach scientific knowledge have, for centuries, misrepresented, marginalized and mistreated people of colour and under-represented communities. The research system has justified racism – and too often, scientists in position of power have benefited from it. That system includes the organization of research: how it is funded, published and evaluated.

It is still the literature produced by this Euro-American group which enjoys wide currency in the Indian universities and other institutions. We are still a long way from working out a proper nationalist archaeology of India. In this essay I have only tried to outline its several possible dimensions.

REFERENCES

(Many additional references have been incorporated in the body of the text.)

Ambedkar, B.R. 1946, *Who were the Sudras?* Bombay.

Banks, I. 1996, 'Archaeology, Nationalism and Ethnicity'. In, J. Atkinson, I. Banks, J.'O. Sullivan (eds.), 1996, *Nationalism and Archaeology, Scottish Archaeological Forum*, pp. 1-11, Glasgow.

Bhargava, P.L. 1971, *India in the Vedic Age*. Lucknow.

Bryant, E. 2001, *The Quest for the Origins of Vedic Culture. The Indo-Aryan Migration Debate*. New York.

Caldwell, R. 1875, *A Comparative Grammar of the Dravidian or South Indian Family of Languages*. London.

Campbell, G. 1866, 'Ethnology of India'. *Journal of the Asiatic Society of Bengal* special no. 1: 1-152.

Chakrabarti, Dilip K. 1968, 'The Aryan Hypothesis in Indian Archaeology'. *Indian Studies: Past and Present* 9: 343-58.

—— 1977, 'India and West Asia – an Alternative Approach'. *Man and Environment* 1: 25-38.

—— 1993, *Archaeology of Eastern India: Chhotanagpur Plateau and West Bengal*. Delhi.

—— 1997, *Colonial Indology: Sociopolitics of the Ancient Indian Past*. Delhi.

—— 1999, *India: An Archaeological History. Palaeolithic Beginnings to Early Historical Foundations*. Delhi.

—— 2001, *Archaeological Geography of the Ganga Plain – the Lower and the Middle Ganga*. Delhi.

Chakrabarti, Dilip K. and Nayanjot Lahiri 1986, 'The Assam-Burma Route to China'. *Man and Environment* 10: 123-34.

—— 1996, *Copper and Its Alloys in Ancient India*. Delhi.

Chakrabarti, Dilip K., R. Tewari and R.N. Singh 1999-2000, 'The Archaeology of the Deccan Route: A Preliminary Report on the Field Work in 1999'. *Pragdhara* 10: 121-33.

Chatterjee, P. 1994, 'Claims on the Past: The Genealogy of Modern Historiography in Bengal'. In, D. Arnold and D. Hardiman (eds.), *Subaltern Studies VIII, Essays in Honour of Ranajit Guha*, pp. 1-49, Delhi.

Croft, A. 1894/1301 Bengali Samvat. Address delivered at the Annual Convocation of the Calcutta University for conferring degrees, on the 3rd February, 1894 *Sahitya Parishad Patrika*, 1(1): 7-26 (translated into Bengali under the title *Amader Visvavidyalay*).

Diaz-Andreu, M. 1996, 'Islamic Archaeology and the Origin of the Spanish Nation'. In, Diaz-Andreu and Champion (eds.), 1996, pp. 68-89.

Dutt, R.C. 1889, *A History of Civilization in Ancient India, Based on Sanskrit Literature*, Vol. 1. Calcutta.

Falkenhausen, L.V. 1995, 'The Regionalist Paradigm in Chinese Archaeology'. In, Kohl and Fawcett, 1995, pp. 198-217.

Grierson, G.A. 1909, *The Imperial Gazetter of India*, Vol. 1. Oxford.

Hassan, F. 1998, 'Memorabilia: Archaeological Materiality and National Identity in Egypt'. In, Meskell, 1998, pp. 200-16.

Hodgson, B. 1849, 'A Brief Note on Indian Ethnology'. *Journal of the Asiatic Society of Bengal* 18: 238-46.

Hutton, J.H. 1933, *Census of India, 1931, Report 1, Part 1*. Calcutta.

Kohl, P.L. 1993, 'Nationalism, Politics, and the Practice of Archaeology in Soviet Transcaucasia'. *Journal of European Archaeology* 1: 181-88.

—— 1998, 'Nationalism and Archaeology: On the Constructions of Nations and the Reconstructions of the Remote Past'. *Annual Review of Anthropology* 27: 223-46.

Kohl, P.L. and C. Fawcett (eds.) 1995, *Nationalism, Politics, and the Practice of Archaeology*. Cambridge.

Lahiri, Nayanjot 1992, *The Archaeology of Indian Trade Routes (up to c. 200 B.C.)*. Delhi.

Lillios, K.T. 1995, 'Nationalism and Copper Age Research in Portugal during the Salazar Regime (1932-1974)'. In, Kohl and Fawcett, 1995, pp. 57-69.

Meskell, L. 1998, ed. *Archaeology unde Fire, Nationalism, Politics and Heritage in the Eastern Mediterranean and Middle East*. London.

Mookerji, R.K. 1956, *Ancient India*. Allahabad.

Muller, F.M. 1854, 'Ethnology *v.* Phonology'. In, C.C. Bunsen (ed.), *Outlines of the Philosophy of Universal History Applied to Language and Religion* 1, pp. 349-53. London.

Narayan, B. 1998, 'Determining Relations: Memory, History and Politics'. *Studies in Humanities and Social Sciences* 5: 113-28.

Ozdogan, M. 1998, 'Ideology and Archaeology in Turkey'. In, Meskell, 1998, pp. 111-23.
Poliakov, L. 1974, *The Aryan Myth*. London.
Pope, G.U. (ed.) 1879, *A Description of the Character, Manners and Customs of the People of India, and of Their Institutions and Religions*. Madras.
Rajan, K. 1997, *Archaeological Gazetteer of Tamil Nadu*. Thanjavur.
Renfrew, C. 1994, 'The Identity of Europe in Prehistoric Archaeology'. *Journal of European Archaeology* 2: 153-73.
Risley, H.H. 1903, *Census of India, 1901*, Vol. 1. Calcutta.
Said, E. 1978, *Orientalism*. London.
Santra, Tarapada 1407 B.S. (2000), *Banglar Anchalik Itihas Charcha: Ekti Samiksha. Puravritta* 1: 70-114.
Schnapp, A. 1996, 'French Archaeology: Between National Identity and Cultural Identity'. In, M. Diaz-Andreu and T. Champion (eds.), 1996, *Nationalism and Archaeology in Europe*, pp. 48-67, London.
Sinha, Surajit 1962, 'State Formation and Rajput Myth in Tribal Central India'. *Man in India* 42: 35-80.
Singh, B. 1995, *The Vedic Harappans*. Delhi.
Sorensen, M.L.S. 1996, 'The Fall of a Nation, the Birth of a Subject: The National use of Archaeology in Nineteenth-century Denmark'. In, Diaz-Andreu and Champion (eds.), 1996, pp. 24-47.
Tewari, R., R.K. Srivastava, K.S. Saraswat and K.K. Singh 1999-2000, 'Excavations at Malhar, District Chaundauli (U.P.) 1999: A Preliminary Report'. *Pragdhara* 10: 69-98.
Thapar, R. 1989, 'Imagined Religious Communities? Ancient History and Modern Search for a Hindu Identity'. *Modern Asian Studies* 23: 209-31.
—— 1997, *Ancient India*. Delhi.
Trigger, B. 1995, 'Romanticism, Nationalism, and Archaeology'. In, Kohl and Fawcett, 1995, pp. 263-79.

3

Recent Research on the Indus Civilization (c. 2010–2021)

I. THE PURPOSE, CONTENTS AND THE ACADEMIC CONTEXT OF THE PRESENT ESSAY

The main purpose of this essay is to critically review the major areas of research on this civilization during the last decade with occasional references to the preceding period.

We begin by emphasizing that the Indus civilization was the fountainhead of the great Indian tradition (section II). Then (section III) we pass on to a few major topics which have been researched well in the last decade. It is important that we specify these topics because without the scaffolding of this well-defined frame no research review is likely to possess clarity. Section IV deals with the 'Saraswati' drainage as a geo-archaeological issue and we focus on a number of important publications which examine the issue from the point of view of geosciences. To put this geological literature in its perspective, we draw attention to some early academic literature on the Sarasvati system (Section V) and also to major references to the Sarasvati in the *Rigveda* (Section VI). Section

VII is devoted to the remote-sensing imageries and some more geological literature on the Sarasvati.

The problem of aridity and its relationship with the Indus decline has been a fertile ground of speculations in recent years and in Section VIII we attempt a threadbare discussion of the issue.

Uptil now, our focus was on geology, climate, Rigvedic references and the relationship between aridity and civilizational decline. From Section IX onward we shift to the rest of the issues on which there is some ongoing research: Harappan or Indus metallurgy (Section IX); Harappan agriculture and animal remains (Section X); Harappan skeletal studies (Section XI); some recently excavated Harappan sites (Section XII); some Harappan burial sites (Section XIII) and a review of the general Harappan situation (Section XIV).

Section XV takes up the issue of the entire sequence of Harappan development between the Sutlej and the Yamuna. The issue of ancient DNA, as discovered very recently at Rakhigarhi, comes in Section XVI and finally, in Section XVII, we offer some critical comments on the miscellaneous features of the ongoing Harappan research.

At the end, this research review is followed by our comments on certain key issues of the Indus civilization, critically reviewing in this context how the Indus research has proceeded in various phases since 1924, the year in which the civilization was identified.

II. INDUS CIVILIZATION IS THE FOUNTAINHEAD OF THE GREAT INDIAN TRADITION

To us, the Indus civilization was the fountainhead of India's Great Tradition. We make this claim for the following reasons.

Let us first stress the significance of its geographical space and chronological span. On map the geographical space may be said to run from Shortughai in the Oxus valley in Afghanistan to Daimabad in the Godavari valley of

Maharashtra on the one hand, and from Sutkagendor on the border between Pakistani and Iranian Baluchistan to the banks of the Ganga below the Manasa Devi hill of Haridwar on the other. Even if one takes Afghanistan out of this space, the north-south axis of its distribution spans the length from the site of Manda in Jammu to Daimabad in Maharashtra. In recent years there have also been reports of pottery of the Indus affinity from near Jalgaon in Maharashtra. When one adds to this geographical fact, the distribution of OCP-Copper Hoards, an artefact assemblage which certainly belongs to the late Harappan chronological and cultural orbit, if not to the earlier mature Harappan tradition itself, this geographical space may be said to have incorporated the whole of the Ganga-Yamuna Doab down to Sringaverapura near Allahabad. The thought of its geography alone is enough to convince anybody that this civilizational tradition marks the most important and largest civilizational growth in the subcontinent.

The second point to consider in this context is the chronological column represented by this civilizational growth and tradition at sites like Bhirrana and Rakhigarhi, which Amarendra Nath has recently analysed and is supported by Anindya Sarkar, Arati Deshpande Mukherjee et al. Basically, the chronological and cultural columns of these sites sum up the growth story of the Indus tradition from around 7000 BC to c. 1200/1300 BC. These sites do not stand alone; the combined archaeological testimony of the entire northern and northwestern segment of the subcontinent, including the indisputable proof of the beginning of agriculture in the Aravalli belt of Rajasthan-Gujarat, tells the same story.

We assert that the civilizational growth of this geographical and chronological magnitude could not have left any part of the subcontinent untouched in its quest to procure various kinds of resources. In bits and pieces this has been clear for a long time; one remembers Edwin Pascoe's famous chapter on the natural raw materials in the first volume of John Marshall's

Mohenjodaro report where it is said that amazonite of the site was likely to have come from the Nilgiris in the deep south.

The imprint of this civilization on the later civilizational tradition of India is well-known and has been adequately emphasized in the essay on the legacy of the Indus civilization on later Indian cultures in the volume *Protohistoric Foundations* (2014) and also in many earlier volumes, the most important of which is the first volume of Marshall's report on Mohenjodaro.

The final and the most significant point is that the vast space and time represented by this civilization neatly fits in with the literary, cultural and philosophical tradition of India which is visible in the column of Vedic texts and the innumerable later texts traditionally rooted in the Vedic texts. We must realize that the corpus of Vedic texts was, once one forgets its so-called Aryan association, was an Indian literary tradition, and whatever may be its date, it has to fall in the date-bracket of protohistoric cultures before the beginning of the early historic urban growth in the Ganga plain. This point has been repeatedly emphasized in many of his recent publications by B.B. Lal and we find no conceivable reason to dispute this unless we accept the theory of Aryan migration at the end of the Indus civilization. As we shall find later, some archaeologists have, in fact, tried to correlate some recently discovered Harappan burial remains with some burial practices described in the corpus of Vedic texts. There has apparently been a concern among some Indian archaeologists to find an echo of the Mahabharatic epic tradition in the burial assemblage of chariots at Sanauli. We do not believe in any straight correlation between the epics and the recently discovered Harappan finds, but at the same time the probability of the epic Mahabharatic tradition hanging somewhat loosely over the late Harappan context in the Doab and parts of Haryana cannot altogether be ignored. In any case, there is increasing evidence in the recent times that the Harappan tradition was slowly transforming itself in the Doab heartland and that there is no archaeological hiatus between the late Harappan phase and the first phase of the early historic urban transformation. The two radiocarbon dates of the recent Harinagar copper hoard find in Bijnor district are 2200-2000, thus putting this hoard in the mature Harappan period itself (Vikrama and Pradhan 2017), although towards its end.

At the present stage of knowledge, the equation of the archaeological time-space column to the literary column represented by the Vedic literature and its successor literary tradition seems to be unavoidable. At the same time, there is a great need of exercising caution in relation to the details of this situation. The Indus literary tradition is undeciphered and thus not understood, and one must resist the temptation of interpreting the various scenes represented on the Indus seals in terms of Vedic texts, although in the case of the representation of unicorn on the Indus seals the hypothesis offered by I. Mahadevan appears to be the most logical of all such hypotheses. This does not mean that Mahadevan's other hypotheses in the Indus context have to be given the same weightage, but that is a different matter.

Even if the Indus script is satisfactorily discovered, it is unlikely that we shall be confronted with a vast mass of literary data. The very fact that quantitatively there is a very great unevenness in the number of the actual representation of individual Indus signs seems to mean that there was probably a vast mass of the Indus or Harappan literature written on perishable materials. That the tradition of writing on perishable materials such as birch and palm leaves continued in India down, at least to the close of the 19th century AD, is a well-documented historical fact. B.B. Lal has further pointed out the identical representation of a particular type of wooden tablets known as *takhtis* on some terracottas of Mohenjodaro, and as this similarity is totally acceptable to all who have seen *takhtis* still in use in many parts of northern India (including the state-run primary schools of Delhi where the children of poor people go), the implication is that there was a regular system of education in the Indus civilization, a fact which is eminently acceptable in the light of what is known about the education system prevalent in both ancient Mesopotamia and Egypt.

It has been necessary to emphasize, repeatedly, the point that the Indus civilization is the fountainhead of the whole length of the indigenous civilizational tradition of India which has continued down to the modern period because the integrity of its civilizational importance is currently being denied by some archaeologists from Pune, Vadodara and other places in the name of various regional pottery elements. We shall discuss the issue in some detail later and all that we would point out here that some Indian archaeologists who cannot look beyond their own sites and areas have now wholeheartedly joined the business of running down the integrity and importance of the Indus civilization, all, of course, in the name of 'science'. The anti-national tradition set by the archaeologists of many Indian institutions in the post-Independence period still runs strong. The only charitable explanation which can be offered is that these archaeologists are not even aware what is or what is not nationalism. Interestingly, this civilization is still listed as 'Indus valley civilization' in innumerable Indian publications, indisputably showing that these Indian authors are in no way aware of the politics of putting emphasis on the Indus valley alone in the title of this civilization.

III. THE SARASVATI DRAINAGE

The current research on this topic has been based mostly on the geosciences, and we summarize here the results obtained by some lead researchers in this field.

III.1. Sanjeev Gupta and His Associates (Singh et al. 2017)

The most important effort to bring in both climate and river behaviour in this field was made by Sanjeev Gupta and his associates in their paper 'Counter-intuitive influence of Himalayan river morphodynamics on Indus civilization urban settlements' in *Nature Communications*, volume 8 article number: 1617, in 2017. Their basic argument is that the Indus urban settlements developed, at least in Haryana and Panjab, in a relict channel of the Sutlej. There is no dispute about the existence of the palaeochannel known as the *Sutlej having been diverted to its present course shortly after ~8 ka or around 6000 BC*. The authors' argument is that "Indus urban settlements thus developed along an abandoned river valley rather than active Himalayan river". Further, the fact that the Sutlej remained confined to its 'present incised course' since about 6000 BC enabled the 'long-term stability for Indus settlements sited along the relict palaeochannel'.

The main physical sources of this study are a number of cores obtained by these researchers to reconstruct the history of the river flowing through the region. *Both the compositions and the chronology of these cores were studied, leading to a number of primary inferences*. What eventually emerged may be clearly understood from the following passage.

> Our study sheds new light on the role of river dynamics on early urbanisation. We find that the locus for the abundant Indus Civilisation urban settlements along the Ghaggar-Hakra palaeochannel was the relict, underfilled topography of a recently abandoned valley of the Himalayan Sutlej River rather than an active Himalayan river. We suggest that this abandoned incised valley was an ideal site for urban development because of its relative stability compared to Himalayan river channel belts that regularly experience devastating floods and lateral channel migration. It is also worth noting that many large Himalayan rivers are typically characterised by high avulsion frequencies, with rivers

commonly revisiting past courses. For example, the Kosi River in the eastern Ganges basin shows an average avulsion frequency of 24 years. However, in the western Ganges basin, rivers such as the Sutlej and the Yamuna flow in incised valleys that are deeply entrenched in abandoned alluvial plains and form regionally extensive sediment routing corridors. We suggest that confinement to incised valleys reduced the propensity for these rivers to frequently re-route. Since complete avulsion of the Sutlej River to its present course shortly after ~8 ka, the Sutlej has remained trapped in an incised valley and has not revisited its former Ghaggar-Hakra course. This has provided environmental stability within the Ghaggar-Hakra palaeovalley, a factor that may have helped to enable the long-term development of Indus urban settlements. Following avulsion of the palaeo-Sutlej to its present course, the relict incised valley became partially infilled by very fine-grained sediments that we interpret as deposition from ephemeral monsoon-fed rivers derived from the Himalayan foothills, likely the equivalent of the modern Ghaggar River and its tributaries. (Sinha et al. 2017)

The implications of the study from the archaeological point of view have been amplified by the following conclusion of these researchers.

In conclusion, our results firmly rule out the existence of a Himalayan-fed river that nourished Indus Civilisation settlements along the Ghaggar-Hakra palaeochannel. Instead, the relict Sutlej valley acted to focus monsoon-fed seasonal river flow as evidenced by very fine-grained sediments in the upper part of the valley-fill record. This and the potential to pond flood waters in the topographic depression formed by the valley likely offered favourable conditions that led Indus populations to preferentially settle along the incised palaeovalley. We find that river dynamics controlled the distribution of Indus sites in the region, but in the opposite sense to that usually assumed: it was the departure of the river, rather than its arrival, that triggered

> the growth of Indus urban settlements here. We posit that a stable abandoned valley, still able to serve as a water source but without the risk of devastating floods, is a viable alternative model for how rivers can nucleate the development of ancient urban settlements. (Singh et al. 2017)

III.2. Support of the above Conclusion by the Inference Arrived at on the Basis of Visual Observations and Historical Sources (Chakrabarti and Saini 2009)

In 2007-08 I moved around extensively in Haryana-Punjab, and although not a scientist, I could feel on the basis of visual observations of sites and their contexts, that the Indus sites and thus this civilization could flourish in the context of a landscape which could not be much dissimilar to what can be observed in the region today. For instance, many village sites of the region lie on sand dunes; a little sand-scraping tells us that the sand dunes formed the physical context of the topography when the ancient settlements were flourishing. In 2009 (Chakrabarti and Saini 2009) I went to the extent of asserting that we should be ready to appreciate the growth and flourishing of the Indus civilization in a climatic context which prevails in this region today. More accurately, this should be something which is indicated by the Haryana district gazetteers reflecting climatic and water-related situation in the 19th century. The only allowance I am ready to give is a better availability of water and the related wetness throughout the area. A close study of the nineteenth century and somewhat later district gazetteers of Haryana-Punjab showed that there were rich, well-watered patches of land in the entire region right up to the extinct course of the Ghaggar in Rajasthan. The availability of water during the monsoon was never in doubt; the gazetteers even speak of ferries running through certain sections during at least the monsoon. This may well reflect the historical situation. There is nothing in the historical records which testifies that the Ghaggar-Hakra flow ever completely dried up. There is a reference to an eastern section of the Sarasvati (*Prachi Sarasvati*) in one of the epigraphic sources, and some literary source refers to an agriculturally prosperous Haryana criss-crossed by irrigation canals. The source of this water was the monsoon water but it was water and this water could adequately nourish the settlements along the Ghaggar-Hakra flow.

The following was written in 2009 (Chakrabarti and Saini 2009: 287-288) and its basic idea seems to have been supported by the conclusions arrived at by Singh et al. 2017.

> The early gazetteers depict conditions towards the end of the nineteenth century and underscore the possibilities of pre-modern agriculture in parts of Haryana. In the British Indian district of Karnal, which was much larger in extent than the present district of the same name, the Ghaggar and the Sarasvati had ceased to flow continuously by the 1880s but still, they flooded their banks in the rainy season, leading in this *Neli* tract to a fine crop of rice, gram and barley. At Sotha (Sotar?) the Sarasvati needed a ferry to be crossed during the rains. The ferry boat was in fact needed for a few months in a year. This means that the Sarasvati monsoonal flood could not be treated casually. Further, the gazetteer refers to the "trace of ancient canals cut from the Ghagar and the Sarasvati".
>
> The Hissar gazetteer of the same period refers to what is called *Sotar* villages in the north of Hissar where no crop was grown except on land which is irrigated from one or the other branches of the Ghaggar. The area produced two crops a year, and rich grass grew in the *Daban* villages on the bank of the Ghaggar.
>
> James Tod wrote that in the area to the north of Bhatnir, there were "many tracts susceptible of high cultivation, having water near the surface, and many large spaces entirely free of sandhills". According to Raverty, the Chitang near Bhadra overflowed its banks regularly during the rains, becoming close to 2 miles or more in width. Near Sirsa, the

Ghaggar monsoonal waters spread out for about 2 miles or more, and considerable quantities of wheat were cultivated. In about 100 square miles of territory around Derawar, Stein hinted at the possible former existence of a network of canals.

On the whole, this is an interesting situation. All these scars or traces of river beds which, as we have seen, mark this vast region from the Siwaliks to the Sind-Kutch estuaries must have been, by virtue of their being river beds, areas of great agricultural potential as long as some water could be taken to them. All these *Naiwals* of Panjab must have had a history of being tilled by the pre-modern cultivators of the area. Panjab before the modern irrigation system or the introduction of canals on a large scale by some of its rulers, including the British, was not a howling wilderness. There were prosperous historical period settlements throughout the modern separate territories of Haryana and Panjab. We have already drawn attention to the evidence of *Yasastilakachampu* of Somadeva in the 10th century, which is one of the most significant testimonies of the beauty of the land whose archaeological geography we have tried to discuss in this volume: the Yaudheya country, where the abundance of irrigation rendered it free from the vagaries of rain, was 'like an ornament of the earth'.

On the whole, the geomorphological past envisaged for the Ghaggar-Hakra stretch by Sanjeev Gupta and his team carries conviction even to a non-scientist like me because this scenario fits in with what can be inferred about the valley from historical sources and visual observation.

The final question is: how does the explanation offered by Gupta and his group fit in with what we know of the Rigvedic references to the Sarasvati, all of which suggest that the river was very much alive and flowing then? If the *Rigveda* was composed before 8000 BP, there is no problem because the Sutlej got confined to her present bed only after 8000 BP. However, such an early date of the *Rigveda* may not be acceptable to all, and all that we can suggest is that even after the Sutlej deserted its Ghaggar-Hakra bed, the river did not lose its basic riverine character in a relatively short period because the monsoonal flow of water was always there, and it is logical to infer that the river continued to flow long after that mainly due to the strength of the monsoonal rain. A close reading of H.G. Raverty tells us that the situation broadly persisted at least till the 14th century, i.e. the time of Firoz Shah Tughlak.

The situation seems to have lasted in some ways till the recent period. Karam Tej Singh Sarao, a Delhi University professor in his sixties, grew up in the Mansa-Bhatinda area of Punjab, and drawing on his childhood memory he recollects that agriculture of the *Manjha* or central division of eastern Punjab revolved around the annual monsoonal Ghaggar floods and that even he found ferries across the monsoonal flow. Equally importantly, the depth of ground water in the Ghaggar bed did not exceed 15-20 feet, and it was easy for the village farmers to have access to it by digging wells. I have also been told that during the construction of a large cantonment at Ambala, a lot of disturbance was made to the original Ghaggar channel of the area. I have not been able to follow up this information, but it may be worth doing so on the basis of the archival sources related to the construction of the Ambala cantonment.

The paper (Singh et al. 2017) gives rise to a host of issues. First, does the situation envisaged by its authors limit itself only to the central portion of the area between the Sutlej and the Yamuna, a portion which has a dense cluster of sites, with some of its density being manifest as far downstream as Kalibangan and Ganweriwala? The issue remains to be settled because Raverty's detailed description of the Ghaggar-Hakra drainage system and its place in the ramification of the Indus river drainage system till the sea suggests that the Ghaggar-Hakra course offered a parallel river system to the east of the Indus drainage. My impression is that what has been clearly argued for the central section of the Ghaggar-Hakra drainage between the current Sutlej and the Yamuna should be valid for the Ghaggar-Hakra system as a whole. However, there is enough scope for local variations in the river behaviour, although this is unlikely to change the overall scenario offered by Sanjeev Gupta and his associates.

III.3. Imran Khan and Rajiv Sinha 2019

A new dimension has been added to the research of Gupta and his associates by Imran Khan's and Rajiv Sinha's research on the system of what they call palaeo-Yamuna. Their conclusions are as follows:

> Geophysical surveys (VES and ERT) were performed in a total stretch of ~50 km across the trace of the palaeo-Yamuna in parts of Haryana plains to establish its subsurface existence and to understand its linkage to the Harappan civilization. The geo-electrical models generated by integrating 1D and 2D resistivity data and calibrated with lithologs and well logs reveal the presence of subsurface thick (>30 m) sand bodies of variable resistivity values, interbedded with silty clay layers. The channel-form geometry of the sand bodies and their stacking pattern confirm that they were deposited by mobile channel belts of a large river, the palaeo-Yamuna, that was once connected to the Ghaggar-Hakra system. A large number of Mature and Late Harappan settlements are located close to delineated palaeochannels but *the results available so far suggest that the demise of the large river and the Harappan civilization are widely separated in terms of timing* (italics added). Our ongoing detailed sedimentological and chrono-stratigraphic analysis will better characterise sedimentary environments and the alluvial stratigraphic development of the palaeo-Yamuna to understand the long-term evolution of the large river system in this region. (Khan and Sinha 2019)

They further add that this palaeo-Yamuna channel was nearly contemporary with the Ghaggar-Hakra channel flowing to its west and 'they together formed a large river system that was abandoned more than 8-10 ka ago'.

The location of the major transect from Karnal to Kaithal and the density of Harappan sites along this transect have been clearly shown by Khan and Sinha in a map attached to their paper. They also draw attention to the studies which are supposed to clearly demonstrate *"that all fluvial activity related to a large river terminated in this region between ~23 and ~12 Ka"*. (italics added)

III.4. A. Chatterjee and J. Ray 2018

Another interesting paper in this context is A. Chatterjee and J. Ray 2018, 'Geochemistry of Harappan potteries from Kalibangan and sediments in the Ghaggar river: clues for a dying river', *Geoscience Frontiers* 9(4): 1203-1211.

> The Ghaggar alluvium is a repository of sediments originated from two distinct provenances. The oldest grey micaceous sand (~70-4.3 ka) originated from the glaciated Higher Himalayas, thus indicating a strong fluvial past of the river. The younger yellowish-brown sand and brown silty clay (16-0 ka) were sourced from the sub-Himalayan rocks, in particular from the Siwalik Group, Kasauli and Dagsahi Formations. Temporarily overlapping depositions of sediments derived from both the Higher Himalayas and the Sub-Himalayas during the late Pleistocene and early Holocene point to the dwindling state of the river and gradual disappearance of its perennial water sources. The depositional ages of the topmost brown coloured silty-clay horizon confirm that the river had already lost its glacial sources and became an ephemeral foothill-fed river by 3 ka. The exact period of the hydrological changes has been narrowed down by the Nd-Sr isotopic finger-printing of the Kalibangan potteries. This study suggests that the local sediments, which were most likely used for manufacturing the pottery, were not derived from the glacier covered parts of the Himalayas but were derived from the foothills of the

> Himalayas. *This in turn suggests that the Ghaggar had already transitioned from being a glacier-fed river to a rain-fed river during the Mature Harappan period.* (italics added) (Chatterjee and Ray 2018)

III.5. A.K. Dave et al. 2019

The palaeo-Yamuna channel or the Chautang palaeochannel has been further studied by A.K. Dave and his associates. As they put it,

> This is the first study that directly dates sediments from the Chautang palaeochannel, which was a likely path for the westward flow of the Yamuna river and it unambiguously establishes that the existence of mighty glacially-fed rivers in NW India and the Harappan civilization were two distinct non-contemporaneous and unrelated events. Analysis of the distribution of Harappan sites along the two main rivers in the region, the Indus (perennial) and the Ghaggar-Hakra (ephemeral) through time suggests that caution should be taken in making linear associations of site abundance to river hydrology. The Harappan settlement pattern indicates that factors other than the presence of a perennial river dictated settlement preference in ancient times. In addition, the chronostratigraphic framework for the Chautang palaeochannel and floodplain suggests that the major change in river dynamics from its past glacially-fed to its present ephemeral state, occurred sometime between >24 and 45 ka and most likely around 40-45 ka. *Since ~24 ka, beyond dune building, the general landscape has not changed.* (italics added)

The inference that the general landscape has not changed beyond dune-building, comes through remarkably well from the present author's study of the primary route from the Dera Ghazi Khan area to the heart of the Indo-Gangetic plain by such places as Hissar, Hansi and Rohtak in *Pakistan Heritage*, volume 2 (2010) (reprinted in the present volume). This is one of the arterial lines of communication in both protohistoric and historic India, and we believe that the site of Harappa derived its primary significance from its location on this communication line. The current researchers on the Indus civilization should be aware of the other but equally valid non-scientific dimensions of enquiries into the past landscapes.

IV. SOME EARLY ACADEMIC LITERATURE ON THE SARASVATI SYSTEM

Map 3 of James Rennell's 'A Memoir of the Map of Hindoostan' (1788) shows a dotted line through the Indian desert under the caption 'combined stream of the Gaggar or Kanker and the Sursooty'. That this was the Sarasvati mentioned in the *Rigveda* was proposed first by the French historical geographer Vivien Saint-Martin in 1858-60. The only early attempt to equate this with the Helmand of Afghanistan came from E. Thomas (1886), but he was ignored by most of his contemporaries including Aurel Stein, who in his famous discussion on the Rigvedic rivers does not even mention this opinion. The early scholarship is primarily centred around the following writings:

Oldham, C.F. 1893. 'The Saraswati and the Lost River of the Indian Desert'. *The Journal of the Royal Asiatic Society*, pp. 49-76.

——. 1874. 'Notes on the Lost River of the Indian Desert'. *The Calcutta Review*, July 1874, pp. 1-27.

Raverty, H.G. 1892. 'The Mihran of Sind and its Tributaries'. *The Journal of the Asiatic Society of Bengal* (*JASB*) 61(4): 155-297, Extra No. 1892, pp. 298-508.

Oldham, R.D. 1886. 'On Probable Changes in the Geography of the Punjab and its Rivers: A Historico-geographical Study', *JASB* 55 (Part 2). 1886, pp. 322-343.

Of these, the most important piece is the one authored by H.G. Raverty who had access to an unpublished survey of the entire system done in 1790. This survey was possibly done by Mirza Afzal Beg, who was an associate of Colonel Wilford, one of the early British writers on Indian historical geography. Raverty extensively cited Islamic sources to argue that the river continued to flow, at least in places, till 14th century AD. It is important that Raverty's analysis of the mediaeval topography of the Ghaggar course should be cross-checked item by item by somebody as proficient in the Islamic sources as Raverty.

This is one aspect of the Sarasvati literature. The archaeological aspects drew attention as early as Colonel Tod's writings on Rajputana, and comparatively recently it emerged as a major concern after the survey of the Pakistani portion of the river in Bahawalpur by Rafiq Mughal. The point is that after Mughal's survey it was possible to argue that this river system witnessed the various stages of growth and decline of the Indus civilisation. It could be further argued that it was in this valley that the Indus civilisation could rise and take shape. The survey in the Pakistani section was followed by Indian surveys in the Bikaner section of Rajasthan, Haryana and Punjab. The distribution stretches up to the Siwaliks. This, in fact, covers a vast area from the course of the Ghaggar-Hakra in Rajasthan to the Himalayan foothills of Punjab. It takes no imagination to realise that, geography-wise, this region was most likely to be the core area of the Indus civilisation.

V. REFERENCES TO THE SARASVATI IN THE *RIGVEDA*

One also has to consider the references to the Sarasvati in the *Rigveda* (*RV*). There are two major references to Sarasvati in *RV*. Book I: Book I.3 (lines 11-12) where Sarasvati has been invoked as the "purifier, the bestower of food and as the inspirer of those who delight in truth, the instructress of the right-minded", and in Book I.13 where she is bracketed with two other goddesses, *Ila* and *Mahi*. The Sarasvati has assumed identity as the goddess of learning by now. In *RV* Book II, the most important reference to Sarasvati occurs in II.41: "best of mothers, best of rivers, best of goddesses ... divine ... abounding in food?" *RV* Book VII.36 uses the epithet "loudly roaring" and calls the Sarasvati "mother of floods? with copious milk, with fair streams, strongly flowing, full swelling with the volume of their water".

RV Book VII.95 has another full verse dedicated to Sarasvati: "pure in her course from mountains to the sea" and seeks her protection as "a tree for shelter". *RV* Book VII.96 also has a full verse dedicated to Sarasvati, calling her the "mightiest, most divine of streams".

VI. REMOTE-SENSING IMAGERIES AND SOME MORE GEOLOGICAL LITERATURE ON THE SARASVATI

Another branch of learning in this field is the evidence furnished by the remote-sensing imageries of the relevant areas. The literature, again, is vast, and the most dependable recent discussion has been offered in the following publication: J.R. Sharma, A.K. Gupta and B.K. Bhadra, 2005-2006. 'Course of Vedic river Saraswati as deciphered from latest satellite data', *Puratattva* 36: 187-195.

An important introduction to the range of geological issues related to the Sarasvati is Valdiya 2017, *Prehistoric River Saraswati, Western India. Geological Appraisal and Social Aspects*, Springer, Switzerland.

N. Khonde et al. 2017, 'Tracing the Vedic Saraswati river in the Great Rann of Kachchh', *Scientific Reports* 7: 5476, basically reports the results of their drilling in the Great Rann of Kutch, which must have received input from the Sarasvati, if active. Their conclusion is the following:

> Nd and Sr isotopic measurements suggest that a distinct source may have been present before 10 ka. Later in Holocene, under a drying climate, sediments from the Thar desert probably choked the signature of an independent Saraswati-like river. (Khonde et al. 2017)

The 'distinct source' suggested by Khonde et al. stands for the Sarasvati channel. It is thus clear that no Sarasvati-like river had moved through the Great Rann of Kutch after 10000 ka. We do not know if this is applicable to the upper reaches of the Sarasvati as well, but here we find a clear echo of what Sanjeev Gupta and other researchers, whom we have previously cited, argued.

For a new assessment of the palaeo-river network of the Haryana-Punjab region, one may cite H.A. Orengo and C.A. Petrie 2017, 'Large-scale multi-temporal remote sensing of paleoriver networks: a case study from northwest India and its implications for the Indus civilization', *Remote Sensing* 9(7). If I have understood the paper correctly, the authors point out the possibility of more sites existing in Cholistan. It is perfectly possible but without groundwork this cannot be accepted at its face value.

If one puts the result of modern research on the Sarasvati system, as expressed by Gupta and his associates (2017), Khan and Sinha (2019), Dave et al. (2019), and Chatterjee and Ray (2018) in the context of the Sarasvati research as a whole since the 18th century, we realize that this river scenario has drastically changed for the Indus civilization. There is no doubt an extensive network of palaeo-channels but these palaeo-channels had ceased to be active by the time the Indus civilization developed. We cannot dispense with the palaeo-channel system entirely because this system must have been to some extent active, at least in parts, during the monsoon. Chatterjee and Ray (2018) try to argue that by 4.3 ka the palaeo-river system which was basically a combination of the palaeo-Ghaggar and palaeo-Yamuna became wholly rain-fed from the Siwaliks, but the process of transition from being related to the high Himalayas to the Siwaliks possibly began some centuries ago, about 16 ka. This was also a long process, long enough to preserve some kind of flow in the channels of the palaeo-Ghaggar and palaeo-Yamuna.

We relate this scenario to what I had pointed out in my study of the Sarasvati problem (Chakrabarti and Saini 2009):

the Indus civilization sites of this region could come up in a setting not too dissimilar to what could be environmentally observed in the region in the late 19th century when the district gazetteers of the region were being compiled.

VII. ARIDITY AND THE PROBLEM OF DECLINE

The issue has been with us for some time, as the relevant section in Chakrabarti and Saini (2009) will testify. We also argued that the climate-civilization relationship was too complex to be pinned down to any straitjacket formula.

VII.1. L. GIOSAN et al. 2018

A starting point in recent times is L. Giosan et al. 2018, 'Neoglacial climate anomalies and the Harappan metamorphosis', *Climate of the Past* 14: 1669-1686.

> We reconstructed the Indian monsoon over the last 6000 years using palaeobiological records from the Arabian Sea. According to modern climatologies, strong winter monsoon winds correspond to rains along a zonal swath extending through the western Himalayas. Changes in the planktonic community structure indicative of cool, productive waters highlight strong winter monsoon conditions between ca 4500 and 3000 years ago, an interval spanning the transition from peak development of the urban Harappan to the demise of its last rural elements. Inferred increases in winter rains during this time were contemporaneous with the regionally documented decline in summer monsoon, which has previously been interpreted as detrimental to the inundation agriculture practised along the Indus and its tributaries. We propose that the combined changes in summer and winter monsoon hydroclimate triggered the metamorphosis of the urban Harappan civilization into a rural society. A push-pull migration can better explain the relocation of Harappans from summer flood-deficient river valleys to the Himalayan piedmont plains with augmented winter rains and a greater reliance on rainfed crops.

A general comment may be made also on the supposed impact of "changes in intensity of the Indian summer monsoon during the Holocene". The late 19th century/early 20th century rainfall data on various Uttar Pradesh districts are available in the respective district gazetteers. One notes that the rainfall may show significant variations from year to year, sometimes up to 20 inches of annual rainfall. The significance of such variations in the life-cycle of the concerned people may not be properly known but certainly such variations did not lead to any major disruption in people's lives. Monsoon failures are known from certain areas of Kutch and Rajasthan. Seasonal displacements of populations and even famines are known to take place because of such monsoon failures. However, people survive from one such 'dry' season to one of adequate rainfall either by migrating from one place to another or by bringing in grain from other areas to cope with the shortage created by the drought. Before one claims that the end of the Indus civilization was due to a decline in the monsoonal rainfall, one had better translate this decline in terms of its actual quantity and the range of its variations.

There are other problems too with the position of Giosan et al. For instance, how do they know that 'inundation agriculture' and not canal irrigation was practised along the Indus its tributaries?

What is very clear to us that even in a science-based study of the Indus civilization, many untested assumptions enter the discussion and that these assumptions are attributable to people who belong to the same academic network as the author of the 'scientific' study.

VII.2. Yama Dixit and Others 2014

There have been various attempts to relate the growth and decline cycle of the Indus civilization to a growth and decline in the monsoonal rainfall, and among the recent such attempts one may mention Yama Dixit's Ph.D. study documenting

Indian summer monsoon variability for the past 6.5 ka at the palaeolake Kotla Dahar in Haryana. According to this study, there was a peak in the evaporation/precipitation ratio at 4.1 ka in the lake catchment area. According to some scholars, the radiocarbon date of about 2000 BC marks a phase of 'deurbanisation' in the Indus distribution zone, and thus there may be a correlation between the decline of the Indus civilization and the onset of aridity. According to the discussion section in Dixit, Hodell and Petrie (2014), "a relatively deep fresh-water lake existed at the site from 6.5 to 5.8 ka", an interpretation consistent with an early to middle Holocene strengthening of the monsoon documented in records from Oman, the Arabian Sea, and the Thar desert lakes. After c. 5.8 ka there was "a progressive lowering of lake level and increasing salinity". There were also indications of "a gradual change toward higher E/P (evaporation/precipitation) conditions between ca. 5.8 and 4.2 ka", a climate trend "consistent with a long-term Holocene decrease in ISM rainfall recorded in marine and speleothem records". The authors' conclusion is that "the resultant age of drying at Kotla Dahar is consistent with the suggested archaeological dates for the onset of Indus de-urbanization within dating uncertainties".

VII.3. Khan and Lemmen 2014

This publication is worth citing because it tries to go beyond climatic factors of Harappan decline and tries to offer some socio-economic variables instead.

> We find that despite a large geographic change of the site distribution, the number of sites and to first approximation – population does not change much between the Early, Mature and Late Harappan phases. Urban area and baked bricks, however, change dramatically in the material culture, as do their social counterparts – administration, elite structure and religion. By concentrating on cities, we point to primarily social reasons as a starting point for further investigations on the decline. (Khan and Lemmen 2014)

VII.4. Soil Profiles and Indus Site Locations: Sayantani Neogi and Her Associates

Soil profiles of four sites, each dated by radiocarbon and OSL, have been studied by Sayantani Neogi as part of her Ph.D. thesis. The sites are Alamgipur, Masudpur I, Masudpur VII and Burj. Said to be occupied first in the late centuries of the third millennium BC, Alamgirpur has been ascribed Mature to Late Harappan label. Masudpur I has been similarly bracketed but Masudpur VII seems to hover around only the Mature level, its corresponding date showing the date-range of 4.9 – 4.6 cal BP. Burj also reflects this span, 4.8-4.5 cal BP. Regarding the earliest date from Alamgirpur, there may be a query. According to the excavator of the site R.N. Singh, there is a deposit of about 1 m below the level from which the earliest radiocarbon sample, about 2200 BC of the site was collected (personal information from R.N. Singh). This fact by itself is likely to add about 300 years more to the beginning of Alamgirpur which may have begun its occupation around 2500 BC and thus the beginning of occupation at the site seems to be as early as the first phase of the mature Indus civilization. It is certainly not a matter of statistical analysis to see which date suits Alamgirpur the most. People who believe that the Indus civilization spread from the west to the east will consider sites like Alamgirpur later in the Harappan time-scale and interpret its dates accordingly. In any case, the basic significance of Sayantani Neogi's work is that it throws light on the geomorphological context in which these four sites developed (Neogi et al., in press):

> This geoarchaeological study has shown that at least some and perhaps many Indus populations living on the Sutlej-Yamuna interfluve had a preference for targeting low terraces and sandbar/ridges on the margins of the ancient floodplains for the establishment of their settlements. Although the immediate environs of only four sites have been investigated, their floodplain edge locations would

> have reduced the risk of settlements being inundated, which would certainly have been affecting the adjacent alluvial plains throughout the Holocene, and are documented up to the present. Significantly, the combination of relatively good soils on these areas of higher ground and the associated naturally and seasonally replenishing alluvial soil system adjacent combined to provide a most important resource that assured agricultural sustainability. Moreover, this earlier-mid-Holocene soil development can only have been associated with a better moisture regime with less risk of drought, and relative landscape stability, ... This combination of factors is probably the essence of the establishment and sustainability of the agricultural system in this region during the Indus periods. This type of relationship between humans, their locale, and good soil development, is an important aspect of Indus cultural adaptations to diverse, variable and changing environments through time, and it is likely that many variations on such adaptations were widespread across the Indus River Basin. Significantly, it appears that the more favourable and stable landscape regimes that had existed throughout much of the earlier-mid-Holocene, had begun to change by the mid-late third millennium BC, when Indus Civilisation settlement sites were distributed across an extensive area. In the past, the landscape was more undulating, with variable soil development on the floodplain margins and *levées* versus the wet alluvial zones alongside former channels. The wide floodplain areas have gradually aggraded with alluvial material, and this process continued during the post-Indus and historic periods. In combination with modern levelling activities, this process has created the ostensibly flat to gently undulating surface topography that is evident today. (Neogi et al., in press; I warmly thank Dr. Neogi for making this available to me.)

Reading Sayantani Neogi carefully between the lines, one realizes that the landform that one sees around modern Alamgirpur cannot have changed much from the days when there was a Harappan settlement of the mid-third millennium BC at the place.

VII.5. TORSA SENGUPTA et al. 2020

Another important paper in this context is Torsa Sengupta et al. 2020, 'Climate change led to the demise of 5000-year-old Harappan settlement at Dholavira: isotopic evidence from gastropod Terebralia Palustris', *Journal of Quaternary Science.*

Oxygen isotopes of small snail showed that there was seasonal mixing of river water in summer and monsoon with seawater that periodically inundated the Great Rann of Kutch. These snails grow in a kind of water that is only possible if glacial melt water mixes in the mangrove. This clearly suggests that a glacier-fed river was debouching in the Rann of Kutch. The summary of the argument is the following:

> Remains of an ancient settlement at Dholavira located in the Rann of Kutch, Gujarat represent the evolution of a Harappan metropolis from the Early to Late cultural phases of the Indus Valley Civilization (IVC 5.2-3.9 ky BP). The hospitable climate that supported the IVC contrasts sharply with the present inhabitable landscape of the Rann. Stable isotopic studies of the carbonate phase of the estuarine gastropod shells Terebralia palustris, found in the recent mangrove sediments as well as the Dholavira ruins, show that they record ambient water composition and temperature. A few of these gastropod shells from the Dholavira site was used to reconstruct the ambient hydrological regime and its seasonality during the Early to Post Harappan times. The highly negative δ18O values of a 4.7 ky old T. palustris (δ18Oshell ~-5.8 ‰) suggest the presence of a glacial-fed river having δ18Owater value of about -12 ‰ (ancient Indus distributary/Sarasvati?). In contrast, the δ18O value of a 4.3 ky old T. palustris (δ18Oshell ~-1.9 ‰), is similar to the values seen in modern-day shells (δ18Oshell ~-1.5 ‰). This indicates drying up of this ancient river at the onset of the global Meghalayan stage drought (4.3-4.1 ky BP). An abrupt desertion of the Dholavira settlement about this time (between Stage-V and VI), is also corroborated by archaeological evidence. The δ18O values

of yet another Dholaviran T. palustris (δ18Oshell ~-2.8 ‰) suggest a return to a comparatively wetter regime near the lower boundary of the Meghalayan stage drought (~ 4.0 ky BP).

VII.6. The Issue of Palaeochannels (K.S. Valdiya et al. 2016)

In 2016 the Ministry of Water Resources, River Development and Ganga Rejuvenation of the Government of India set up an expert committee to review the available information on palaeochannels related to the Sarasvati-Drishadvati river system. The committee under the chairmanship of K.S. Valdiya submitted their report in 2016 itself and was titled *Palaeochannels of Northwest India: Review and Assessment*. The summary of the report stated the following.

> In the dry western part of the Indian sub-continent encompassing Haryana, southern Punjab, Rajasthan and Gujarat, numerous palaeochannels have been identified and comprehensively investigated since early nineteenth century by geomorphologists, geologists, geophysicists, geohydrologists, archaeologists and remote-sensing specialists using high-end techniques. Large number of exploratory wells dug along the palaeochannels in these states to establish extensive networks of surface and buried palaeochannels constituting potential water-bearing aquifers in multiple groups covering the entire plain of the drainage system. The quality of groundwater in these palaeochannels is generally good. The aggregate length of the palaeochannels of all – in parts of Haryana, Rajasthan and Gujarat – is of the order of more than 2200 km. Water is available in quite many of them. More importantly, almost all of them can be artificially recharged and replenished with water. The palaeochannels promising to hold substantial amount of water thus act as storage reservoirs augmenting groundwater resources.

The banks of one of the misfit rivers, the Ghaggar-Hakra-Sarasvati-Drishadvati, is intimately associated with multiplicity of palaeochannels dotted densely with ruins of settlements, including the largest ones such as Ganweriwala (>100 ha) in Cholistan (Pakistan) and Rakhigarhi (>150 ha) in Haryana and such medium to large cities as Kalibangan, Farmana, Karanpura, Baror, Banawali, Bhirrana, Farmana and Mitathal. These settlements belong to the Hakra, Pre/Early Harappan, Harappan, Late Harappan, Painted Grey Ware and Rangmahal cultures. The middle course of the Ghaggar-Hakra palaeochannels (Sarasvati) is thus related with archaeological sites from the fourth millennium BCE to the historical period. However, there was perceptible dwindling both quantitatively and qualitatively in the settlement pattern during the second millennium BCE, which is attributed to the changing water regime. The river that supported these settlements finally disappeared in the late Holocene period.

Applying various geophysical methods of underground mapping, analyzing hundreds of well logs and pertinent data and interpreting satellite imageries, recent workers have demonstrated existence of under-surface sand bodies of palaeochannel systems (adjacent to the Harappan sites). These aquifer bodies represent the past courses of large rivers originating in the Himalaya – one flowing in the period 20 to 15 ka and the other 6 to 3 ka in northern Haryana. The Ghaggar of this region occupies the former course of the Satluj River and the hydraulically related Markanda and Sarsuti rivulets etc. were connected to the palaeo-Yamuna River. Recent studies have identified sediments deposited in the Ghaggar-Hakra palaeochannel that were sourced from the Yamuna and Satluj catchments.

The strontium ratios and neodymium ratios of the constituents of the Ghaggar sediments in the northern Haryana and in the Sirsa-Kalibangan reach in the west unequivocally demonstrate that the sediments of the buried channels were derived from the Great (Higher) Himalaya as well as from the Lesser Himalaya. In the Hakra reach, where among hundreds of settlements, the largest city of the Harappan civilization, Ganweriwala was located, the buried palaeochannel yielded potable water dated 12,900 years BP to 4700 BP. Likewise the palaeochannels in the Jaisalmer area have been supplying potable water. The water in the depth range of 30 to 50 m being 1800 to 5000 years old and in the 60 to 250 m deep aquifers 6000 to 22000 years old. In the lowermost reach, the Ghaggar-Hakra-Nara formed a delta characterized by a network of distributaries. Some of the channels have yielded heavy minerals of Himalayan origin. The facts presented in the pages of this report lead to the conclusion that in the northern Haryana, the Ghaggar-Patialiwali rivulets provided pathways to the western branch of the Himalayan born river (palaeo Satluj) and through the former courses of the Markanda and hydraulically connected Sarsuti rivulets flowed the eastern branch of the Himalayan river (palaeo Yamuna). The two branches combined 25 km south of Patiala, then flowed through the extraordinarily wide channel of the Ghaggar-Hakra-Nara and emptied itself into the Gulf of what is today known as the Arabian Sea.

On the banks of this Ghaggar at Sirsa stands an ancient fort named Sarsuti, the name recalling the rivulet Sarsuti that joins the Ghaggar at Pehowa in Kurukshetra distict. Presumably, the fort represents a tribute to the importance of the rivulet Sarsuti, a corruption of the name, Sarasvati. The name Sarasvati is ingrained in the perception of the people and the Government revenue records show the river Sarasvati extending from Adibadri in the Siwalik foothills to Pehowa and beyond.

VII.7. The Issue of Palaeochannels (A.R. Chaudhri et al. 2021)

After A.R. Chaudhri et al. 2021, 'Saraswati River in Northern India (Haryana) and its Role in Populating the Harappan

Civilization Sites—a Study Based on Remote Sensing, Sedimentology, and Strata Chronology', *Archaeological Prospection, June 2021*

The summary of this research is the following. The crucial historical point here is the fact that the Sarasvati river 'formed a dense web of interconnecting channels' and that 'the Harappan settlements in Haryana and Rajasthan nucleated and prospered in the fertile channel bars and interfluves of this river system'.

> Sarasvati River used to flow from the glaciated peaks of the Himalaya to the Arabian Sea, covering a distance of about 1800 km. It possibly sustained the Harappan civilization in the Indian subcontinent. This river has been studied as a part of the Ghaggar–Satluj–Hakra–Nara channel system in India and Pakistan. This study investigated its independent existence and evolution in the Himalayan foothill terrain and the proximal alluvial plains. Use of satellite imagery, shuttle radar topography mission data, accelerator mass spectrometry 14C dating and optically stimulated luminescence chronology is being made to identify the possible palaeo-path of this ancient river and to characterize the trench sediment log architecture of the Sarasvati River palaeochannels in northern India (Haryana). Our investigations reveal that this river formed a dense web of interconnecting channels which are continuously networked for more than 2,984 km in Haryana and their individual floodplain width varies from 1.5 to 13 km. The Harappan settlements in Haryana and Rajasthan nucleated and prospered in the fertile channel bars and interfluves of this river system. Majority of these habitation sites were located within a radius of less than 500 m from these palaeo-water channel networks. Enormous amount of water was flowing through this channel network until BC 11,147. Sediment characteristics and their chronology reveal that flow of water in the river channel decreased with time as

the glacial cover diminished. The varying thickness of clay beds in sediment logs is indicative of the fluctuations in water flow possibly as a consequence of terrain slope modifications and consequent gradual channel avulsion, climate change, and global drought events. The flow of water continued through the Himalayan foothill input channels of the palaeo-Sarasvati River in Haryana until AD 1402.

VII.8. The Issue of Palaeochannels (A. Chatterjee et al. 2019)

After A. Chatterjee et al. 2019, 'On the Existence of a Perennial River in the Harappan Heartland', *Scientific Reports vol 9—Article No. 17221*

What is important here is that the authors 'present unequivocal evidence for the Ghaggar's perennial past', although that past was confined to 80-20 Ka and 9-4.5 Ka.

> The legendary river Sarasvati of Indian mythology has often been hypothesized to be an ancient perennial channel of the seasonal river Ghaggar that flowed through the heartland of the Bronze Age Harappan civilization in north-western India. Despite the discovery of abundant settlements along a major palaeochannel of the Ghaggar, many believed that the Harappans depended solely on monsoonal rains, because no proof existed for the perennial rivers uninterrupted flow during the zenith of the civilization. Here, we present unequivocal evidence for the Ghaggar's perennial past by studying temporal changes of sediment provenance along a 300km stretch of the river basin. This is achieved using $^{40}Ar/^{39}Ar$ ages of detrital muscovite and Sr-Nd isotopic ratios of siliciclastic sediment in fluvial sequences, dated by radiocarbon and luminescence methods. We establish that during 80-20 ka and 9-4.5 ka the river was perennial and was receiving sediments from the Higher and Lesser Himalayas. The latter phase can be attributed to the reactivation of the river by the distributaries

of the Sutlej. This revived perennial condition of the Ghaggar, which can be correlated with the Sarasvati, likely facilitated development of the early Harappan settlements along its banks. The timing of the eventual decline of the river, which led to the collapse of the civilization, approximately coincides with the commencement of the Meghalayan Stage.

VII.9. The Issue of the Markanda River in the Sub-Himalayan Catchment of the Ghaggar-Hakra Palaeochannel

After A. Singh et al. 2021, 'Larger Floods of Himalayan Foothill Rivers Sustained Flows in the Ghaggar-Hakra Channel during the Harappan Age', *Journal of Quaternary Science 2021, 1-17*

The summary of argument of this publication is the following:

> Here, we estimated the palaeohydrology of the foothill Markanda river in the sub-Himalyan catchment of the Ghaggar-Hakra palaeochannel. Our morphology and chronology results show aggradation of a fan (57.7 ka) during the Late Pleistocene and T-1 to T-5 fluvial terraces (13.1 to 6 ka) during the terminal Pleistocene and Holocene, and deposition of palaeoflood sediments (3.9-3.8 ka) over the T-3 terraces during the Late Holocene. Considering the known uplift rates along the Himalayan frontal thrust and our aggradation rates, we derived channel palaeogeometry and calculated discharge at the site of palaeoflood deposits, we conclude that the Markanda river's peak discharge was several orders of magnitude higher during the late Holocene than the modern day peak discharge of 100-year return period. The palaeoflood deposits represent larger flooding of the foothill rivers that sustained flows in the downstream reaches of the Ghaggar-Hakra palaeochannel during the Late Harappan civilization.

VII.10. P. Clift et al. 2012

A new dimension has been added by P. Clift et al. 2012, 'U-Pb Zircon Dating Evidence for a Pleistocene Sarasvati River and Capture of the Yamuna River', *Geology 40(3)*

The conclusions of the paper are the following:

> The Harappan Culture, one of the oldest known urban civilizations, thrived on the northwest edge of the Thar Desert (India and Pakistan) between 3200 and 1900 BCE. Its demise has been linked to rapid weakening of the summer monsoon at this time, yet reorganization of rivers may also have played a role. We sampled subsurface channel sand bodies predating ca. 4.0 ka and used U-Pb dating of zircon sand grains to constrain their provenance through comparison with the established character of modern river sands. Samples from close to archaeological sites to the north of the desert show little affinity with the Ghaggar-Hakra, the presumed source of the channels. Instead, we see at least two groups of sediments, showing similarities both to the Beas River in the west and to the Yamuna and Sutlej Rivers in the east. The channels were active until after 4.5 ka and were covered by dunes before 1.4 ka, although loss of the Yamuna from the Indus likely occurred as early as 49 ka and no later than 10 ka. Capture of the Yamuna to the east and the Sutlej to the north rerouted water away from the area of the Harappan centers, but this change significantly predated their final collapse.

VII.11. A. Chatterjee and J.S. Ray 2017

An important paper in this context is A. Chatterjee and J.S. Ray 2017, 'Geochemistry of Harappan pottery from Kalibangan and Sediments in the Ghaggar River: Clues for a Dying River', *Geoscience Frontiers 9(4)*

The argument of the research ran like the following:

> The ephemeral Ghaggar-Hakra River of northwestern India has always been considered to be the remnant of an ancient

> perennial glacier-fed river (Vedic Saraswati). The exact reason and timing of major hydrological change of this river remains speculative. The river's purported association with the zenith of the Harappan civilisation remains a conjecture because the timings of its fluvial past are still being debated. In this study we have made an attempt to resolve this issue using geochemical provenance of sediments from some dated horizons in the Ghaggar flood plain and that of the material used in the potteries from the Mature Harappan period (4600 to 3900 yr BP) at Kalibangan. Sampled sedimentary horizons were dated by radiocarbon and optically stimulated luminescence (OSL) methods. Results of our study from the Ghaggar alluvium indicate that the river did have glacial sources during the early Holocene. However, the data from the potteries suggest that during the Mature Harappan period, the sediments in the Ghaggar as used by the potters did not have a higher Himalayan provenance and hence, were not derived from glaciated Himalayas. These findings imply that during the time of the Mature Harappans, the Ghaggar had already become a foothill-fed river.

VII.12. R. SINHA et al. 2013

Another paper worth citing is R. Sinha et al. 2013, 'Geoelectric resistivity evidence for subsurface palaeochannel system adjacent to Harappan sites in northwest India', *Quaternary International*, 308-309, 66-75.

The authors have concluded the following:

> It has been proposed that a major palaeo-river channel course, the Ghaggar-Hakra, flowed in the interfluve between the modern Yamuna and Sutlej rivers in the western Ganges basin during the Late Quaternary. This palaeochannel course has been associated with extensive Bronze-age Harappan civilisation archaeological sites that are located with the channel. The abrupt abandonment of urban centres at <"3500 BP has been explained as a consequence of river

> diversion, although alternative explanations for cultural decline have also been offered. A major problem with earlier interpretations has been that little information exists on the geology of the palaeochannel system. Electrical resistivity soundings were used to map the large-scale geometry and architecture of the palaeochannel system. A thick and extensive sand body is present in the subsurface in parts of north-western Rajasthan, Haryana and Punjab. The dimensions of the palaeochannel bodies imply that these are the deposits of a large river system, though detailed sedimentological analysis is necessary to validate this. Two of the resistivity transects are close to important Harappan sites, Kalibangan and Kunal, suggesting a possible link to archaeological site distribution. However, detailed chronological constraints are required to establish such links. Nevertheless, this study reports the first geophysical evidence for the subsurface geometry of Ghaggar-Hakra river system.

VII.13. R. Sinha, A. Singh and I. Khan 2020

Yet another interesting paper in this context is R. Sinha, A. Singh and I. Khan 2020, 'On non-contemporaneity of the Saraswati river and the Harappan Civilization in NW India: Constraints from subsurface chrono-stratigraphy'. In S. Acharya, K. Ghosh and A. Kar eds. *Saraswati: The River Par Excellence*, Kolkata Asiatic Society.

The approach of the paper and its conclusions are both summarized below in the words of the authors. The approach puts the problem and the method in proper perspective and the final summary puts the scholarly view clearly.

Approach of the paper

> Until recently, one of the biggest problems in resolving this issue has been that the subsurface existence of the Saraswati remained speculative due to a lack of high-resolution sedimentological and chrono-stratigraphic data. This

chapter is aimed at compiling the available information on stratigraphy and sedimentology of the subsurface sediments in this region to understand the evolution and particularly the timing of cessation of the large river and to critically examine its linkage with the Harappan Civilization. Some of the issues that we have chosen to address specifically are: a) Stratigraphic data based on geophysical surveys and drill cores to establish the subsurface existence and alluvial architecture of a large river system in NW India, considered as the largest concentration of sites of the Harappan Civilization. b) Sedimentological and chronological data on the subsurface sediments that have emerged from the recent work to constrain the timing of the river activity in this region. c) Sediment provenance data to fully establish the source of the subsurface deposits of a large river. d) Reconstruction of landscape morphodynamics in consequence of the drainage reorganization in this region and its linkage with the Harappan Civilization.

The long debate on the contemporaneity of the mighty Sarasvati River with the Harappan Civilization should probably be put to rest now. The growing evidence from both the major tributaries of the Ghaggar-Hakra system (Sarasvati) seem to suggest that the major rivers avulsed from this valley at least 18-8 ka ago while the urban peak of the Harappan Civilization continued until 3.3 ka. *There is a gap of at least 15-5 ka between the demise of the major rivers namely, the paleo-Sutlej and paleo-Yamuna, respectively, and the urban peak of the civilization. A much smaller monsoon-fed system, possibly a network of them, much like the modern Ghaggar system, probably continued to flow through most of the mid-Holocene period and some of these occupied the same valley as that of the mighty Sarasvati. The climatic transition after the mid-Holocene period finally led to the drying up of the river network and lakes in NW India and the fluvial deposits of the mighty river were covered by aeolian sediments in most parts, thereby generating the modern landscape.*

Although scholars have published extensively on the Sarasvati system and reached various technical solutions, all no doubt important in themselves, the foregoing paper by Rajiv Sinha, Ajit Singh and Irfan Khan has a special importance because of its historical implications. That a network of monsoon-fed system came to replace the once-mighty Sarasvati river network by the time the Harappan civilization was in its mature form and the subsequent onset of aridity generated the modern landscape of the area fits in with what I see and perceive in the landscape of Harappan spread in Rajasthan, Punjab and Haryana. If one reads Raverty's description of the system, one gets an idea of the very extensive character of a more or less extinct drainage system which still retained sufficient water during the monsoon period. The only problem that one can see here is the description of a full-flowing stream in the *Rigveda*. According to this publication the river 'avulsed' around 8000 ka, roughly 6050 BC, and it is probable that the particular portion of the *Rigveda* which deals with the Sarasvati dates either from a period a little earlier than the 'avulsion' or from somewhat later in the 6th millennium BC. Again, this publication does not go against the present author's idea that the Harappan civilization flourished in a landscape which could be seen in the gazetteers of the late 19th century. As I do not have the faintest idea of the geosciences, I cannot assess the various publications I have cited either on the basis of their methods and results; I have only expressed my opinion regarding what is historically possible.

VIII. HARAPPAN METALLURGY

Evidence of arsenic and zinc alloying has been noticed among the copper artefacts found in the Harappan context at Bagasra (Patel and Ajith Prasad 2015). Hoffman and Miller (2014) offer a detailed study of the various technological and typological problems related to the study of copper-bronze materials of the Indus civilization, although their various conclusions need not be accepted at their face value. As far as the site of Harappa is concerned, their conclusion is the following:

> The results from the beginning stages of analysis of the copper assemblage from Harappa indicate that during the Harappan Phase, the city was obtaining copper raw material primarily from sources to the west or south of the site in Oman, Baluchistan, and Waziristan. The artefacts from Harappa also demonstrate this pattern. While there is some evidence for the possible utilization of copper from northern Rajaśthan at Harappa, it is neither firm nor indicative of a high degree of use, contrary to previous hypotheses regarding the source of Indus period copper (Hoffman and Miller 2014).

In 2009 F. Begemann and S. Schmitt-Strecker published in German ('uber das fruhe kupfer Mesoptamiens') a paper in *Irania Antiqua* 44: 1-45, which is interesting from the Indian point of view. Its abstract is quoted below.

> A lead isotope study on the early copper of Mesoptamia reports on copper-base artifacts ranging in age from the 4th millennium BC (Uruk period) to the Akkadian at the end of the 3rd millennium BC. Arguments are presented that, in the (tin) bronzes, the lead associated with tin used for alloying did not contribute to the total in any detectable way. Hence, the lead isotopy traces the copper and cannot address the problem of the provenance of tin. The data suggest as possible source region of the copper a variety of ore occurrences in Anatolia, Iran, Oman, Palestine and, rather unexpectedly (by us) from India. During the earliest period the isotopic signature of ores from Central and North Anatolia is dominant; during the next millennium this region loses its importance and is hardly present any more at all. Instead, southeast Anatolia, central Iran, Oman, Feinan-Timna in the rift valley between Dead Sea and Red Sea, and sources in the Caucasus are now potential suppliers of the copper.

> Generally, an unambiguous assignment of an artefact to any of the ores is not possible because the isotopic fingerprints of ore occurrences are not unique. In our suite of samples bronze objects become important during ED III (middle of the 3rd millennium BC) but they never make up more than 50% of the total. They are distinguished in their lead isotopy by very high 206 Pb-normalized abundance ratios. As source of such copper we suggest Gujarat/ Southern Rajasthan which, on general grounds, has been proposed to have been the most important supplier of copper in ancient India. We propose this Indian copper to have been arsenic-poor and to be the *urudu-luh-ha* variety which is one of the two sorts of purified copper mentioned in contemporaneous written texts from Mesopotamia to have been in circulation there concurrently. (Begemann and Schmitt-Strecker 2009)

That there was contact between the Indus valley and Mesopotamia in the Early Dynastic III period is proved by the occurrence of two types of Indus carnelian beads in the Royal Graves at Ur around 2600 BC. Whether some Indus copper was reaching Mesopotamia during this period is still uncertain.

Among the thousands of metal artefacts reputedly found at Dholavira, 65 metal artefacts – 35 of lead/lead ores, 14 of silver and 16 of copper/copper ores – were subjected to lead isotope and other analyses (Bisht et al. 2015). These sampled objects came from contexts representing all major areas of the site and most of its chronological stages. What has been inferred is that the Amba Mata deposit at the Gujarat-Rajasthan border near Mount Abu and the Kanrach valley of southern Baluchistan were significant source areas with some copper from northern Rajasthan and Oman. It may be noted that much of such inferences is speculative, especially the case of Omani copper at Dholavira. K. Raghuvans (2013) offers a systematic study of the 'ancient mines and metal processing activities in the Sekhawati region of Rajasthan' and refers in that context to a study of the sources of copper at the site of Harappa. This study supposedly infers that the sources of the major supply of copper to Harappa lay mainly to the west of the site, although north Rajasthan is not completely ruled out.

> A preliminary investigation of lead isotope analysis was carried out by Hoffman, Randal and Raghubans (2005) to determine the provenance of copper ore during Harappan period. The copper sample were derived from Harappa and were compared with seven regional copper source areas, i.e. Ganeshwar and Singhana in Rajasthan, Chagai hills in Baluchistan, Shin Kai copper deposit in Waziristan, Iran and Oman. The analysis resulted that Harappans perhaps acquired most of copper ore from the west of Harappa and some of its copper ore was also obtained from Rajasthan.

The general scientific opinion is that such inferences based on lead isotopic analysis require, before they can be accepted with a degree of certainty, is that the ore bodies are sufficiently well characterised isotopically and that the suite of lead isotopes is sufficiently distinct from other ore bodies. One is not sure if the lead isotope analysis of ores and objects in these cases fulfil satisfactorily the above criteria. Thus, the idea that site of Harappa was getting most of its copper from the West, i.e. from Baluchistan and Afghanistan, may be an exaggeration, although entirely in keeping with the assumption of certain modern Western scholars that major Harappan sites in Pakistan were aligned more to the west than to the east.

Excavations at Khanak (Singh et al. 2016) have significantly contributed to the study of Harappan metallurgy by isolating what was certainly one of its prominent sources of tin. The 2.65 m deep cultural deposit at the site has been divided into

Early and Mature Harappan, yielding steatite beads, terracotta cakes, beads of lapis lazuli, carnelian, agate, jasper, terracotta bangles, terracotta animals, terracotta crucibles and slag. The metallic analysis of some relevant material has clearly established the utilization of tin at the site. Slag samples contain tin. The traces of 'melt' found inside the crucibles and potsherds show tin. Also, a copper celt of the late phase of Early Harappan shows 2.02% tin. Singh et al. (2015) conclude that the Harappan settlers at Khanak "used locally available polymetallic tin ores from nearby areas and were practicing extractive metallurgy particularly of tin and probably of copper-bronze".

IX. HARAPPAN AGRICULTURE AND ANIMAL REMAINS

In the field of agriculture an important publication is Kashyap and Weber (2010) on the 'Harappan plant use revealed by starch grains from Farmana, India'. First, for the uninitiated they define what a starch grain is:

> starch grains are plant microfossils with distinctive features such as size and shape, and exhibiting certain physical features ... which are genetically controlled. These features, when carefully studied, can be used to identify plant taxa.

At Farmana, starch granules were extracted "from 50 different surfaces including surfaces of pottery vessels, stone tools and dental calculus of human burials". The following primary plants have been identified: wheat, barley, rice, among large grained cereals; setaria, panicum and sorghum millets among the small grained cereals; gram (*vigna*), horsegram and eggplant among pulses and vegetables; cucurbits and mango among fruits; and ginger, turmeric, sedge, *dioscorea* and garlic among root tubers and spices.

There has been an attempt to reinforce the idea that with the beginning of arid conditions around 4200 years BP there was a shift in agriculture towards millet in Gujarat by A. Pokharia et al. (2017) in the context of Khirsara (Kathiawar). The site is said to belong throughout its duration for about 700 years (~4600-#3900 years cal BP) to the Mature Harappan, but with three phases. Phase IA (~4600-4300 years BP) yielded both winter crops (barley, wheat, field-pea, grass-pea, linseed) and summer crops (green/yellow/bristley, horse gram and green gram). Barley appears to be the main crop whereas the small-grained millets were low in abundance. The abundance of barley and wheat declined in the transitional phase (~4300-4100 years cal BP) but the small-grained millets (green/yellow bristley, foxtail, sorghum, finger millet) seem to have increased their abundance. 'In the later phase of the mature Indus cultural era' (~4100-3900 years cal BP) barley and wheat are supposed to have declined significantly whereas the millets including sorghum seem to have dominated the agricultural produce. According to Pokharia and his group "botanical evidences suggest that the ~4200 years BP arid event may have forced a shift in agriculture towards millet type (also C-4 type) crops at Khirsara and other human-occupied sites in the region".

Regarding this shift towards millet type, one wonders if it would be possible for these scholars to translate the much-talked-about arid event in the background in terms of the actual inches of annual rainfall. Significant rainfall variations are not unknown in the subcontinent: in Mewar the maximum annual rainfall was nearly 44.5 inches in 1893 whereas it was just under 10 inches in 1899 (Chakrabarti 2019: 145-146). No new drought-resistant crop was recorded to have been adopted by Mewar cultivators then. The quantity and distribution of annual rainfall certainly influence the character of agriculture in an area but whether major shifts in agriculture take place only because of the diminished quantity of rainfall is perhaps an uncertain point. It appears that some scientists believe in straight correlation between the amount and distribution of annual rainfall in an area and its agricultural character. The reality is likely to be far more complex, as many comparatively recent situations suggest. Historically speaking, it should be possible to find an echo of what Possehl once wrote about the preference for millets in the Harappan economy of Gujarat in Pokharia's claim for a shift towards millets, although I would not like to give any credence to these ideas of these scholars.

Another set of crop data comes from J. Bates' report of finds from the sites excavated by Cameron Petrie and his group in Haryana (Bates et al. 2016).

> Rice (Oryza sp.), several varieties of millet (Echinochloa cf. colona, Setaria cf. pumila and Panicum sp.) and a range of tropical (also called kharif or summer) pulses (Vigna mungo, Vigna radiata, Vigna unguiculata, Macrotyloma uniflorum) were found alongside barley (Hordeum vulgare), wheat (Triticum sp.) and rabi (winter) pulses (Lens cf. culinaris, Pisum sp., Cicer sp., Lathyrus sp.) at all three sites .... Rice spikelet bases were also recovered from a range of contexts at both sites ..., including deposits that have been dated to Early Harappan, Mature Harappan, Late Harappan and PGW periods on the basis of relative comparanda .... Following the discovery of rice grains at these sites, a programme of directly dating rice grains was carried out as part of a wider programme of dating the use of summer crops at Masudpur I and VI .... These dates demonstrate that rice was being exploited in both Mature and Late Harappan period, and the recovery of rice grains and spikelet bases from stratigraphically earlier contexts that were direct dating through dates on other crop species show that rice was also used as early as the Early Harappan period.

The explanatory part of the data with regard to rice seems to be interesting.

> ... excavations also demonstrate that the exploitation of rice by Indus populations appears to pre-date the arrival of O. sativa sp. japonica and wet rice farming. Furthermore, the weeds suggest that rather than a shift towards wetland cropping during the Late Harappan or PGW periods, as has been previously hypothesised, a complex pattern of exploiting both wet and dry land species is seen in the Early, Mature and Late Harappan periods and also in the post-Harappan PGW phase at these settlements. The analyses of the rice grains, spikelet bases and weeds suggest therefore that the relationship between agricultural strategy and domestication is more complex than has been previously suggested and that rice domestication without paddy fields may have occurred in northern South Asia between c. 6000 BCE (Lahuradewa) and the arrival of Chinese rice c. 2000 BCE.

There has been a whole lot of rigmarole about the origin of rice cultivation in India in recent years, especially after the claim of Saraswat and others that the rice obtained from the earliest level of Lohuradeva, dated in the 7th millennium BC was domesticated rice. This upset the grandiose China-and southeast Asia-based theory of scholars like Peter Bellwood who prefer to see the beginning of rice cultivation in India in terms of language and cultural migration from that direction (for criticism of this idea, Chakrabarti 2008). Bates and her mentors apparently belong to this school of thought, and this is the reason of such rigmarole, garbled as 'science'.

Interesting light on the use of animals at Bagasra has been thrown by a study of the enamel formation of its animal remains by B. Chase and his associates (2014).

> In general, small stock spent the period of enamel formation near to Bagasra and grazed on a seasonally variable diet consisting of both wild and agricultural food prior to slaughter upon reaching their full weight. In contrast, several of the large stock included in the study either spent

> the period of enamel formation further afield from the site or were foddered with agricultural products grown in these areas prior to slaughter at Bagasra towards the end of their useful life as suppliers of milk and traction.

This is a normal practice in the Indian context but it has been useful to have this practice verified at Bagasra.

IX.1. More on Harappan Agriculture and Food

One relevant publication in the context of Harappan agriculture is: J. Bates, *2019*, 'Oilseeds, spices, fruits and flavour in the Indus civilization', *Journal of Archaeological Science: Reports* 24: 879-887. This lists non-staple food plants known in the Harappan civilization and "models that move beyond agriculture and diet to think about how people considered these plants as parts of their daily life, with caveats regarding taphonomy and culturally contextual notions of functions". One cannot be sure if historically this kind of exercise is relevant.

One may at this point draw attention to two publications which are interesting not because they throw light on Harappan food per se but on the scientific technique to understand it.

Aksheyata Suryanarayan et al. 2021, 'Lipid residues from pottery from the Indus civilization in northwest India', *Journal of Archaeological Science* 2021. It is based on her Ph.D. thesis, 'What is cooking in the Indus civilization? Investigating Indus food through ceramic lipid residue analysis'. A Cambridge University release offers insight into the methodology of the work:

> As the first large-scale investigation into Indus foodstuff and vessel-use using lipid residue analysis, the thesis first tests the viability of the method in the South Asian context. It compares lipid yields from pottery recovered from collections, washed pottery from recent excavations, and unwashed pottery from fresh excavations. It then integrates

> the molecular and compound-specific isotopic data with available bioarchaeological evidence from the study region to reconstruct which products were used in vessels at different sites. The results indicate that overall, lipid residues are typically poorly preserved in Indus vessels, but the acidified methanol extraction technique provides a good lipid recovery rate. No significant differences in lipid yield are observable between washed pottery samples and those collected directly from the field, which suggests that washed pottery may serve as a good source for samples for future lipid residue analysis. However, it is difficult to interpret lipid evidence ...

A clearer idea is obtained from another university release of the same university, dated 9/12/2020 under the caption 'fatty residues on ancient pottery reveal meat-heavy diets of Indus civilization'.

> This study is the first to investigate absorbed lipid residues in pottery from multiple Indus sites, including the Indus city of Rakhigarhi, as well as other Indus settlements of Farmana and Masudpur I and VII, allowing comparisons to be made across settlements and across time. The identification of specific compounds in the lipid extracts enables the detection of different plant or animal products, such as fatty acids, previously used in the vessels. Additionally, isotopic analysis of fatty acids enables the differentiation of different types of animal meat and milk. These analyses enable an understanding of vessel use and what was being cooked in them.
>
> Suryanarayan said:
>
> Our study of lipid residues in Indus pottery shows a dominance of animal products in vessels, such as the meat of non-ruminant animals like pigs, ruminant animals like cattle or buffalo and sheep or goat, as well as dairy products. However, as one of the first studies in the region there are interpretative challenges. Some of the results were quite

> unexpected, for example, we found a predominance of non-ruminant animal fats, even though the remains of animals like pigs are not found in large quantities in the Indus settlements. It is possible that plant products or mixtures of plant and animal products were also used in vessels, creating ambiguous results.
>
> Additionally, despite the high percentages of the remains of domestic ruminant animals found at these sites, there is very limited direct evidence of the use of dairy products in vessels, including in perforated vessels that have been previously suggested to be linked to dairy processing.

Similar isotopic methods of study were adopted by Kalyan Sekhar Chakraborty in the case of animals from the excavated site of Kotada Bhadli: Kalyan Sekhar Chakraborty et al., 2018, 'Enamel isotopic data from the domesticated animals at Kotada Bhadli, Gujarat, reveals specialized animal husbandry during the Indus civilization', *Journal of Archaeological Science: Reports*, 21 (2018): 181-199

> This pilot study based on the oxygen and carbon isotope data from cattle/buffalo, sheep, and sheep/goat teeth from .... Kotada Bhadli (2400–2000 BCE) suggests that this settlement was indeed engaged in specialized seasonal herding of the domesticated animals. Comparing these data with published data on cattle/buffalo, sheep and goat from the nearby Harappan settlement of Bagasra indicates that a distinct form of sedentary animal husbandry was practised at the site of Kotada Bhadli, the nature of which is considerably different from that practised at the permanent settlement of Bagasra. At Kotada Bhadli both wild flora and agricultural waste were utilized as fodder, depending on their seasonal availability. Such seasonal availability, and the diversification of fodder selection may suggest a regional adaptation to the local climate by the agro-pastoralists during the Late phase of the Mature period (2300–1900 BCE) of the Indus Civilization. The strontium isotopes from the

> tooth enamel suggest that domesticates consumed at Kotada Bhadli were most likely raised locally, with a grazing catchment not extending far from the settlement. The results also suggest that at least in Gujarat during the Mature period of the Indus Civilization, carbon isotope values along with tooth morphology might be used to distinguish between sheep and goats, due to human practices involving the deliberate use of millets as fodder for sheep but much less so for goat.

Study of isotope analysis of lipid residues of sherds from Kotada Bhadli led Kalyan Sekhar Chakraborty to the postulate of dairy farming at the site. Kalyan Sekhar Chakraborty et al., 'Compound specific isotope analysis of lipid residues provides the earliest evidence of dairy product processing in south Asia', *Scientific Reports* (2020) 10: 16095.

> In this paper, by analyzing the absorbed lipid residues from fifty nine ceramic sherds recovered from an agro pastoral settlement that was occupied during the peak of the Indus period around mid to late third millennium BCE, we provide the earliest direct evidence of dairy product processing, particularly from cattle and possibly from some water buffalo. By providing direct evidence of animal product processing, we identify the use of primary domesticated animals and other resources in the diet during the Indus Civilization.

The methodology of Chakraborty's work is interesting, as the following extract clearly reveals. He worked while being affiliated to the University of Toronto, Missisauga.

> Chakraborty worked with Professor Greg Slater of McMaster University to determine that dairy was being produced. Pottery is porous and absorbs some of the food cooked inside it. Chakraborty looked for lipids because they don't dissolve in water. Centuries later, it's still possible to identify which types of fat are present using a technique called stable isotope analysis.

Using an organic solvent to dissolve the residues, Chakraborty and Slater were able to identify which lipids were present. They analyzed palmitic and stearic acids – both abundant at archaeological sites. Depending on the carbon isotopes present, it's possible to determine if the lipids in the residue came from plants, fish or ruminant animals.

They were also able to determine which types of ruminant animals were being used for dairy production. Cows and water buffalo ate a diet that consisted primarily of millet, while sheep and goats grazed on nearby grasses. These plants have different photosynthetic processes that produce different acids. From their analysis, the researchers were able to determine that the dairy residues came from animals that had eaten millet.

Finally, the most important recent paper in the present context is: R. Agnihotri et al., 'Macroscopic, biochemical and staple isotopic investigations of seven multi-nutritional food-balls from Indus archaeological site Rajasthan (India)', *JAS Reports vol. 37, 2021*. The abstract of the paper states the following:

During excavation of a Harappan archaeological site 4MSR (29°122 24.483 N, 73°092 20.163 E) from western Rajasthan (India), seven closely spaced similar sized spheroids (food-balls) were recovered. Detailed microscopic, biochemical (organic), elemental and stable isotopic composition of the spheroidal-material was studied. δ13C value of organic fraction (–22.5‰) indicated agricultural origin of organic matter. Significant excesses of Magnesium (Mg) and Calcium (Ca) and Potassium (K) further supported organic (food material) dominance in the spheroids. Gas chromatography mass-spectrometry (GCMS) analysis showed dominance of plant derived organic compounds in the spheroid sample. Microscopic stain analysis using safranin and iodine dyes confirmed bulk of the spheroids was composed of organic material. Majority of starch granule morphotypes found in

> spheroid-material were made of legumes and cereals dominated by Mung (*Vigna radiata*). Siliceous phytoliths, Ca and Mg oxalate crystals along with a few Mg sulphate crystals were also observed in spheroids composition. We surmise these spheroids were mainly made up of food grains comprising both cereals and legumes. The concept of offerings for some ritual or multi-nutritive compact food-balls for instant nutrition as food-supplements, perhaps prevailed during that period. The presence of bull figurines, hand held copper adze and a Harappan seal in the vicinity of these seven food balls signify that humans revered all these commodities due to their utility and importance to them.

Spheroid balls of this type, made of cereals, legumes and oilseeds, are produced in most Indian households either as delicacies or as ritual offerings especially in cases where the idea of *pindadana* is invoked. *Pindas* of this type are offered in the memory of ancestors in Hindu *Sraddha* ceremonies. In fact, the holding of such *Sraddhas* does not require any special place because I myself have offered such *Pindas* in the memory of my ancestors while sitting on a river-bank. In a newspaper report (www.freepressjournal.in) the excavator Sanjay Manjul in fact says that it could be akin to *pindadana*. I would say that the mixing of oilseeds, especially black sesame seeds (*til*) in these food balls is almost a sure indication that these were *pindas* offered to ancestors.

The questioning of R. Agnihotri et al. article by J. Bates et al., 'The challenge of the unique and unprecedented, comment on Agnihotri et al. 2021', *Journal of Archaeological Science Reports*, 31 October, 2021, does not seem to carry any weight at all and may be ignored by Indians.

X. SKELETAL STUDIES

In the case of the excavated skeletons at Harappa, the following pathological conditions were observed by earlier scholars: low prevalence of iron-deficiency anaemia, degenerative joint disease, a low frequency of enamel defects and a moderate caries rate. Further, according to the same group of scholars, "there was no evidence for any biological discontinuity among the Cemetery R-37 populations and later cemetery populations at the site", the later cemeteries being the two strata of cemetery H. Later G. Robbins Schug et al. (2012) studied the skeletal remains from Harappa kept in the Anthropological Survey of India in Kolkata mainly for signs of trauma and diseases. She reports the general result of this type of research on 90 individuals kept in a different place: "there was no evidence for traumatic injury in the 90 individuals studied previously".

Trauma has been divided into postcranial and cranial injuries. Postcranial trauma at Harappa affected only three of the 160 individuals studied. The postcranial injuries affected wrist, hand and foot bones and were "consistent with either accidental or violent injuries". Nine individuals suffered cranio-facial trauma – 2 immature individuals, 4 adult females and 3 adult males. Seven of the nine individuals studied "were injured more than once, indicating interpersonal violence was a recurrent feature of life for some individuals at Harappa". An interesting part of this enquiry is the examination of skeletons from what was apparently a mass grave or ossuary of Area G. More cases of this type of cranio-facial trauma have been noticed here, which has not been considered surprising in view of the possible disintegrating process of the earlier organized urban structure of the site. A notable find of Schug and her group is the occurrence of both leprosy and tuberculosis at the site (Schug et al. 2013). Whether the occurrence of these diseases was related to the declining phase of the civilization or the product of general medical conditions lasting through this civilization is a point which cannot be settled without investigations on a far larger scale. As things stand, none of the results of Schug's enquiry can be said to have led to an integrated causal mechanism of Harappan decline.

An emerging but still uncertain area of enquiry is the strontium isotope analysis of tooth enamel found in skeletons and determining on that basis the presence of people from different areas at a particular site. Such a study has been available in the case of the contact between the Indus civilization and Ur but without specific results (Kenoyer et al. 2013).

XI. NEWLY EXCAVATED SITES

The number of Harappan sites which have been excavated since 2014 are not many, and many of them are small sites where the main purpose of excavations was to collect samples for scientific analysis. Another noteworthy development is the publication of Dholavira and Rakhigarhi excavation reports, both of which, although very important, do not seem to have contributed much to the addition of fresh knowledge about these sites. An important 'new' site is Karanpura, excavated in 2012-14 (Prabhakar and Majid 2014). Located on the bank of the dried-up course of the modern Chautang or the ancient *Drishadvati*, this site is about 16 hectares in extent, of which the Mature Harappan phase occupies the larger area. The extent of its Early Harappan occupation was smaller. The mud bricks used in the Early Harappan phase fell in the general, although not universal, ratio of 1: 2: 3. The normal Early Harappan brick size at this site was 14 x 28 x 42. Copper implements were present throughout. The pottery comprised red pottery with chocolate slip on the neck and shoulder, bi-chrome pottery, and red pottery with incised decorations. The bead industry included lapis lazuli, agate, bloodstone, shell, etc. as raw materials. A phase, apparently succeeding that of the Early Harappans, comprised terracotta nodules, steatite disc beads and Mature Harappan pottery forms. This has been called a transitional phase between the Early and Mature Harappans. The Mature Harappan settlement at the site was a bipartite settlement which had a mud brick fortification for one division clearly. There were well laid-out house blocks along the fortification wall which was separated from the houses by a street running all along. There were typical Mature Harappan pottery forms and a bead industry of steatite, amazonite, etched carnelian, etc. Black sandstone was among the grinding materials. Domestic fowls stand out among the domesticated animals which comprised cattle, sheep, goat, etc. Graffiti occurred extensively, especially on the chocolate-slipped red pottery. One graffiti example showed two stylized animals looking at each other. Copper mirror, arrowheads, rings and bangles constituted the copper industry. There was a chert weight and there was also one seal showing unicorn.

Among the recently excavated sites in the Rajasthan-Haryana sector one may also mention Masudpur in Hissar (Petrie et al. 2009), Burj near Fatehabad in Haryana (Singh et al. 2010) and Dabli vas Chugta (Singh et al. 2012). No new settlement type was discovered, but at the site of Lohari Ragho there was an extensive occurrence of grinding stones, which seemingly suggests that "intensive crop processing was being carried out at the settlement", although one cannot yet be sure of the phase when this was being carried out (Singh et al. 2018). Alternately, this could be a place which was a grindstone production centre from which they used to be exported to the neighbouring sites. Among the other sites, mention may be made of Janan in the Khadir island of Kutch, which has yielded some Early Harappan and Mature Harappan material and an extensive stone blade industry (Rajesh et al. 2018).

XII. BURIAL SITES

The addition of a few new burial sites to the inventory of Harappan sites in Haryana and western U.P. is an important feature of this research period, with two major points having been located so far: the Farmana belt of Rohtak in Haryana, and Sanauli near Baghpat in western Uttar Pradesh. The major focus of the first centre is Farmana (Shinde et al. 2008), a site of more than 18 ha which shows a road with houses on either side. The most noteworthy complex comprises 26 rooms, 3 or 4 kitchens, 3 or 4 bathrooms and a central courtyard. The burial site yielded 70 burials in the form of primary, secondary and symbolic remains. The skeleton of a middle-aged woman was found associated with 3 shell bangles, 2 copper bangles, and copper earrings. The burial area of her remains also yielded copper beads and ornaments of the feet. Farmana is a Mature Harappan site and within the distance of 2 to 5 km from the site there are burial remains at Bedwa-2, Puthi Seman-2 and Bhaini-Surjan-1, all of which "can be assigned to the late phase of Mature Harappan to Late Harappan period" (Dangi and Samunder 2013).

The burial at Sanauli near Bagpat yielded about 116 burials in the first phase of excavations beginning in 2004. On the basis of pottery the Sanauli burial complex has been ascribed to the Late Harappan stage. One of its excavators, M.N. Prabhakar, reports the following:

> The evidence at Sanauli indicates its long usage as a cemetery as different stratigraphic contexts indicate in the absence of absolute dates. Further, the findings from this also brought to light the probable interactions with the 'Copper Hoard' culture due to the presence of an antenna sword from one of the burials. Another antenna sword was also discovered from the site prior to the excavation by the villagers. The general arrangement of burials at Sanauli clearly indicates continuity from the Harappan phase in terms of placement of bodily remains, associated burial furniture, with the exception that dish on stand was placed below the hip portion of the dead ones.

The results of further excavations at the site, about 120 m away from the earlier excavated area, have been reported by S.K. Manjul and Arvin Manjul who conducted these excavations on behalf of the Archaeological Survey of India in *Puratattva 48 (2018)* under the heading 'Recent excavation at Sanauli, district Bagpat, UP: a landmark of Indian archaeology'. To understand the nature and significance of these excavations, one may try to follow them in some detail. First, a 10 m x 10 m trench was laid out and further extended in the east, west and the south for 5 m more. The total number of burials unearthed were eight, of which there were three burials in coffin, three secondary burials including one 'twin burial' and two symbolic burials. The latter contained no human skeletal remains but bones of dog and bird were found in the same pit. The details of the coffin and other burials are as follows.

Burial Pit 1: the decomposed remains of a wooden legged coffin were found associated with pottery and other grave goods arranged systematically in the grave pit. The skeleton lay supine in the coffin whose top and the skeleton itself were found disturbed by later activities. The floor of the grave pit was found to be of olive green sticky clay.

Burial pit 2: although disturbed, the position of bones and burial pottery indicates an orientation from the northwest to the southeast.

Burial pit 3: a legged coffin (wooden) is placed in the centre of this secondary burial with a chariot, a shield, a sword, pottery and other burial goods being arranged on all sides. The coffin yielded only a part of the bone remains and was in this sense a fragmentary burial. The vases and bowls were kept near the head and two wide mouthed storage jars close to the legs. A copper object which has been tentatively interpreted as a helmet, two channel-like (copper?) objects and a copper dagger were found placed beneath the coffin. A copper antennae sword was placed in an east-west alignment on the yoke of the chariot. A bowl-shaped copper helmet with flared rim was put on the northern side of the coffin. A highly ornamented shield shaped like a human torso was placed on the pole of the chariot.

An interesting object found in this pit is what has been described as a "chalice-shaped copper pot having tortoise base". This is a big shallow copper bowl with flared flat rim, small stem and tortoise base, the stem and the base being made of solid copper cast in one piece with the upper part 'jointed'. Two stick tops "probably used for capping the top of commanding stick" have been found beneath the coffin near the tortoise-shaped copper pot. These two 'stick tops' are said to be made of electrum. A long wooden shaft of whip has been found from the northern side of the coffin. The lash, possibly made of some flexible organic material, has decomposed. Five gold beads were recovered from near the coffin. These are disc-shaped gold beads, the like of which has been recovered from Mandi in Muzaffarnagar. Paste and steatite beads decorated the sides of the coffin.

Burial pit 4: this is a secondary or fractional burial with 6 cylindrical steatite beads being found in the pit.

Burial pit 5: this is a symbolic burial without any skeletal find. Its burial goods comprise pottery, two antennae swords and two copper channels, all systematically placed inside the pit. It is possible that that this symbolic burial belongs to two persons. One of the jars contains tiny fragments of bones. One of the antennae swords (70.5 x 5 x 0.7 cm) is hilted, the hilt being 19 cm long and 3.5 cm in diameter. The hilt is made of wood but covered with copper strips. Between the hilt and the blade there is a V-shaped pommel. Two copper channels have been found along with these swords. There is also a long, semi-circular sheet of copper with finished edges.

Burial pit 6: in the centre of the pit is a legged wooden coffin (259 x 72 x 95 cm), the legs being 50 cm long.

> The lid of the coffin is highly decorated and carved out in high relief. At the starting possibly a crown or royal insignia was depicted and followed by eight anthropomorphs. The high relief carving was done in wood and after that thin copper sheathing was provided with the help of small nails ... during excavations we have found large quantities of nails in situ. At present wood is fully perished and copper sheathing is also deteriorated badly. A human skull has been exposed partially below the first and second anthropomorphic figures. All eight figures are depicted in similar style with minor difference in shoulder part and *ayudha* holding in hand. The depiction is of a human, head adorned with the headgear of half rounded horn turning inwards and probably a *pipal* leaf in centre .... These figures are one of the finest examples of wood and metal craftsmanship .... The legs of coffin were also decorated with copper strips and triangles. Copper sheathing was provided both on outer as well as inner side of coffin. A beautiful foliage design has been exposed on the outer side of the coffin.

What has been outlined above is only a summary of the major finds at the end of the first year of the renewed excavations at Sanauli in 2018-19. The first phase of excavations at the same site in 2004-05 revealed 116 burials but none with the association of chariots. However, there is no reason to assume that these two phases of work at Sanauli represent two separate archaeological cultures. On the basis of pottery types and the finds of antennae swords, anthropomorphs and other material such as gold and semi-precious and steatite and faience beads they may be convincingly ascribed to the late Harappan assemblage found in the Doab. The so-called Copper Hoard element, of which indisputable signs have been noted at Sanauli, has long been known to be a part of the mature/late Harappan tradition, although, according to Manjul and Manjul, the excavators of Sanauli 2018-19, the Copper

Hoard elements provide the evidence of "their co-existence with mature Harappans". The Copper Hoard site of Harinagar near Bijnor in the Doab has been radiocarbon dated 2200-2000 BC, and thus the roots of this Copper Hoard tradition may be earlier than what is generally assumed to be 'late Harappan'. Sanauli, however, is not yet radiocarbon dated and one hopes that with further excavations the picture will be better understood. At the present stage of knowledge there is no point in getting excited by the occurrence of electrum as the raw material of two 'stick tops' of burial 6 and the thought that the nearest source of electrum was western Anatolia.

The same may be said about V. Shinde's and his group's excavations at the burial ground of Rakhigarhi (Shinde et al. 2018). Their description of the excavated burials in the specific cemetery area of the site also lays down the definitional criteria of the different types of burials found here. For instance, they "sub-categorized the Rakhigarhi cemetery's primary burials into typical and atypical cases. Typical cases, entailing burial of supine-positioned bodies inside of a plain pit were found in much greater numbers than were atypical, exceptional cases such as brick-lined graves, multiple bodies or prone-positioned burial. The Harappan people's common practice was, at least as far as Rakhigarhi cemetery indicates, the burial of the body without any process of reduction." Secondary burials were defined as "the final disposal of the body parts long after death, regardless of inhumation or cremation, decomposition, or earlier relocation". Symbolic burials were cases where "the body was not placed inside the burial at the time that the grave was first constructed." Such burials could contain sacrificed animal bones or other grave goods. The burials were found at different depths, and "the carbon dating of the samples at the depths of 9.1 and 20.6 metres yielded calibrated dates of 2273 +/- 38 years BCE and 2616 +/- 73 years BCE, respectively."

Careful notes have been taken of the differences between burials, leading to possible inferences regarding the social position of the buried persons. For instance, four brick-lined graves were noticed at Rakhigarhi where "the brick-lined burials were among the most elaborately constructed graves, implying a high social or ritual status for the deceased". All the four skeletons belonged to differently aged females. There were three cases of prone-positioned burials where the extended skeletons were found lying with their face down and one of them was that of a female. There was a single case of multiple individuals inside a single pit, showing a mix of primary and secondary burials. One expects that with detailed studies of this type a comprehensive picture of the Harappan burial practices will slowly emerge. Further, it has been reputedly claimed that a single Rakhigarhi skeleton has yielded ancient DNA. Although various speculations in this regard have appeared in the popular press, one would rather wait for its definitive publication and analysis (see later in this essay).

XIII. A GENERAL ASSESSMENT OF THE INDUS SCENARIO: PETRIE et al. 2017

The paper, 'Adaptation to variable environments, resilience to climate change, investigating land, water and settlement in Indus northwest India', by C. Petrie and his associates in *Current Anthropology* 58(1) 2017 offers a systematic review of the developments in those spheres of Indus studies in which the members of this research group have been involved. The first major point which is underlined is that the Indus sites display both an environmental and hydrological diversity. In view of the sheer geographical spread of this civilization in the map of the sub-continent and the various environmental and hydrological diversities that one can observe in the same areas even now, this is undoubtedly a logical statement. Whether the area around Rakhigarhi had only small watercourses or a major palaeo-channel known as the Drishadvati running through it is a debatable point but both wells and ponds must have played a role in the irrigational landscape of this site. The second major point of crop diversity is also undoubtedly acceptable, but the way in which this is currently being interpreted may be open to disagreements. That there was a broad division between the areas growing winter crops and summer crops can be hypothesized sheerly on the basis of the modern agricultural landscape of the total area. However, to argue that "there was an increased use of summer crops from the beginning of the second millennium BC onward" and that "this agricultural diversification may have been a response to ecological challenges" is hardly logical. This neat correlation between a supposed ecological challenge and shift towards the cultivation of millets in the context of Gujarat was tentatively made by Gregory Possehl in the case of his Ph.D. study of some Harappan sites in Kathiawar and has since then been uncritically cited by his followers both in the West and in India. The main reason why various crops have spread in comparatively recent times to various areas outside their main areas of occurrence, such as wheat in modern West Bengal, is that they have become acceptable in the modern context mainly because of economic reasons associated with some change in food habits. To read anything more in this may not be an acceptable exercise. However, the way in which the occurrence of rice and millet in the pre-Harappan contexts of Banawali, Balu and Kunal, all in Haryana, has been "discounted because of a lack of quantifications in the final publications and a lack of direct absolute dates" is reflective of the negative attitude of the concerned authors to one of the most celebrated Indian students of botanical remains in archaeology, K.S. Saraswat. Rice, as studies related to Lohura Deva, far to the east in the Gorakhpur area, has shown, developed as a crop long before the emergence of the Indus civilization and the migration of this crop to the Indus domain in Haryana-Punjab should by no means be accepted as 'out-of-context'. For instance, Sind has been a major rice-growing area of the sub-continent and I would say that this is likely to be valid for the protohistoric context as well. I say this not on the basis of any 'science' but only on the basis of the historical perception that in India the major crop-pattern of the given areas has been historically stable. I would also argue that the emphasis on multi-cropping during the Indus phase does not need any 'science' to prove or disprove it because without multi-cropping the agricultural landscape of the concerned areas would not have sustained the growth of a civilization like the Indus civilization in them. The fact that the occurrence of rice in the early Harappan context in the Indus region will negate the idea of a straight wheat-barley-based cultural sequence from Mehrgarh onwards, which eventually culminated, so to speak, in the growth of the Indus civilization in the Indus plain eminently suits those scholars, according to whom, this civilization spread from the west to the east. The problem does not fall in the domain of 'science' but in the domain of the socio-politics of the Indus or Harappan studies.

Petrie et al. also emphasize the elements of regional variation, assuming that this evidence "supports the suggestion that the widespread attestation of classic Indus material is actually a veneer that overlay a considerable degree of cultural diversity".

One might not like the use of the word 'veneer' in this context. By any dictionary definition 'veneer' connotes a surface layer to hide the cruder layers underneath, both the parts being separate and commonly detachable. To many of us Indians, the Indus civilization, although with many locally diverse contexts in the background, grew up as a cultural, economic, social and perhaps even political tradition, that was the high/great tradition of India through the ages. Not for a moment was it a detachable or superficial 'veneer'.

XIV. THE PROCESS OF DEVELOPMENT OF THE INDUS CIVILIZATION IN THE SUTLEJ-YAMUNA DOAB: AMARENDRA NATH 2018

I have been detailing so far in this section some aspects of research on a few separate areas of the Indus civilization since c. 2010. An important issue now will be to determine if any research has currently thrown any new light on the process of development of this civilization, especially outside the area which has been considered the traditional area of its growth. *From this point of view, Amarendra Nath's essay (Nath 2018) 'chrono-cultural clue to the rise of the Harappans in the Satluj-Yamuna plain' is a major point of departure.* The most important section of this article is what has been called 'chrono-cultural perspectives of the Harappans' based both on the dates and cultural sequence of the sites of Alamgirpur, Balu, Banawali, Baror, Bhirrana, Binjor, Dhalewan, Farmana, Girawad, Hulas, Kalibangan, Karanpura, Kunal, Mitathal, Ropar and Rakhigarhi. Nath is a major excavator of Rakhigarhi and thus the site provides the most important point of this detailed study. The first exercise in this direction came from K.N. Dikshit and B.R. Mani on the basis of the dated sequence at Bhirrana but Amarendra Nath has strengthened the general argument and the corresponding dates.

Amarendra Nath, one of the main excavators of Rakhigarhi, has pointed out recently (Nath 2018) that chronologically the intervening area between the Sutlej and the Yamuna shows extensively a stratigraphic profile of sites, which suggests that here we have a continuous phase of civilizational development beginning with a pre-metallic stage and that this dated sequence is not later than any of the dated sequences of the Indus civilization elsewhere. *The implication is that this is one of the primary areas where the Indus civilization took shape*. This is a very bold scenario but if we consider the emerging data and research with an open mind, this seems to be a likely scenario. The chronological table offered by Nath for Bhirrana derives partial support from the dates derived from the animal bones of the site and obtained by Anindya Sarkar and his colleagues (Sarkar, A. et al. 2016).

The importance of the Rakhigarhi sequence, as reported by is excavator Nath is that it is a very long and well-dated sequence giving clues to the development of the Indus civilisation at its every step. The phase 1 of Formative or Early Harappan stage is clearly put between c. 4000 and 3500 BC. The Mature Harappan period, the earliest Rakhigarhi date of which is c. 2600 BC and the last about 1800 BC, does not quite fit in with the available terminal date of Early Harappan (phase 2) at the site, roughly 3500-3000 BC. Uninscribed seals and a public drainage system appear in phase 2 itself, and it is likely that the full-fledged development of the civilization took place around 3000 BC itself.

The key-stone of Nath's analysis is the dated sequence of Rakhigarhi, a 300 ha site which he himself excavated. The C-14 sequence fits in with the evolving cultural scenario from what has been called 'pre-formative early farming traditions (Mesolithic/Neolithic)' or Period I to Period III or Mature Harappan. All these three periods have been divided into 'phases'. Period I has three phases, Phase 1 yielding circular structures of perishable materials, possibly wattle-and-daub, and a metal-free assemblage comprising ill-fired plain dull red pottery, bone tools, lithic flakes, polished stone celts, sling ball and possibly stone bead-polisher. The presence of wheat and barley has been surmised, although there is no direct evidence yet, and there are bones of cattle, sheep, goat and bird. Radiocarbon dates bracket the phase squarely in the mid-6th millennium BC. Phase 2, placed basically in the second half of the 5th millennium BC, continues the same cultural assemblage but with some elaborations – metal-free, ill-fired dull red ware but some with painted band over rim and shoulder, mud applique or rusticated red ware, chocolate-slipped red ware, thick mud platforms, short cylindrical steatite beads, stone querns and sling ball. Phase 3 falls in the first half of the 5th millennium BC and remains still metal-free, although accompanied by mud-bricks and wattle-and-daub walls impressed with rice-husks. Domesticated pig, sheep, goat and cattle occur along with some elaboration of earlier pottery types. The earliest and latest specific C-14 dates from the three phases of Period I at Rakhigarhi are: 5570 +/- 70 BC and 4080 +/- 40 BC, both calibrated. This metal-free 'period' lasted apparently for 1500 years at Rakhigarhi.

Nath's summary of the cultural sequence of Rakhigarhi in conjunction with its dates is worth re-emphasis. The tentative time-frame of 'pre-Formative or Mesolithic/Neolithic' at this site is c. 5500-5000 BC for its Phase 1 and c. 5400-4500 BC for its Phase 2. Phase 3 is put between c.4500-4000 BC. Interestingly, this phase 3 of the 'pre-formative phase' has yielded 'fragments of wattle and daub imbedded with impressions of rice husks', which unmistakably indicates that the tradition of rice cultivation was well rooted by this time. One hopes that this will put paid to laboured ideas regarding rice cultivation in India.

The supporting evidence of Nath's interpretation of the Rakhigarhi sequence and its chronology has emerged from a number other sites in the region, notably Kunal and Bhirrana. Kunal has been subjected to fresh excavations with the following periodization now being in place: Period IA – Pre-Harappan, Period IB – Early Harappan, Period IIA – transitional to Harappan, Period IIB – Mature Harappan, and Period III – Painted Grey Ware. These excavations initiated in 2016-17 have provided new C-14 dates ranging between ca 6000 and 3000 BCE for the early deposits and dates ranging in the third millennium BCE for Harappan deposits. There are basically the following periods at Bhirrana: Period IA or Hakra Ware culture, inclusive of the evidence of copper-smelting and dwelling pits; Period IB or Early Harappan including a large house complex with a courtyard; Period IIA or 'Early Mature

Harappan' with no evidence of fortification, and Period IIB or Mature Harappan with evidence of fortification. Stratification-wise, the C-14 dates from Bhirrana have been placed in 5 sets by Nath: the first set of dates between c. 7500 and c. 6000 BC, the second set between c. 6000 and c. 4500 BC, the third set between c. 4500 and 3000 BC, the fourth set between 3000 and 2600 BC and the 5th set between 2600 and 1800 BC.

XV. ANCIENT DNA: A BURIAL FROM RAKHIGARHI

Most of the current theories regarding the population history of the subcontinent have been flawed in two ways. First, no ancient DNA has yet been available, and secondly, the present studies in this regard have been characterised by a marked predilection to seek support for one or other anthropological/ linguistic/historical theory in this field. Those like the present author who views any attempt to relate sophisticated scientific studies like DNA analyses to mostly subjective 19th century speculations regarding population history totally unwarranted and anti-historical, find no consolation in the championing of various unsubstantiated theories regarding India's population history. Further, it must be realized in the context of a multi-lingual and multi-cultural landmass like India, attempts to equip different ethno-linguistic groups with their own DNA trajectories are fraught with grave danger, injecting elements of different types of conflicts among these ethno-linguistic groups.

The publication titled 'an ancient Harappan genome lacks ancestry from Steppe pastoralists or Iranian farmers' and published in *Cell* 179 (first on September 5, 2019) under the authorship of a large scientific group, whose members for correspondence are V. Shinde, V.M. Narasimhan, Niraj Rai and David Reich has brought about the first whiff of change in this scenario. The skeleton, from which it became eventually possible to extract DNA is mentioned as '16113 burial with the skeletal code RGR7.3, BR-01, HS-02', came from the cemetery at Rakhigarhi, one of the largest Indus civilization sites, falling now in the state of Haryana. It is a female skeleton and the authors' observation is the following:

> After building a mitochondrial DNA consensus using damage-restricted sequences, we determined that its haplogroup was U2b2, which is absent in whole mitochondrial genomes sequences available from about 400 ancient Central Asians; today this specific haplogroup is nearly exclusive to South Asia.

Another related finding is that

> in South Asia as in Europe, the advent of farming was not mediated directly by descendants of the world's first farmers who lived in the fertile crescent. Instead, populations of hunter-gatherers – in Eastern Anatolia in the case of Europe and in a yet-unsampled location in the case of South Asia – began farming without large-scale movement of people in these regions.

The authors finally conclude:

> Our analysis of data from one individual from the IVC, in conjunction with 11 previously reported individuals from sites in cultural contact with the IVC, demonstrates the existence of an ancestry gradient that was widespread in farmers to the northwest of peninsular India at the height of the IVC, that had little if any genetic contribution from Steppe pastoralists or western Iranian farmers or herders, and that had a primary impact on the ancestry of later South Asians. While our study is sufficient to demonstrate that this ancestry profile was a common feature of the IVC, a single sample – or even the gradient of 12 likely IVC samples we have identified – cannot fully characterize a cosmopolitan ancient civilization. An important direction for future work will be to carry out ancient DNA analysis of additional individuals across the IVC range to obtain a quantitative understanding of how the ancestry of IVC people was distributed and to characterize other features of its population structure.

Those who are convinced about the essentially indigenous archaeological growth-sequence of the subcontinent without reference to the admittedly nebulous ideas and theories in this field (cf. Chakrabarti 2006, 2009) will have no difficulty in understanding the significance of the above-mentioned Rakhigarhi Indus Civilization female skeleton. In the present essay itself, we have drawn attention to Amarendra Nath's idea of a steady and indigenous sequence from the beginning of agriculture to the growth of the Indus Civilization in the present Punjab-Haryana belt. We feel that with the ongoing research and the consequent availability of a large number of dates, this picture is getting relentlessly clear.

XVI. INDUS CIVILIZATION AND WEST ASIA

The only important new piece of evidence seems to have emerged from Ebla, a site not far from the coast in Syria, roughly northeast of the famous site of Ugarit and also the centre of a kingdom rich in international contacts and trading. Its high noon came to an end around the late 3rd millennium BC. Hama in Syria is another third millennium BC site from where E.C.L. During-Caspers once reported an object which could be Indus-inspired in origin (for discussion, Chakrabarti 1990). The context of the find is a temple dated to a central-late phase of EB IVB, ca. 2200-2100 BC. The long-barrel cylinder bead of orange-red translucent carnelian, about 11 cm long originally, "comes from a layer over a floor located immediately west of the rear wall of Temple HH3" (Peyronel 2015: 217-220). These beads occur, along with another variety of Indus beads, i.e. etched carnelian beads, mostly in Mesopotamia but also in Iran and elsewhere.

> The Mesopotamian evidence is mainly related to funerary assemblages dating from ED III and Akkadian periods (ca. 2500–2200 BC) and the beads are often part of precious necklaces or ornaments consisting also of gold and lapis lazuli elements .... The situation in Northern Mesopotamia

> and Syria appears completely different: isolate exemplars of long-barrel carnelian beads are extremely rare and the findings from Ebla and Brak suggest a deliberate burying as ritual offerings in cultic compounds and a chronological attribution later than the ED III period, which is the phase of flourishing circulation of the type in Southern Mesopotamia.
>
> They might testify direct contacts between Southern Mesopotamia and the northwestern regions related to different historical events during the last centuries of the 3rd millennium BC and, at the same time, they could indicate that these foreign and precious beads were sometimes included in the local ritual actions with specific symbolic meanings. (Peyronel 2015)

Another important publication in the area of Indus contact with central Asia is by Dennys Frenez, 'manufacturing and trade of Asian elephant ivory in Bronze Age Middle Asia: evidence from Gonur Depe (Margiana, Turkmenistan)', *Archaeological Research in Asia 15 (2018): 13-33*. Direct evidence of Asian ivory task and manufacture of ivory objects is available in the Bronze Age setting of the site, meaning that such ivory tasks were a trading item and that practitioners of ivory craft were present in the region along with the ivory trade reaching out to this region from the Indus area. Considering the much documented presence of a wide variety of Indian trade goods and traders all over central Asia in various pre-modern contexts, this is an eminently acceptable hypothesis.

XVII. DISCUSSION

The present decade (2010-2019) has witnessed significant developments in the scientific studies of the Indus civilization. The most important aspect of these developments is that the palaeo-river channels of the Sutlej in the Ghaggar bed and of the Yamuna in the bed of the Chautang have both been proved to have lost their flows by the time the Indus civilizational tradition developed in this region. It is improbable that the rivers completely dried up. Whatever monsoonal flow from the Siwaliks they could retain was no doubt retained and formed no doubt the base of the canal irrigation system which, as the historical evidence testifies, was at the heart of the agricultural prosperity of Haryana. The landscape, at least on the Chautang or palaeo-Yamuna side, has been argued to have remained unchanged since about 24 ka. With some variations, the point has been proved to be true of the landscape related to the Ghaggar as well.

The impact of this find or realization is mind-boggling in a sense. The scholarly literature on this has been copiously cited earlier in this essay. Instead of a vast network of free-flowing palaeochannels representing the Ghaggar and Yamuna networks of the main rivers and their tributaries, we are confronted by a vast and stable plain of somewhat moribund rivers which could come alive only during the monsoon. Basically, this was the situation till the late 19th century when the material for the Haryana gazetteers was being compiled. It was this setting which witnessed the development of the whole Harappan civilizational tradition in this sector.

This setting was also characterized by some aridity and a phase of dune formation. This is an easy point to realize by anybody who knows well the sites of the region. Attempts to link the onset of aridity with the process of 'de-urbanisation' cannot be allowed much ground because the monsoon rainfall has frequently fluctuated in Indian history without necessarily leading to the human settlements of the afflicted areas being wiped off. The maximum annual rainfall was nearly 44.5 inches in Mewar in 1893 whereas it was just under 10 inches in 1899 (Chakrabarti 2019: 145-146).

A major problem of the Indus, and generally ancient Indian studies, is that the results of science-based research are equated by the concerned researchers to the dominant historical ideas related to it. In a sense it is getting increasingly somewhat like the publications on modern DNA studies of ancient populations. The implications of such DNA studies are almost invariably related to the generally early (mostly 19th century) linguistic premises regarding India's language history and the various ideas of migrations involved in it. What also requires some emphasis in the Indus context is that one of the best ways to interpret Indian archaeological data is to interpret them in the light of what has traditionally been India.

A great limitation of various science-based studies of the Indus civilization is that the researchers are not concerned merely with their findings; they feel it obligatory to explain their findings in the light of the various theories in circulation in the field. Many of these theories may not have much basis and are in most cases no more than mere opinions, but this does not normally deter 'scientists' to offer their own explanations as long as these explanations fit with the ideas of their own 'reference groups'. As far as nationalist Indian archaeologists and historians are concerned, there are a few points they cannot compromise on. First, this is a product entirely of the Indian soil and lies at the root of the later Indian high tradition. Secondly, there is a deep-seated continuity between the Indus and later Indian historic civilization. Trying to bring in imaginary groups of people known as Aryans will not simply do. Thirdly, the basic ideas to explain the civilization must emerge from the traditional Indian ground and must fit in it. Invocations of great anthropological ideas merely for the sake of invoking them will simply not suffice anymore.

The reconstruction of a well-dated and steady archaeological column leading to the development of the Indus civilization in the Sutlej-Yamuna Doab, which we have discussed in detail following the cited evidence, is another landmark development in the current study of the Indus archaeology. Although it is not yet done, it is rather important that we try to integrate this emerging evidence into the neighbouring centre of early agriculture and metallurgy in the Aravallis. Although the significance of the Aravalli centre from this point of view has been adequately stressed (Chakrabarti 2019, for a detailed recent discussion), due credit must be given to Arunima Kashyap for her 6th-5th millennia BC dating for the two phases of Bagor and the presence of agricultural products in both of them (see Chakrabarti *ibid*).

It may be added as a general background that the development of the Indus civilization has so far been visualized as the culmination of the process of domestication of barley and wheat which apparently began at sites like Mehrgarh in central Baluchistan in the 8th millennium BC. With the emergence of the Gorakhpur area of eastern UP as an independent centre of rice domestication going back to c. 7000 + BC and with the find of domesticated rice at in the Early Harappan contexts of sites like Balu and Kunal in Haryana, it became apparent that there could be yet another strain of agricultural development based on the cultivation of rice behind the growth of the Indus civilization and that this growth area lay to the east of the Indus valley. Equally importantly, the Aravalli area of Rajasthan along its broad alignment from northeastern to southeast Rajasthan and its extension in Gujarat has been argued to be a separate and independent centre of agriculture and metallurgy. *Thus, the situation regarding the genesis and development of the Indus civilization to the east of the Indus belt has become more complex and multi-hued in recent years.* The traditional assumption that the Indus sites in the east were the result of the dissemination of this civilization from the basin of the Indus with such classical sites as Mohenjodaro and Harappa has justifiably been questioned in recent years. The 'eastern zone' falls more or less in what has been known as the Ghaggar-Sarasvati valley in eastern Punjab and Haryana and extends all over the upper section of the Ganga-Yamuna Doab stretching up to the Ganga flowing below the Siwaliks at Haridwar. The Mature Harappan, as the evidence from Hulas and Alamgirpur shows, was present in the Doab and co-existed and interacted with the OCP-Copper Hoard tradition which has so far been interpreted as essentially the Doab tradition co-existing with the late Harappan tradition of the Doab. The presence of Mature Harappans in the Doab puts the feature of Harappan-Copper Hoard co-existence further back. Considering that the OCP-Copper Hoard tradition stretches as far south as Sringaverapura on the bank of the Ganga near Allahabad, one has to take into consideration the fact that through the OCP-Copper Hoard distribution, the Harappan tradition too was likely to have merged into the mainstream Gangetic tradition of the country. This has been a major, although generally unappreciated, development in the archaeology of India in recent years. What is singularly distressing in this regard is that some Indian archaeologists are currently great believers, without convincing reason, in the idea that the Harappan civilization and the OCP-Copper Hoard tradition were two separate entities.

In the beginning of this essay we have outlined how the Indus civilizational tradition may be said to be the fountainhead of the stream of high culture of India. We believe that this is amply evident in the manifold legacies this civilization has left behind. These legacies have, in fact, been adequately sketched in the essay on 'legacy' in *Protohistoric Foundations.* At this point, it may be worth emphasizing that some Indian archaeologists have currently begun to detract from the fact that the Indus civilization was the fountainhead of the continuing Indian tradition. This they do by harping on the theme that the Harappan civilization denoted an 'imported element' among the regional cultures of the period, especially among the regional cultures of Gujarat. The recurrent attempts of some archaeologists of Pune and Vadodara to think of the Harappan manifestation as something imported or extraneous to their regional cultural scenes are nothing but attempts on the part of this group of Indians to view the Harappan element away from the mainstream Indian tradition. Dhavalikar, for instance, compared the Harappan settlements in Gujarat to the so-called British 'factories' set up by the East India Company along the Indian coast, implying that the Harappan settlements in Gujarat were as much intrusive in the Gujarat landscape as the British factories were in Surat.

Nobody will deny the prevalence of regional elements in the Indus civilization, although I am not quite sure if there is any other feature except pottery which will isolate the regional styles of this civilization. The tradition was set up by G. Possehl who first coined the term 'Sorath Harappan', a term which has since then repeatedly used by his camp followers from Pune and Vadodara who do not hesitate these days even to use such ridiculous terms as *Anarta Culture* to denote the Harappan culture confined to the Mehsana and other related sections of northern Gujarat. I cannot escape the same sense of revulsion when some enthusiasts of the Archaeological Survey and elsewhere declare a separate 'Bara culture' in the vast zone of Punjab and Haryana. This scholarly tendency is somewhat like denying the existence of Hinduism as an overarching religion on the ground that it is divided into the groups of Saivite, Vaishnavite, etc.

To explain why some Indian archaeologists are apparently keen to dilute the notion that the Indus civilization was the most important of the early civilizational legacies of the country, one would have to analyse in some detail the basis and character of Indian higher education, as far as it is concerned with history. This remains outside the scope of the present essay, but emphasizing India's civilizational legacy within a nationalist framework has never been an important part of Indian higher education. In the case of archaeology and even the history of modern India, the basic reference point is not an indigenous narrative but only an examination of what Western scholars have theoretically postulated about this and comparable situations in India and elsewhere. In places like

Pune and Vadodara and many other institutional contexts even archaeological discoveries have been primarily judged by what some Western archaeologists have offered by way of theories regarding Indian developments.

Till the Indus script is satisfactorily deciphered, it would be unwise to indulge in any kind of 'linguistic archaeology' (for reviews, Chakrabarti 1997, 2008, 2014) although the literary column of the Vedic literature has to be incorporated in the Indus archaeological column without being in any way specific about it.

Finally, while we welcome the increasing boundaries of science-based research in this field, we remember at the same time that our main task is to arrive at some kind of truth – the basic ground reality, if we can call it that – regarding the Indus civilization. Pre-conceived theories and support for scholarly ideas belonging to one's own archaeological or scholarly colour-based fraternity are unlikely to go far in this quest for truth, although this seems to be the general academic situation these days in Indian archaeology. Some Indian archaeologists who are fairly thoughtless about acquiring a proper historical understanding of the Indus Civilization are no less responsible for this situation than Western archaeologists.

REFERENCES

(Many additional references have been incorporated in the body of the text. Further, this review has carefully avoided all linguistic appreciations of the Indus texts, however clever and mathematical they may be.)

Bates, J., C.A. Petrie and R.N. Singh 2016, 'Approaching Rice Domestication in South Asia: New Evidence from Indus Settlements in Northern India', *Journal of Archaeological Science* 30: 1-9.

Bisht, R.S. et al. 2015, 'Pb Isotope Analysis of Lead, Silver and Copper Artifacts from Dholavira', *Heritage* 3: 1-18.

Chakrabarti, Dilip K. 1990, *The External Trade of the Indus Civilization*, Delhi: Munshiram Manoharlal.

—— 1997, *Colonial Indology: Sociopolitics of the Ancient Indian Past*, Delhi: Munshiram Manoharlal.
—— 2006, *The Oxford Companion to Indian Archaeology*, Delhi: OUP.
—— 2008, *The Battle for Ancient India*, Delhi: Aryan Books.
—— 2009, *An Archaeological History of India*, Delhi: OUP (2nd edition).
—— 2014, *Nation First: Essays in the Politics of Ancient Indian Studies*, Delhi: Aryan Books.
—— 2019, *Ancient Rajasthan*, Delhi: Aryan Books.
Chakrabarti, D.K. and S. Saini 2009, *The Problem of the Sarasvati River and Notes on the Archaeological Geography of Haryana and Indian Panjab*, Delhi: Aryan Books.
Chase, B. 2014, 'Pastoral Land-use of the Indus Civilization in Gujarat: Faunal Analysis and Biogenic Isotopes at Bagasra', *Journal of Archaeological Science* 50: 1-15.
Chatterjee, A. and J. Ray 2018, 'Geochemistry of Harappan Potteries from Kalibangan and Sediments in the Ghaggar River: Clues for a Dying River', *Geoscience Frontiers* 9(4): 1203-1211.
Dangi, V. and Samunder 2013, 'New Evidences from the Harappan Cemetery of Seman 6, District Rohtak, Haryana', *Heritage* 1: 402-423.
Dave, A.K. et al. 2019, 'Revisiting the Contemporaneity of a Mighty River and the Harappans: Archaeological, Stratigraphic and Chronometric Constraints', *Quaternary Geochronology* 49: 230-235.
Dhavalikar, M.K. 1995, *Cultural Imperialism: Indus Civilization in Western India*, Delhi: Books and Books.
Dixit, Yama, D. Hodell and C.A. Petrie 2014, 'Abrupt Weakening of the Summer Monsoon in Northwest India ~4100 yr Ago', *Geology* 42(4): 339-342.
Giosan, L. et al. 2018, 'Neoglacial Climate Anomalies and the Harappan Metamorphosis', *Climate of the Past* 14: 1669-1686.
Hoffman, B. and H. Miller 2014, 'Production and Consumption of Copper-base Metals in the Indus Civilization', in C. Thornton and B. Roberts (eds.), *Reader in Global Early Metallurgy*, New York: Springer, pp. 697-727.
Kashyap, Arunima and Steve Weber 2010, 'Harappan Plant Use Revealed by Starch Grains from Farmana, India', *Antiquity* 84 (Project gallery).
Khan, Imran and Rajiv Sinha 2019, 'Discovering Buried Channels of the Palaeo-Yamuna River in NW India using Geophysical

Evidence: Implications for Major Drainage Reorganization and Linkage to the Harappan Civilization', *Journal of Applied Geophysics* 167: 128-139.

Khonde, N. et al. 2017, 'Tracing the Vedic Saraswati River in the Great Rann of Kachchh', *Scientific Reports* 7: 5476.

Giosan, L. et al. 2018, 'Neoglacial Climate Anomalies and the Harappan Metamorphosis', *Climate of the Past* 14, 1669-1686.

Manjul, S.K. and Arvin Manjul 2018, 'Recent Excavation at Sanauli, District Bagpat, UP: A Landmark in Indian Archaeology', *Puratattva* 48: 220-225.

Nath, A. 2018, 'Chrono-cultural Clue to the Rise of the Harappans in the Sutluj-Yamuna Plain', *Puratattva* 48: 93-129.

Neogi, S. et al., in press, 'Offsite Geoarchaeology from the Indus Sites of Haryana and Uttar Pradesh: Placing the Sites into their Environmental Context', *Quaternary Research*. (I thank Dr. Sayantani Neogi most warmly for making this paper available to me.)

Oldham, C.F. 1893, 'The Saraswati and the Lost River of the Indian Desert', *The Journal of the Royal Asiatic Society*, pp. 49-76.

Oldham, R.D. 1886, 'On Probable Changes in the Geography of the Punjab and Its Rivers: A Historico-geographical Study', *JASB* 55 (Part 2), 1886, pp. 422-23.

Orengo, H.A. and C.A. Petrie 2017, 'Large-scale Multi-temporal Remote Sensing of Paleoriver Networks: A Case Study from Northwest India and Its Implications for the Indus Civilization', *Remote Sensing* 9(7).

Petrie, C.A. et al. 2017, 'Adaptation to Variable Environments, Resilience to Climate Change, Investigating *Land, Water and Settlement* in Indus Northwest India', *Current Anthropology* 58 (1).

Petrie, C.A., R.N. Singh and A.K. Singh 2009, 'Investigating Changing Settlement Dynamics on the Plains: The 2009 Survey and Excavations at Masudpur (Hissar District), Haryana', *Puratattva* 39: 38-49.

Peyronel, L. 2015, 'A Long-barrel Carnelian Bead from Ebla: A New Evidence for Long-distance Contacts between the Indus Valley and the Near East', *Studia Eblaitica* 2: 217-220.

Pokharia, A.K. et al. 2014, 'Archaeobotanical Evidence of Millets in the Indian Subcontinent: Some Observations on Their Role in the Indus Civilization', *Journal of Archaeological Science* 42: 442-455.

—— 2017, 'Altered Cropping Pattern and Cultural Continuation with Declined Prosperity Following Abrupt and Extreme Arid Event at ~4200 yrs BP: Evidence from an Indus Archaeological Site Khirsara, Gujarat, Western India', *PLoS One* 12 (10).

Prabhakar, M.N. and J.C. Majid, 'Preliminary Results of Excavation at Karanpura, a Harappan Settlement in District Hanumangarh, Rajasthan', *Man and Environment* 39(2): 13-41.

Prabhakar, V.N. 2013, 'Ceramic Typology of the Late Harappan Cemetery at Sanauli, Uttar Pradesh', *Heritage* 1: 78-103.

—— 2014, 'Possible Convergence of Historic Literature and Archaeology: Examples of Harappan Burial Practices and Customs', *Heritage* 2: 152-183.

—— 2015, 'A Survey of Burial Practices in the Late/Post-urban Harappan Phase During the Second and First Millennium BCE', *Heritage* 3: 54-83.

Raghuvans, K. 2013, 'Ancient Mines and Metal Processing Activities in the Sekhawati Region of Rajasthan', *Heritage* 1: 138-170.

Raverty, H.G. 1892, 'The Mihran of Sind and Its Tributaries', *The Journal of the Asiatic Society of Bengal* (hereafter *JASB)* 61(4): 155-297, Extra No. 1892, pp. 298-508.

Sarkar, A. et al. 2016, 'Oxygen Isotope in Archaeological Bioapatites from India: Implications to Climate Change and Decline of Bronze Age Harappan Civilization', *Scientific Reports*, Volume 6 (article number 26555).

Schug, G.R. et al. 2012, 'A Peaceful Realm? Trauma and Social Differentiation at Harappa', *International Journal of Palaeopathology*.

Schug, G.R. et al. 2013, 'Infection, Disease and Biosocial Processes at the End of the Indus Civilization', *PLoS One* 8 (12): 1-20.

Shinde, V. et al. 2019, 'An Ancient Harappan Genome Lacks Ancestry from Steppe Pastoralists or Iranian Farmers', *Cell* (2019) *https://doi.org/10.1016/ j.cell. 2019.08.048*

Shinde, V. et al. 2008, 'A Report on Excavations at Farmana 2007-08', in, T. Osada and A. Uesugi (eds.), *Linguistics, Archaeology and Human Past*, pp. 1-116.

—— 2018, 'Archaeological and Anthropological Studies on the Harappan Cemetery of Rakhigarhi, India', *PLoS One* 13 (2).

Singh, A. et al. 2016, 'Geochemistry of Buried River Sediments from Ghaggar Plains, NW India: Multiproxy Records of Variations in the Provenance, Palaeoclimate, and Palaeovegetation Patterns in the Late Quaternary', *Palaeogeography, Palaeoclimatology, Palaeoecology* 449: 85-100.

—— 2017, 'Counter-intuitive Influence of Himalayan River Morphodynamics on Indus Civilization Urban Settlements', *Nature Communications*, Vol. 8.

Singh, R.N. et al. 2010, 'Geoarchaeological Survey and Excavations at Burj, Fatehabad, Haryana', *Puratattva* 40: 94-101.

—— 2012, 'Survey and Excavations at Dabli Vas Chugta, Hanumangarh District, Rajasthan', *Puratattva* 42: 133-147.

—— 2016, 'Report on Tin Metallurgy at Khanak, a Harappan Site in Bhiwani, Haryana', *Puratattva*: 104-113.

—— 2018, 'Living in the Hinterland I: Survey and Excavations at Lohari Ragho', *Puratattva* 48.

4

Key Issues

Major Themes in Different Phases of Harappan Research*

I. CHANGING PERSPECTIVES

It was by 1924 that the archaeologists of the Archaeological Survey of India, led by its Director General John Marshall, realized that they were confronted with a Bronze Age civilization in the north-western part of the subcontinent on the model of the Bronze Age Mesopotamia. The seals of this civilization bearing pictographs had long been found in the excavations in the Bronze Age levels at different Mesopotamian sites, and the same type of seals with the same type of pictographs turned up in the Archaeological Survey of India excavations, first at Harappa in undivided Panjab and then at Mohenjodaro in Sind. After these excavations, scholars not merely located the primary area of such finds in the Indus valley but also realized that this particular area of the subcontinent had possessed a Mesopotamia-like ancient civilization with which the Mesopotamian cities were in

---

* The literature of this section will be known to students of Indian archaeology. Detailed referencing has been avoided here.

contact. The first definitive report on the civilization was published in 3 volumes in 1931 by John Marshall under the title *Mohenjodaro and the Indus Civilization*. The Indus seals had, in fact, been found in India herself much earlier than the realization that they represented on their own a distinct civilization. They were located at least at three sites: Harappa where the first excavations were conducted but from where Alexander Cunningham reported seals in the late 19th century; Kalibangan in Rajasthan where, early in the 20th century, L.P. Tessitori, an Italian investigator of the Rajasthani bardic literature, found seals; and Bhuj in Kutch where Le Grand Jacob, British Resident in 1851-56, found them but they lay forgotten till D.R. Bhandarkar, after the civilization was identified, recognized them for what they were worth. Thus, interestingly, long before the civilization was recognized as a civilization, its traces were found in Panjab, Rajasthan and Gujarat, broadly indicating its general area of distribution. Considering that Marshall's publication on Mohenjodaro in 1931 was the central point of the first phase of Indus discoveries, the key issues during this phase were the following. First, what was the language the people of this civilization spoke? As the script was not deciphered, there could not be any firm answer to the problem. A philologist from Kolkata, Suniti Kumar Chatterji, guessed, without any solid ground, that its language was likely to have belonged to the Dravidian family. The second issue hovered around its possible relationship with India that was described in the Vedic texts, whether it was pre- or post-Vedic. In the Marshall volume it was declared as pre-and-non-Vedic. The third issue was chronology. The baseline was the date of the Mesopotamian contexts in which the Indus seals were found, but the problem lay on the Indus side itself. Was there any way of knowing the levels of Mohenjodaro and Harappa from where such seals went to the Mesopotamian sites and thus, was there any way of relating the dates of the Indus seal-bearing levels of Mesopotamian sites to the internal sequence of the Indus sites? Speculation held the field and Marshall dated Mohenjodaro between 3250 and 2750 BC. The issue of chronology was also related to the issues of origin and decline. On decline, Marshall had no specific clue but on origin he was specific that its origin lay deep in the Indian soil. The final issues were related to social organization and religion. The sector by sector work at Mohenjodaro showed a broad homogeneity of general planning and house types, without any sharp emphasis on social divisions. The city itself profited from rigorous planning and a well-managed water and sanitation system, something that traditional Indian towns have not enjoyed for a long time. This caught people's imagination and the picture of a prosperous bourgeois settlement without sharp class divisions slowly gained ground. Further, in a detailed analysis of the relevant material Marshall showed the unmistakable reflection of many key elements of modern Hinduism in the Indus finds. What is also interesting is that in the excavations in the higher citadel area of Mohenjodaro, the Great Bath carried the impression of sanctity attached to water and a tank as a part of the extended ground of a probable temple nearby. The 'Indian' character of this civilization came through in the first phase of ground research itself and it was in the same phase that the broad nature of its geographical spread was made clear: from Baluchistan to Ropar in east Punjab and from Baluchistan to the Peninsular and the mainland Gujarat. The second major phase of Indus research may be fixed around 1946 when the report of the Archaeological Survey of India excavations at Harappa under Mortimer Wheeler was published. This excavation led to two major conclusions. First, the citadel at Harappa was found fortified, suggesting that there was not much of bourgeois democracy in the ruling character of the place, and that the skeletons found helter-skelter in the upper levels of the site might be interpreted as the material evidence of an invasion by people who in the absence of any firm identifying evidence could be coaxed into the idea of their being traces of an onslaught by the Rigvedic Aryans. The text of the *Rigveda* was supposed to bear the echoes of such an invasion. Wheeler also wrote a general book on the Indus Civilization, the first edition of which was published in 1953. In this book he built the structure of a civilization which was born due to the migration of the idea of civilization from Mesopotamia and died due to the supposed invasion by the Rigvedic Aryans. To give strength to the idea of Mesopotamian influence on the origin of the civilization, Wheeler brought down the basic chronology of the civilization from c. 3250 to c. 2700 BC of Marshall to c. 2500 to 1500 BC, the latter point devised to fit in the traditional date of the *Rigveda* in about 1500 BC. He tried to argue that there was no acceptable evidence of Indus-Mesopotamia contact before Sargon of Akkad who himself was placed around 2325 or 2371 BC. Thus, the two chronological points offered by Wheeler were supposed to fit in with the dates of two historical events, i.e. the date of Sargon of Akkad and the invasion by the Rigvedic Aryans. Regarding origin, Wheeler and one of his contemporaries, D.H. Gordon, ascribed the motivating factor either to the migration of the idea of civilization from Mesopotamia or to the movement of the ruling group from that direction. The problem of origin was not an issue in the earlier phase; Marshall took it for granted that the civilization lay deeply rooted in the Indian soil. But except at Amri no proof of a preceding culture was found during that time. It is this evidence of an antecedent phase that kept on increasing in the second phase. Some evidence became available in the pre-fortification phase of Harappa itself, and in the post-Wheeler days, much clearer evidence became available at Kot Diji near Khairpur in Sind. Meanwhile, the sequence of Baluchi protohistoric sites began to be closely looked at, and gradually the idea of a long-range cultural sequence that began in Baluchistan and culminated in the Indus civilization began to take shape among scholars. Chronology came into focus after the first crop of radiocarbon dates from the Harappan sites was published in 1964. Assuming, quite wrongly, that the radiocarbon dates were historical dates, some scholars, notably D.P. Agrawal, lent support to Wheeler's dating of the civilization to 2500-1500 BC. The Aryan angle was seriously dented when it was pointed out by George Dales that the skeletons found in the upper level of Mohenjodaro did not belong to the same time and thus could not represent any single group of invaders. An equally blunt criticism of the idea came from the physical anthropologist D.K. Sen who showed that the earlier classifications of skeletons from Indus civilization sites into a few racial and linguistic categories were no longer valid in terms of progress of anthropological science. This second phase of research may be said to have continued into the 1980s. By this time a whole lot of primary data on the distribution and sequence of many of the Indus sites from virtually all distributional areas had emerged. The fact that this civilization had emerged from its long period gestation in the Indian soil itself had solidified itself beyond any doubt by this time. Another idea that got buried was that of the mythical Aryans moving in at its end. By the1980s even ardent champions of the theory of Aryan migration had to accept the fact that archaeologically at least there was not even an iota of evidence of migration of a new set of people at the end of the Indus civilization. Excavations of different major sites, such as Lothal and Kalibangan, went on at full speed and the science-based research on many excavated material items, especially metallurgy, greatly expanded. The Ganga-Yamuna Doab emerged as an important area of study where the Ochre-Coloured-Pottery and Copper Hoards of certain specific types were found to belong to the Harappan tradition of at least the late phase, if not the earlier one. In view of the fact that this OCP-Copper Hoard combine extended up to the modern Allahabad region put the idea of Harappan roots in the Ganga-Yamuna Doab in a new perspective. Similarly, the identification of Harappan script signs at Daimabad in the Godavari valley of Maharashtra showed the Harappan thrust towards the Deccan. Distribution and origin were the two key issues in the second phase of research, and both of them were no longer issues by the time this research phase ended. The Aryans also continued to haunt scholars during this second phase but by the time this phase ended, the professional archaeologists could no longer seriously hold the idea. Another key issue of this phase was the consolidation of the idea of the Ghaggar or Sarasvati flow from the Siwaliks to the sea along a distinct channel to the east of the Indus course. The existence of this channel has been known since at least the late 18th century but the discovery of many sites of different phases of the Indus civilization along a network of river channels in Bahawalpur gave this concept of a separate riverine flow to the east of the Indus a concrete historical shape, which was also strengthened by the discovery of a large number of sites in Indian Punjab, Haryana and Rajasthan. As the Sarasvati as a river has been repeatedly extolled in the Vedic literature, especially in the *Rigveda*, this emergence of the Sarasvati as a historical entity also led to a renewed interest in seeking the archaeological correlate of the Vedic texts in the Indus civilization or, as some scholars began to argue in the 1980s, 'Indus-Saraswati civilization'. From about 1990 to about 2010, the Indus research may be said to have undergone its third phase. The results of excavations at major sites like Dholavira and Rakhigarhi began to yield fruit. Dholavira with its components of different fortified segments and Rakhigarhi with its huge area divided into sectors with a huge burial ground began to lend different colours to the character of Indus settlements. Their stratigraphy left no room for doubt that the civilization, as reflected in its fortifications and seals, can be traced at such sites phase by phase. This is also the phase when the sites of Kunal and Bhirrana, both in Haryana, strengthened the idea of this part of the Sarasvati valley as a distinct core area of the emergence of the Indus civilization through different stages of development. In a sense, to fully understand how the civilization took shape and evolved right from its beginning to its end was a key issue of this phase. It was also in this phase that the results of American excavations at Harappa with an impressive number of radiocarbon dates became known. The fact that these dates proved that the civilization continued right up to c. 1200/c. 1300 BC without any break in continuity was an important realization. The second key issue of this phase was the emergence of the idea of the Aravalli system as an independent area of both food-production and metallurgy. It is singularly regrettable that the significance of this idea has not yet sunk in Indian archaeological consciousness, although Anupama Kashyap provided indisputable evidence of this early agriculture and metallurgy at the site of Bagor.

A third issue broke into the foreground: are the sites in the Ganga-Yamuna Doab all late Harappan and on decline? The probable date of c. 2500 BC for the beginning of Alamgirpur and the find of a rich material assemblage including a rich array of gold and silver objects including high-end stone beads at Mandi have put such ideas in doubt.

It should be clear from the brief survey above that the issues of this civilization have changed from time to time, or, as we have tried to show, from phase to phase. This is something to be expected in every research field. The issues never go away. Once a particular issue gets settled, another moves in.

II. CONTROVERSIES AND ARGUMENTS

Controversies and arguments may be invariably intertwined in every field of research but the theoretical issues in the background vary from subject to subject or, more specifically, from one academic discipline to another. Archaeological explorations and excavations lead to the accumulation of data related to the material life of the past societies. The basic contexts in which these data are found and various analyses of the material components of the data are mostly beyond dispute, but what is not beyond dispute is the way we arrive at their historical interpretation. In many cases we choose to depend on past ideas and formulations which may not necessarily be beyond criticism. Secondly, our past ideas and formulations regarding ancient societies do not always depend on a range of cast-iron facts. Mostly there will be a wide choice of possible interpretations and the particular point of view that an archaeologist takes in such circumstances may be nothing more profound than his personal or subjective preferences for a particular set of beliefs. Thirdly, historical disciplines like archaeology have also been subject to ideas which, because of long-time interest and belief in them, have almost acquired the status of truth, and unless one has the intellectual strength to challenge them, one is likely to get bogged in various kinds of ideological quagmire. In the field of ancient Indian archaeology and history the most deadly of all such quagmires is belief in a correlation between material remains, i.e. archaeology, and the elements of race and culture, language being an important component of the last. This aspect of ancient Indian historical and archaeological studies has been closely examined since the late 1980s, especially by the present author who pointed out in an essay included in his *Theoretical Issues in Indian Archaeology* (1988) and in subsequent publications like *Colonial Indology: Sociopolitics of the Ancient Indian Past* (1997) and *The Battle for Ancient India* (2008) that the prevailing tendency to interpret cultural changes in the Indian archaeological sequence in terms of diffusion from various parts of Asia, notably West and Central Asia, was due to the general acceptance of the idea of correlation between archaeology, race and culture. The basic assumption is that the assumed complex of biological features called race, the particular language family to which the bearers of these biological features belong and the remains of the material life of these people are all interrelated. Subsequent research has shown that these correlations are all meaningless. First, race as a category has ceased to exist in modern anthropological studies. Secondly, biological features in no way determine the life we lead, and thirdly, the material basis of life which different human groups possess have got nothing to do with the language they speak. In the case of archaeological contexts where there is no direct evidence of script and language, all the suppositions regarding the probable language of these prehistoric people are absolutely unprovable and all speculations in this regard have to be considered purely speculative. This sense of logic has not, however, deterred archaeologists and ancient historians to opt for different language-families as the possible language-families prevalent in the Indus civilization. Two theories currently hold the field. First, the idea that the people of this civilization spoke a language of the Dravidian family has been readily accepted by the people of the southern part of the subcontinent. The script of this civilization is un-deciphered and till the script is satisfactorily deciphered, it is absolutely impossible to ascribe any language family to this civilization. Certain scholars are also proponents of the idea of the Indus civilization people being speakers of a language of the Indo-Aryan family. The argument in favour of this idea is that the present distribution area of the civilization falls in the belt of such language-speakers and there is no evidence to support the hypothesis that the Dravidian speakers of this belt have been replaced by Indo-Aryan speakers. The assumption is that an Indo-Aryan language has been in use in this belt since the time of the Indus civilization. It must be emphasized that all speculations in this case, i.e. the probable language-affiliation of the Indus civilization, are mere speculations, and there can be no conclusive verification of its language history until the script can be read and understood. At this point it is also relevant to ask why the idea of Aryans has so strongly entangled itself with this civilization. It is also important to put emphasis on another related point: can we understand this civilization without reference to the archaeologically untestable language families such as Aryans and Dravidians? Here we unequivocally enter the domain of socio-politics of Indian archaeology. The Aryan idea is important to some scholars because if the Aryans entered the country as an important part of the post-Harappan, then that would mean that the Vedic literature which forms the bedrock of later-day Hinduism was an intrusive phenomenon in the course of ancient Indian history. Hinduism, the Aryan hypothesis would imply, was apparently as much intrusive in Indian history as the later religions of Muslims and Christians were. The idea of Aryans moving in at the end of the Harappan civilization cannot fit in the national narrative of ancient Indian history. It may be difficult for the general students of ancient India to realize this: the entire Aryan narrative has been built right from the days of its inception in the middle of the 19th century AD on an endless series of unsubstantiated assumptions, both linguistic and archaeological. The people who argue on the other hand that it was India which was the Aryan homeland and sent them out to the other relevant areas of the world, forget that the very idea of a group of people calling themselves Aryans is a racist concept and should have no place in modern historical research.

Another area of controversy relates to the origin of the Indus civilization. While John Marshall in his Mohenjodaro report was convinced that the civilization was deeply rooted in the Indian soil, there has been a consistent attempt since then to explain its origin in terms of a direct or indirect diffusion from Mesopotamia. In different forms the idea still persists among a section of Indologists and archaeologists. When the Italian Indologist Verardi thinks of the possibility of the existence of a Ziggurat in the stupa mound of Mohenjodaro, he implies this or when the American and other

Western archaeologists like G. Possehl think of its origin primarily in terms of Bronze Age interaction with central Asia, they aim primarily to perpetuate this idea. This idea has also different shades of meaning. For instance, when there are attempts to date the Civilization somewhat later than the classic efflorescence of Mesopotamian civilization, it is this attitude which is echoed because if the Indus civilization is later in origin than that of Mesopotamia, the idea of a migration from Mesopotamia to the Indus becomes more acceptable. Many Indian and foreign books on the history of India seem to accept this premise without demur. Recently however, this has found an interesting expression in Mukhtar Ahmed's book *Pakistan: An Archaeological History*. Dr. Ahmed, although not a professional academic, took enough interest in south Asian archaeology to write a long book on it. According to him, even a cursory look at the archaeological data will show that the territory now called Pakistan always fought shy of what is now called India and leaned more towards central Asia in terms of culture and genetics. This is certainly a novel hypothesis but the supposed central Asiatic affinity of the Harappan civilization figures in the writings of many Indian archaeologists either directly, as it does in some writings of JNU archaeologists like Shireen Ratnagar whom Mukhtar Ahmed cites approvingly or indirectly in the writings of those Indians or non-Indians who find real or imaginary evidence of central Asian contacts in the Indian archaeological scene. For instance, a group of people have long been trying to relate some 'seals' of the Ahar culture of southeast Rajasthan to the Bactro-Margiana culture of Bactria in north Afghanistan and the territory to its north in modern Turkestan. The fact that these so-called seals of the Ahar culture may be nothing more than dies or casts to prepare sweets is of no concern to these scholars. Such dies or casts are still easily available with the sweetmeat-sellers of modern West Bengal. More areas of uncertainty and controversy remain. As the Aravalli system of Rajasthan to Gujarat has emerged as a separate and independent area of agriculture and metallurgy, what is the relationship of this zone with the Indus-Sarasvati belt of Sind, Punjab and Haryana? Now that an early belt of rice agriculture has emerged in eastern U.P. and the related region, how did it affect the cultural developments up to the Indus-Sarasvati zone? The fact that rice was known as early as Early Harappan at certain sites of Haryana is a conclusive proof that there was a dissemination of rice agriculture from its core area in the east to the west. Further questions remain. Archaeological excavations of recent years have clearly established that the classic form of the Indus civilization has had a series of developmental stages, including the major stages of evolution of seals, at such sites as Dholavira, Rakhigarhi, Bhirrana, Kunal and others. There is not even the slightest scope of claiming that the origin of this civilization did not lie in the Indian soil. However, it is important to demarcate the precise level at which the transition to writing and thus civilization took place. For instance, script signs have been found in the Early Harappan level at a number of sites. Will this mean that the Early Harappan level should be considered from now on a part of the decidedly civilized level of the Harappans? There is no great clarity about the issue as yet. Another controversy which dogs this context is the problem of decline, including the acceptable criteria of decline and its features. A fair amount of science-based research has begun to take place in this direction, especially to understand the issue of aridity/non-aridity during the time when the civilization developed, flourished and declined. It is also clear that the recent propensity to attribute Harappan decline to the onset of aridity may be nothing more than eagerness to read much more in the climatic curve than what can be allowed in view of the examples from later Indian history. If long-term developments in human history could be reduced only to the problem of better or lesser rainfall, there would not be any question of complexity in such developments. In fact, in a subject like archaeology which involves essentially the traces of the material life of the past societies, the employment of science-based techniques may only expand the range of possible explanations. They usually do not offer cut-and-dried solutions. This is true of not merely aridity/non-aridity but also of a host of other features such as metallurgy, pottery, etc. In recent years people have gone overboard to specify the origins of the people behind this civilization. What is ignored is that the physical features and the so-called origins of the concerned people are not really historical issues because these issues should not really matter in the process of historical developments. Although the purpose of archaeology is not to prove or disprove literary traditions of a country or region, in the case of India, because of its deep-rooted tradition of Vedic and epic texts, the issue cannot be ignored altogether. The issue has assumed some urgency or sharpness in the current situation because of two developments. First, now we have a complete sequence of cultural developments from the very beginning of food-production to the growth of historic cities in different parts of the country, especially in all its core areas. On the one hand, we have this developmental sequence, and on the other we have a whole series of Vedic and epic texts which form our literary tradition. A large part of this tradition is supposed to pre-date our documented history and can also be argued to be entirely Indian in origin. If so, here are two columns – the column of archaeology and the column of literary tradition. If we do not insist on finding specific item-based correlations between archaeological stages and those of the literary data, we have to admit that our literary development took place within the ambit of the archaeological development itself. Whatever we know of the Indus civilization has to be fitted into the known frame of Vedic textual developments. As long as we do not get into the specifics – and we cannot get into the specifics till the Indus script is read – this seems to be the most logical hypothesis so far regarding the place of the Indus civilization as the fountainhead of the great Indian tradition.

Among other things, one may recall the presence of Siva *linga* and thus of Siva in the Indus tradition. After the find of a 'Siva *linga* set in *yoni-patta*' in the form of a terracotta from the mature Harappan level at Kalibangan, the presence of Siva along with the associated female form of *Gouri* cannot in any case be disputed in the Indus tradition. In fact, there was a time when nobody doubted Marshall's contention of the stone Siva *lingas* being found among the excavated finds of this civilization. It was accepted all around, and on this basis it became even customary to call Siva as a non-Aryan god. The way attempts were made in comparatively recent years by scholars like Sankalia and Doris Srinivasan to displace Siva from his position in the Indus scheme had more to do with the determination of these scholars to take the Indus civilization out of the basic ethos of the Indian tradition than with any substantive academic argument. The terracotta *yoni-patta* of Kalibangan further shows that Siva's female consort, *Gauri* or *Parvati* was also present in the Indus scene, and together, Siva and Parvati unequivocally underline that as a pair of divine luminaries they have been presiding over the pre- and non-Islamic religious universe of India since the Indus civilization assumed its form. Now that the Indus civilization – the entire column of its development and subsequent transformation – has emerged as the archaeological counterpart of the long Vedic literary tradition we have, the significance of Siva and Parvati in the Indus scheme has, in fact, become undeniable.

III. THE POLITICS OF THE HARAPPAN STUDIES

There are four major political and ideological issues behind the Harappan studies. The first began soon after the discovery of the Harappan civilization in 1924 and related to its supposed language. S.K. Chatterjee proposed that it was Dravidian and the idea gained so much acceptance among the people of Tamil Nadu and the protagonists of the Dravidian movement that it is currently considered almost a sacrilege by them to dispute this notion. The idea has not yet lost its grip, at least in Tamil Nadu. In a paper titled "Dravidian proof of the Indus script via the Rig Veda: a case study" presented at the Roja Muthiah Research Library, Chennai, I. Mahadevan argues that the Indus language is correctly identified as an early form of Dravidian (as reported in the Hindu of November 15, 2014). Mahadevan's argument ran like the following:

After the collapse of the Indus civilisation a section of the Indus Valley population had migrated to south India and the "the Indus Dravidian influenced the South Dravidian languages". The earliest traces of such migratory influence are found in the 'Old Tamil'. The results also supposedly show that "the descendants of the Indus civilisation adopted the Indo-Aryan speech and that there was a long gap of time between the Indus civilisation and the early Vedic culture," said Mr. Mahadevan. The 'Vedic Age' succeeded the Indus civilisation and the *Rigveda* "itself is a product of the composite culture", said the scholar, who began studying the Indus script way back in 1968.

The idea that it spoke a form of the Indo-Aryan developed somewhat later and is now widely accepted among those who believe that this civilization lies at the fountainhead of India's Sanskritic tradition. Much scholarly endeavour was spent in the early years to argue that the Indus civilization was pre- and non-Vedic. Although this was what John Marshall (1931) argued in the Mohenjodaro report, his colleagues in the Survey including R.P. Chanda were not happy about it and suggested in fact a Rigvedic strain in it. The issue was not, however, in any way political during that period. A Rigvedic affinity of the Indus civilization was argued by B.N. Dutta who at one point was a part of the international communist movement. The argument was stronger in P.V. Kane's Presidential lecture to the Indian History Congress, which was published in 1953. However, the belief in the pre- and non-Vedic character of the Indus civilization did not die. It was, in fact, reinforced by Mortimer Wheeler's interpretation of the archaeological stratigraphy of his Harappa excavations in 1946, on the basis of which he argued that the city fell prey to some invaders whom he identified with the so-called Aryans and their supposedly fort-destroying activities mentioned in the *Rigveda*. Wheeler's interpretation found wide acceptance among Independent India's archaeologists. There were some Indian archaeologists who differed from Wheeler's opinion, and among them K.N. Sastri should be mentioned. I cannot comment why Wheeler's opinion found such a ready acceptance among Indians who were in fact prepared to argue that the sun of civilization for India always rose in the West. This simple fact throws a lot of light on the absence of nationalism which has generally characterised Indian archaeological studies since Independence. Again, it would be wrong to think that the idea of an incoming foreign group destroying the Indus civilization has ceased to be influential even today. In a series of emails Dr. Varun Singh, basically a medical scholar, has drawn attention to the implications of an article by Robbins Schug (2012)

> A new study claiming to look at the incidence of traumatic injury in the people of Harappa, claims to have found high incidence of trauma, more than any other city in antiquity (Robbins Schug et al. 2012). This high incidence of trauma was based on a finding of trauma markers in 4% of the skeletal remains studied or in 15.5% of crania. They chose to study remains obtained during field sessions from 1929 to 1948. Those from 1967-68 and 1986-89 field sessions were excluded as were the findings of Dr. Nancy Lovell from the analysis. Claiming to examine if Harappa indeed was a 'peaceful realm' and a rare example of a state without social differentiation or structural violence, their findings, they felt, suggested otherwise. Violence was considered the most

> likely cause for the traumatic injuries. In the final summing up, they bemoan the dispelling of the Aryan Invasion myth and claim that the downplaying of violence at Harappa, by experts like Kennedy, might have been a factor in the rejection of the myth.

Schug's paper which Varun Singh cites is: 'A peaceful realm? Trauma and social differentiation at Harappa?' published in *International Journal of Palaeopathology* 2 (2012): 136-147 with two Indian co-authors, Veena Mushrif-Tripathy of the Deccan College and Anekram Sankhayan of the Anthropological Survey of India. Needless to say, this is basically Schug's work which Tripathy and Sankhayan may be said to have facilitated.

The second issue relates to its origin. While John Marshall in his Mohenjodaro report was convinced that the civilization was deeply rooted in the Indian soil, there has been a consistent attempt since then to explain its origin in terms of a direct or indirect diffusion from Mesopotamia. In different forms the idea still persists among a section of Indologists and archaeologists. When the Italian Indologist Verardi thinks of the possibility of the existence of a Ziggurat in the stupa mound of Mohenjodaro, he implies this or when the American and other Western archaeologists like G. Possehl think of its origin primarily in terms of Bronze Age interaction with central Asia, they aim primarily to perpetuate this idea. This idea has also different shades of meaning. For instance, when there are attempts to date the Civilization somewhat later than the classic efflorescence of Mesopotamian civilization, it is this attitude which is echoed. Many Indian and foreign books on the history of India seem to accept this premise without demur. Equally interestingly, there has been a long resistance on the part of many sub-continental and other archaeologists to the gradually growing belief that the Harappan sites in the east may in many cases be not later than those in the west. In fact, the beginning of the Indus civilization in the east can be as early as its development in the West. The situation has not yet become very clear but already there are distinct signs in this regard.

Also associated with this development is the increasing evidence that the Aravalli belt in Rajasthan was a separate and possibly independent centre of the growth of agriculture and metallurgy in the sub-continent, and the possible contribution of this belt to the Harappan civilizational development cannot in any way be ignored. The developments further east cannot also be ignored. The early rice farming in the central Ganga plain must have led to significant cultural impetus to the Harappan development, as the finding of cultivated rice in several early Harappan contexts of Haryana indicate. The Harappan civilization cannot be the product of a single arrow-line development from the beginning of agriculture in Baluchistan and there are already indications of significant inputs from various areas in the east. An interesting recent development is the evidence of tin-smelting dating back to the early Harappan and mature Harappan period at the site of Khanak in the tin-bearing belt of Tusham in Haryana. The fact that the considerable tin-bearing deposits of Tusam in Haryana could play a major role in the problem of tin in the Harappan civilization was at some point highlighted by the present author. Also, on accompanying Dr. Bikash Pawar of Rohtak to the site of Khanak near Tusam and having seen the signs of ash and early and mature Harappan relics there, the present author requested Professor R.N. Singh of Banaras to excavate this site and assess if it was smelting locally available tin. As Professor Singh informs him, the hypothesis has been vindicated by the occurrence of tin-smelting remains at the site.

The third issue is about its position vis-à-vis the Vedic literature. If one considers it as pre- and non-Vedic, the assumption is that the growth of Hinduism was an intrusive religious development in India brought in by the incoming

Aryans at the end of this civilization. When both Indians and foreigners express a kind of shock, as historians like Upinder Singh do, at the very mention of Hindu elements in the Harappan religion, they implicitly give credence to this notion. John Kay is a British historian who was sponsored to write a book on the early history of Indian archaeology by the Archaeological Survey of India and National Cultural Fund. Many internet authors cite approvingly his view on Harappan religion:

> The religion of Harappans is unknown. No site has certainly been identified as a temple and most suppositions about sacrificial fires, cult objects and deities rest on doubtful retrospective references from Hindu practices of many centuries later. Such inferences may be as futile as, say, looking to Islamic astronomy for an explanation of the orientation of the pyramids. In short, these theories are all fanciful and do not bear scrutiny.

The basic conclusion of Kay is that Harappan religion was non-Hindu.

The fourth issue is expressed by those who doubt that the Indus Civilization was the fountainhead of the continuing Indian tradition. This they do by harping on the theme that the Harappan civilization denoted an 'imported element' among the regional cultures of the period, especially among the regional cultures of Gujarat. The recurrent attempts of the Deccan College Directors like M.K. Dhavalikar and Vasant Shinde and the M.S. University of Baroda archaeologists like V.H. Sonawane and Ajith Prasad to think of the Harappan manifestation as something imported or extraneous to their regional cultural scenes are nothing but attempts on the part of this group of Indians to view the Harappan element away from the mainstream Indian tradition. Nobody will deny the prevalence of regional elements in the Indus civilization, although I am not quite sure if there is any other feature except pottery which will isolate the regional styles of this civilization.

The tradition was set up by G. Possehl who first coined the term 'Sorath Harappan', a term which has since then repeatedly used by his followers from Pune and Vadodara who do not hesitate these days even to use terms such as Anarta Culture to denote the Harappan culture confined to the Mehsana and other related sections of northern Gujarat. I feel the same sense of revulsion when some enthusiasts of the Archaeological Survey and elsewhere declare a separate 'Bara culture' in the vast zone of Panjab and Haryana. This scholarly tendency is somewhat like denying the existence of Hinduism as an overarching religion on the ground that it is divided into the groups of Saivite, Vaishnavite, etc. Not merely foreign scholars but also Indian historical luminaries like Romila Thapar have been somewhat tireless in emphasizing this. Judging by the way things are going, there will no doubt be Indian scholars who will argue that there was no overarching civilization called the Indus civilization.

On the whole, the politics of the Harappan studies offers a fairly confusing scene. All that I would say is that the Aryan issue is not the only element of contention in this scenario. Even the so-called Aryan issue is not beyond asking some preliminary questions. Whereas the Vedic literature is a corpus of Indian texts what is there to relate it to anything significant outside the borders of the sub-continent? Why linguistics should be important in working out hypothetical cultural configurations? Does linguistics have any independent way of dating any point of linguistic evolution and divergence? I am aware that some archaeologists believe in 'linguistic archaeology', but irrespective of where it is practised – Pune where a seminar on linguistic archaeology recently took place, or Cambridge where in the McDonald Institute for Archaeological Research, it has been a seminar theme on multiple occasions – is there an iota of material proof in this regard? Can one imagine what the cultural conflict scenario will be in a country of innumerable languages as in India where every language group will claim a slice of the archaeological past? I have long held the belief that the Aryan idea is a wholly racist concept and should not be an academic issue at all. The corpus of Vedic texts is a corpus of Indian texts, and considering the geographical spread and chronological span of these texts, it is only natural that this should reflect the state of the Indus civilization in its various phases. Many years ago, the late Swami Sankarananda and one my teachers, S.R. Das, used to say that there would be no problem if the late Vedic stage could be identified with the mature form of the Indus civilization. I do not know enough of the later Vedas to support or negate this assertion, but there cannot be any doubt, despite the persistence of various old ideas in the Indus scene, that the Indus civilization was in fact the fountainhead of the mainstream Indian tradition which, we are forced to admit, is essentially the Hindu tradition. The detailed proof may still take some years in emerging but what has already emerged is enough to make a positive claim in this regard.

The basic politics of the Harappan studies, some of which has been discussed in my *Who Owns the Indian Past? The Case of the Indus Civilization* (India International Centre, Delhi, 2009), is to de-link this civilizational tradition from the main tree trunk of the present Indian culture. Whatever form it may take, this is an anti-national attitude, and it is interesting that a good many Indians have not hesitated to adopt this attitude.

The archaeology column beginning around 7000 BC and represented at sites of Bhirrana, Rakhigarhi, Kunal, etc. has become clear only within the last three or four years. The sequence right up to the end of the second millennium BC is clear and there is absolutely no significant sign of influx of new people in this archaeology column. On the literary side, whatever may be the date of the *Rigveda* and the successive phases of the Vedic literature, the latter taking us close to the period of Buddha, this has to be accommodated between the dates suggested by the archaeology column. Thus, finally we are in a position to claim that chronologically and even geographically both archaeology and literary columns fit together. There is no way we can deny that the column of the tradition which emerged as the Harappan civilization at the end is anything but the long column of the Vedic tradition which continues in Hinduism till today. Various scholars have argued this from time to time but the archaeological situation then was not quite coherent and persons like me waited for the time when the logic of the situation would become unassailable. Among these scholars I would wholeheartedly single out Bhagwan Singh and bow to him because he was strong enough in his conviction to write his book *The Vedic Harappans* (1995) where he tried to point out item-by-item similarities between the Harappan civilization and the Vedic tradition in the fields of agriculture, commerce, trade, industry, pottery, town-planning, construction, etc.

More recently, B.B. Lal (2005) has unequivocally stated that "it is abundantly clear that all the objections against a Harappan-Vedic equation are baseless "(p. 151, *The Rigvedic People: Invaders/Immigrants or Indigenous*).

From the point of Indian history the problem may be said to have begun now. The Harappan writing is undeciphered and even when it gets deciphered, it is unlikely that there will be a mass of clear literary data. The Vedic literature also has many problems regarding the interpretations of its various portions. There will also no doubt be infinite disputes regarding the interpretations of scenes represented on the Harappan seals. Many uncertainties will, of course, remain in these fields but the very fact that now we can visualize our archaeological column of a tremendously long period between c. 7000 BC and c. 600 BC in terms of what is offered by our literature is certainly a momentous turning point.

5

The Location of Harappa

I. INTRODUCTION

In 2007-8, I undertook a field-study of the distribution of archaeological sites in the Indian states of Haryana and Punjab (Chakrabarti and Saini 2009). Three aspects of this distribution, which have some bearings on the distribution of sites and routes of communication in the Pakistani Punjab, are the starting point of the present essay.

The first aspect is that the most important orientation of the distribution of Harappan sites in Punjab (India) and Haryana lies along the alignment which can be traced between Delhi, Rohtak, Jind, Hansi, Hissar, Sirsa, Abohar and Fazilka. Beyond Fazilka the route enters Pakistan. I shall take up the ramifications of this route after it enters Pakistan. This alignment was important in Haryana and Indian Punjab not merely in the Harappan context but also in the context of the early historic and later periods.

The second aspect is the alignment which leads from the Delhi area to Amritsar and then, Lahore. This alignment also can be detected easily both in the Harappan and later periods. However, the old alignment did not go up to modern Amritsar. It went up to Ferozepur, beyond which it entered the modern Pakistani territory. What happened to it after it proceeded beyond Ferozepur? This is another theme of my present essay.

The third aspect is the distribution of Harappan and later historic sites in the present Indian Punjab districts of Amritsar and Gurdaspur. An implication of this distribution is that sites of these periods should also be found in the areas across the border. If I remember correctly, no Harappan site has yet been reported in the adjacent Pakistani belt of Lahore, Gujranwala and Sialkot, to mention only the prominent places of this belt. There is however no reason why the distribution of the Harappan sites cannot extend up to the Sialkot zone. In fact, the location of Manda, south of Jammu on the Indian side of the border should have alerted us to the probability of the existence of Harappan sites in the area near Sialkot. Further, the area near Sialkot lies in the foothills of the Siwaliks. On the Indian side, the Harappan sites are known to have existed right up to the Siwaliks. Sites like Rupar near Chandigarh have long been known, and I have found sites with the pottery of the Harappan tradition in Hoshiarpur and Nawanshahr. There is no reason at all to imagine that the Pakistani side of the Siwaliks did not contain any Harappan site. The painted pottery sites of the Ferozepur district fall in a border area with Pakistan, and again, one can expect such sites south of Lahore. Ferozepur itself easily leads to Pak Pattan on the Pakistani side.

More important than this issue of Harappan distribution is the issue of the early historical route which went from Rajagriha in Magadha (modern south Bihar) in eastern India to Takshashila near Rawalpindi. What could be its alignment in Pakistani Punjab?

II. THE LOCATION OF HARAPPA AND OTHER ISSUES

In a large tract of Haryana covering Panchkula, Ambala, Yamunanagar, Kurukshetra, Karnal and Panipat, no mature Harappan site has yet been reported. The broad trajectory of the mature Harappan distribution in Haryana seems to be Sirsa, Fatehabad, Hissar, Hansi, Bhiwani, Rohtak and Jhajjar, with only one site, Balu, in the Jind-Kaithal stretch. This was the broad line of movement from Sirsa to the area of Delhi in the historical periods too, and here we can only observe this general similarity without trying to offer any specific explanation. At Badli, east-southeast of Jhajjar, R.C. Thakran (pers. comm. April 2008) has excavated a mature Harappan level, and the location of this site suggests a mature Harappan thrust towards the Yamuna.

In the case of this route which goes up to Abohar and Fazilka and then enters modern Pakistan, with its original alignment towards Bahawalpur and Multan, one has to enquire what happens to it after entering Pakistan. The same question has to be asked about the route which goes to Ferozepur from Ludhiana and to Amritsar from Ludhiana via Jalandhar.

If one follows the Delhi-Hissar-Sirsa alignment, one can turn from Hissar in the direction of Bhadra and Nohar in Rajasthan to catch the course of the Hakra. Or, one can go beyond Hissar up to Sirsa and turn in that area to the direction of Bhatnir or Hanumangarh to reach the Hakra course there. The Hakra alignment is followed up to Anupgarh to reach the Bahawalpur segment of Pakistan. This well-marked, although extinct, river corridor can give access from different points along it to Multan (through Bahawalpur) and even Dera Ghazi Khan (through Khanpur). One can reach Bahawalpur either from Mirgarh or from Fort Derawar, and for accessing places in the Dera Ghazi Khan sector, Fort Derawar or Fort Marot seems to be convenient. Uchchh or ancient *Uchchapuri* lies on this route in this sector, and so does the Buddhist monastic site of Sui Vihar. The point is that to reach Multan and Dera

Ghazi Khan, and even Dera Ismail Khan lower down, from the Hissar-Sirsa zone, the Hakra course up to Fort Derawar and Fort Marot is one of the convenient alignments. The importance of Bahawalpur as a communication hub has been emphasized in the following fashion:

> At this juncture, we may note that the historical importance of the Bahawalpur tract need not be seen only in terms of the possibility of a perennial river flowing through this region. Bahawalpur was of great significance in the trade and trade route network also because of its geographical position, connecting the Indus plains with the Punjab and Rajasthan and further south, with Gujarat. In fact, the region, at the end of the nineteenth century, used to enjoy commercial transactions with Karachi, Lahore, Bombay and Calcutta. The chief centres of commerce were Bahawalpur, Ahmadpur East, Allahabad, Khanpur and Hasilpur, and part of the commerce used to go to Afghanistan and Turkestan. (Lahiri 1992: 119)

The spaces which have been specifically mentioned (including Allahabad between Khanpur and Ahmadpur East) are all approachable from the area between Forts Derawar and Marot.

If one does not follow the Hakra alignment and yet try to reach Multan from the Hissar-Sirsa segment, one has at least two alternatives. If one follows the Delhi-Hissar-Sirsa-Abohar-Fazilka alignment up to the modern Pakistan border, the first major place that one gets on the other side, after crossing the Sutlej, is Dipalpur. If one follows the alignment beyond Sirsa up to Ferozepur through Bathinda, there is Kasur on the other side of the Sutlej in this territory. The importance of both these places – Dipalpur and Kasur – in the route network has been emphasized by Cunningham (Majumdar-Sastri 1924) and others. Dipalpur was an important place under Firoz Shah Tughlaq in the 14th century. To the southwest of modern Dipalpur, Cunningham (Majumdar-Sastri 1924: 244-245) noted 'a high ruined mound' which also had a number of smaller associated mounds. He noted the presence of Indo-Scythian coins in the ruins, and on the whole he thinks that the Dipalpur mounds to be three-quarters of a mile long and half a mile broad. Pak Pattan or Ajudhan lies 28 miles southwest of Dipalpur. Cunningham writes:

> For many centuries Ajudhan was the principal ferry on the Sutlej. Here met the two great western roads from Dera Ghazi Khan and Dera Ismail Khan; the first via Mankera, Shorkot and Harappa; the second via Multan. (Majumdar-Sastri 1924: 250)

One may take up the issue of Ajudhan/Pak Pattan and Dipalpur at a greater length on the basis of the *Montgomery District Gazetteer 1883-84*. On Pak Pattan the Gazetteer (pp. 182-186) writes:

> Pak Pattan is a place of great commerce, collecting wheat, pulses from surrounding villages, *gur* and sugar from Hoshiarpur and Jalandhar, cloth pieces from Calcutta and Bombay, *majith* and fruits from Afghanistan.

On Dipalpur, the Gazetteer (p. 180) states:

> The place is frequented by traders from Dera Ismail Khan and other places towards the frontier, on account of the main road from Okara to Fazilka passing through that place.

The question of these routes also brings us to the question of the location of Harappa. The *Montgomery District Gazetteer of 1883-84* (pp. 147-148) describes the principal roads of the district and the place of Harappa in that road network:

(1) The Customs line road, running from Jamlera on the Multan border, nearly parallel to the Sutlej through Pak Pattan and Haveli to Rohela Ghat, opposite Fazilka in the Sirsa district.
(2) The Lahore and Multan trunk road, running close to the Ravi, on the left bank of the river. Traffic on this road has

greatly decreased since the opening of the railway in 1865; many of the *sarais* along it are in a bad condition and others have been closed altogether. But the road itself is in very fair order.

(3) The road leading from Jhang, via Kamalia, Harappa, Kabir and Pak Pattan to the Sutlej. Speaking of it, Lieutenant Elphinstone says:-
"Numerous caravans of merchants from Afghanistan frequent this route during the cold weather. They seldom dispose of their merchandise in the district, but, as far as I could ascertain, this route is generally selected by merchants who are anxious to arrive at their principal mart, Delhi, without the delay which would otherwise attend the unpacking of their wares at intermediate stations".

(4) The road from Harappa through Montgomery, Dipalpur and Busirpur to the ferry at Rahela Ghat.

(5) The road from Pak Pattan to Chunian, passing near Dipalpur and through Shergarh.

(6) The road from Jhang through Gugera and Satghara to Wan Radharam, running thence to Ferozepur.

(7, 8, and 9) The roads connecting Montogomery and Pak Pattan, and Gugera and Pak Pattan, and Gugera and Dipalpur.

It is thus clear that Harappa played a role both in the trade with Multan from the Delhi-Sirsa side and in the trade with Jhang and the frontier from the same direction. Harappa was also linked with Kot Kamalia and Shorkot, both to its west and both possibly important on the road to the Jhang area. Cunningham (Majumdar-Sastri 1924: 235-238) calls Shorkot "a huge mound of ruins" which he dated on the basis of the Indo-Scythic coins of Punjab. Kamalia also is "a small but ancient town situated on an isolated mound on the right or northern bank of the Ravi". Cunningham linked both these places to the progress of Alexander's invasion through the Punjab.

It would be fair to emphasize that Raverty (1892: 399, note 421) strongly criticised Cunningham for claiming Pak Pattan to be a traditional ferry point across the Sutlej because of the varying history of the course of this river. This does not take away the fact that Pak Pattan figured significantly in the relevant route network. The Punjab route network in this part has also been highlighted by H.K. Trevaskis (1928) who, as the Inspector General of Registration and Director of Land Records of the province sometime in the last quarter of the nineteenth century, had reasons to be closely familiar with it. Of the three major routes from the frontier, two came from Dera Ismail Khan in the north and Dera Ghazi Khan in the south, along the axis of the frontier hills. They crossed the Indus in their respective areas and crossed the Chenab and Shorkot and Multan. The northerly route or the one coming from Dera Ismail Khan then crossed the Ravi at Tulamba and Harappa, where it joined the southerly or the Multan route (coming from Dera Ghazi Khan) and crossed the Sutlej at Pak Pattan, and followed the Sirsa-Thanesvar alignment. The third frontier route emanated from the Bannu sector which lies further up the axis of the hills from Dera Ismail Khan. This route crossed the Chenab at Chiniot and entered the Lahore area.

III. WAS THE PRESENT LAHORE-RAWALPINDI ALIGNMENT AN ANCIENT ALIGNMENT?

We have noted that if one follows the Delhi-Sirsa alignment up to Ferozepur via Bathinda, one gets Kasur on the other side of the Sutlej in Pakistan. According to Cunningham, Kasur was an ancient city which occupied about one square mile. From Kasur Dipalpur is easily accessible and thus it was also linked with the trade network running through the area. Through Patti, 'another large brick town of considerable antiquity' (Majumdar-Sastri 1924: 230-233), Kasur was linked with Lahore, but despite Cunningham's suggestion that it was linked in tradition with Lava, one of the two sons of Rama, nothing ancient has yet been associated with Lahore. One is not sure if the modern Amritsar entry to Lahore is ancient or if the modern Lahore-Rawalpindi alignment is a truly ancient alignment.

If this is not an ancient alignment, which alignment towards Taxila from the east was ancient? In the ancient context Ferozepur seems to be a more important communication hub than the Lahore-Amritsar zone. *The Ferozepur District Gazetteer 1883-84* (p. 13) has the following on Ferozepur:

> Both town and territory of Ferozepur bear every appearance of having been not only long located, but having been at one time rich and populous. The numerous old walls and sites of villages throughout the present waste lands show that they were once cultivated; and the extensive ruins about this town prove it to have been a large and substantially built city.

There seems to be a problem regarding the antiquity of the present Lahore-Taxila alignment. Lahore is not an ancient place and in Cunningham's account of the region, neither is any place near it convincingly so. The only mound worth consideration is Ransi but this place lies about 25 miles to the west of Lahore and not on the straight Lahore-Sohdara alignment, Sohdara reputedly representing an ancient crossing of the Chenab. Between Sohdara and Taxila there are major ancient sites such as Jhelum and Manikyala.

It is possible that Sialkot marked a major halting place between the eastern sector of the Punjab, of which Amritsar and Lahore may be said to mark the westernmost fringe, and Taxila. Sialkot's identification with the ancient city of Sakala, celebrated as the capital of Menander in *Milindapanho*, is not in doubt (Law 1969), and Cunningham himself (1882: 44-46) described its ancient ruins measuring more than a mile in length and half a mile in breadth. The citadel on the northern side stands on a 700 ft square and 49 ft high ancient mound.

There is a road from Sialkot to Pathankot via Gurdaspur, and that passes by the high mound of Kalanour and a few other mounds that we have noticed in the Gurdaspur area. We suggest that that this route provided access from Pathankot to Sialkot or ancient Sakala, and that this route led further on to Taxila. From the east, the route to Taxila could have gone through Sakala which lies only a short distance to the north-northeast of Sohdara, the ancient crossing of the Chenab.

It may be noted that there was no straight route from Pathankot to Sakala or Sialkot. The reason is that if one proceeds straight to Sialkot from Pathankot, one has to push through the landscape of the Siwalik foothills, which is frequently interrupted by boulder-carrying streams which fan out widely on reaching the plain. The route went via Gurdaspur and Kalanour. The alignment would have been the following: Pathankot > Gurdaspur> Kalanour > Narowal> Pasrur> Sialkot.

That this hypothesis, which we have deduced both geographically and archaeologically, is logical, is suggested by the route taken by Jivaka, the famous physician contemporary with the Buddha, from Taxila to Mathura. From Taxila he travelled through Bhadramkara, Udumbara and Rohitaka, the first two places being Sialkot and Pathankot respectively. Also in the *Ramayana*'s account of the route to the Kekaya territory in western Punjab (Jalalpur near Lala Musa), the route went through Sakala (for these references, see Moti Chandra 1977: 15-16).

IV. CONCLUDING OBSERVATIONS

The present essay has located the position of Harappa on the vast network of routes between the modern Delhi area on the one hand and Multan, Dera Ghazi Khan and Dera Ismail Khan on the other. I have pointed out the traditional importance of this site as a place where the Ravi was crossed and how the route caught the Fazilka-Abohar-Sirsa alignment which, through places like Fatehabad, Hissar, Hansi, Jind, and Rohtak in modern Haryana, led up to the area around Delhi in the Yamuna valley. Having reached the Yamuna valley in this section, it was easy to move down the valley to Mathura in the historical period.

This essay has also stretched the probable distribution of Harappan sites in the Lahore, Gujranwala and Sialkot sectors of Pakistan in view of their distribution across the border in India. Equally important is its argument that the old route from east India to Taxila went through Sialkot, the site of the ancient city of Sakala, from the side of Indian Pathankot which also was a major early historic settlement, although the old site has been destroyed now. It, however, existed in Cunningham's time.

For the last three decades I have been trying to understand the basic archaeological geography of vast sections of India and how the different sections were actually integrated into a network of communications on the ground. My study of the Ganga plain (Chakrabarti 2001; 2007) occupied me for 14 years (1991-2001, 2003-05), and in 2007-08, I extended it up to the Amritsar border. Meanwhile, I examined the routes which linked the Ganga plain with the Deccan (Chakrabarti 2005), and the routes which linked the various parts of the Deccan and the southern peninsula (Chakrabarti, 2012).

*An earlier version of the paper was published in *Pakistan Heritage 2.*

REFERENCES

Chakrabarti, D.K. 2001, *Archaeological Geography of the Ganga Plain: The Lower and the Middle Ganga*, Delhi: Permanent Black.

—— 2005, *The Archaeology of the Deccan Routes: The Routes from the Ganga Plain to the Deccan*, Delhi: Munshiram Manoharlal.

—— 2007, *Archaeological Geography of the Ganga Plain: The Upper Ganga (Oudh, Rohilkhand and the Doab)*, Delhi: Munshiram Manoharlal.

—— 2010, *The Ancient Routes of the Deccan and the Southern Peninsula*, Delhi: Aryan Books.

Chakrabarti, D.K. and Sukhdev Saini 2009, *The Problem of the Sarasvati River and Notes on the Archaeological Geography of Haryana and Indian PaṄab*, Delhi: Aryan Books.

Chandra, Moti 1977, *Trade and Trade Routes in Ancient India*, Delhi: Abhinav Publishers.

Cunningham, A. 1882, *Report of a Tour in the Panjab in 1878-79*, Calcutta: Superintendent of Government Printing.

Lahiri, N. 1992, *The Archaeology of Indian Trade Routes*, Delhi: Oxford University Press.

Law, B.C. 1969, 'Sakala, an Ancient Indian City', *East and West* 19: 401-409.

Majumdar-Sastri, S.N. 1924, *Cunningham's Ancient Geography of India*, Calcutta: Chuckervertty and Chatterji.

Raverty, H.G. 1892, 'The Mihran of Sind and its Tributaries', *The Journal of the Asiatic Society of Bengal* 61(4): 155-297, Extra No. 1892, pp. 298-508.

Trevaskis, H.K. 1928, *The Land of the Five Rivers, an Economic History of the Panjab from the Earliest Times to the Year of Grace 1890*, Oxford: Oxford University Press.

6

Concluding Remarks

The question posed by the famous parliamentarian Ram Manohar Lohia in Indian Parliament in 1966 and the positive comments on his opinion by the education minister of the time M.C. Chagla in the same session of the parliament have not yet been answered: why historians, both Indians and Westerns, view the course of Indian history bereft of any innovation without foreign influence of some kind or other. Nor have we tried to offer an explanation for this curious and self-abnegatory historical attitude on the part of the Indians in the course of this book. We, however, have pointed out the century-old persistence of such beliefs from the time of the Cambridge Sanskritist E.J. Rapson to that of the Deccan College archaeologist H.D. Sankalia and most of his fellow-archaeologists and students in Pune, Vadodara and wherever Indian archaeology is studied in India and elsewhere in the world. I am not surprised by the opinions of people like Rapson; it is only to be expected that Western India-experts will be contemptuous of the natives and natives' history, especially if this history is investigated by the independent-minded natives themselves. It is this situation which is expressed well by Rajiv Malhotra by what he calls 'Hinduphobia in the academia', the American academia in the case of Malhotra. Its corresponding situation in archaeology is the linkage of the Western 'south Asian' archaeologists among themselves and the south Asians with whom they have to keep in touch for various reasons. This has long been crystal clear in the field of the archaeology of the Indus civilization. The linkage among the Western archaeologists themselves is clearly based on the colour of the skin.

The present volume is, in a sense, the sequel to the present author's *Nationalism in the Study of Ancient Indian History* (2021) which dwelt on the various cross-currents of political attitudes and ideas including nationalism in the study of ancient India since its beginning. The present volume deals with Indian archaeology from this point of view. It is a collection of a few inter-related essays. The first one takes as its starting point the nationalistic questions raised in Indian Parliament in 1966 and shows that these questions fell on deaf ears among the important Indian archaeologists of the time. The second essay elaborates some general dimensions of Indian archaeology from the nationalistic perspective, dwelling specifically on a host of issues, especially those offered in the name of combating or challenging Hindutva archaeology. The relationship between the dominant politics of the time and certain major religious sites of the subcontinent has also been highlighted in this context. The third essay, the one on the recent research on the Indus civilization, underscores the various trends of this research and their socio-political connotations. What is clearly noticeable is a marked increase in the spate of geo-archaeological research conducted by the geology professionals. The crucial issue is to focus on whether the Sarasvati channel and the network of channels associated with it were in full flow when the Indus civilization achieved its full and mature form or not. Most of this research would deny this element of contemporaneity but what seems to be clear is that the Sarasvati system always retained a channel fed by the monsoon flows from the highlands and was thus helpful to the growth of settlements and irrigation canals, the latter clearly mentioned in some literary sources. The basic situation seems to have prevailed till the pre-modern period. Another point we would like to put stress on is the element of strong probability that the basic landscape of the Punjab-Haryana region has not significantly changed since the growth of the Indus civilization in this belt. A third major argument of the paper lays stress on the significance of the growth of the Indus civilizational column and the acknowledgement of its logical merger in the literary tradition represented by the Vedic texts. The core identity of the ancient Indian civilization rests on these twin columns, although one understands the innumerable difficulties in relating one to the other in various matters of detail. The major problem lies in the fact that the column of the Vedic literary tradition does not yet admit of well-demarcated chronological line-ups and there are also many uncertainties regarding textual interpretations such as precise connotations of various Vedic terms. The reason why we are so sure of dovetailing the present archaeological situation with the textual testimony is two-fold. First, over the entire northern half of the country, if not over the most of the country, the archaeological sequence beginning with food-production and thus village-life not merely goes back to c. 7000/c. 7500 BC or thereabouts but also shows a steady column of village-based developments including the growth of the Indus civilization and its transformation in the Doab till c. 1200 or c. 1000 BC. That between these two points of time, c. 7500 BC and c. 1000 BC the whole of the country, including the northeast and the deep south, became agriculture-based, developed something no less than the Indus civilization, and was well on its way to the development of the early historic cities and states, is no longer a matter of doubt from the point of view of archaeology. This is comparatively a very recent development and has been possible largely because of the dates from Rakhigarhi, Kunal and Bhirrana. Relevant dates have no doubt been obtained from various parts of the country but the dates from the three sites mentioned earlier are particularly important because they make us aware of a new dimension of the Indus civilizational growth in Punjab-Haryana. They also indicate that certain parts of modern Haryana are well within the growth of the Indus civilization. The dates from Rakhigarhi, Kunal and Bhirrana have been strengthened by Anindya Sarkar, Arati Deshpande Mukherjee et al., 'Oxygen isotope in archaeological bioapatites from India: implications to climate change and decline of Bronze Age Harappan civilization', *Science Report* 2016. They report

> ... a high resolution oxygen isotope (δ(18)O) record of animal teeth-bone phosphates from an archaeological trench itself at Bhirrana, NW India, preserving all cultural levels of this civilization. Bhirrana was part of a high concentration of settlements along the dried up mythical Vedic river valley 'Saraswati', an extension of Ghaggar river in the Thar desert. Isotope and archaeological data suggest that the pre-Harappans started inhabiting this area along the mighty Ghaggar-Hakra rivers fed by intensified monsoon from 9 to 7 ka BP. *The monsoon monotonically declined after 7 ka yet the settlements continued to survive from early to mature Harappan time. Our study suggests that other cause like change in subsistence strategy by shifting crop patterns rather than climate change was responsible for Harappan collapse.*

The second reason is that despite all uncertainties regarding the chronologies of the various sections or stages of the Vedic literature, there is no way we can put their terminal points outside this archaeological column between c. 7500/c. 7000 BC and applicable to virtually the entire northern half of the subcontinent. This understanding of these two columns representing the same historical development in the country has become clear only with the dates and sequences from various recently excavated sites of Rakhigarhi, Kunal and Bhirrana along with a series of internally consistent radiocarbon dates from these sites. This series of dates has been supported by the studies on Bhirrana bones by Anindya Sarkar et al., and I would find no reason to brush this dated sequence aside on the ground of the uncertainty of dates. One hopes that the uncertainties of textual explanations will be taken care of by future research but what is not acceptable from the point of view of Indian nationalism is any attempt to question the integrity of the Indus civilizational column or the Indus civilization itself. From the perspective of an Indian nationalist this has to be considered a thoroughly unacceptable game. The fourth essay deals with a specific archaeological issue, that of the location of Harappa, and we discuss it not from the point of view of any 'science' but on the basis of what we know and understand about the interconnections and routes covering the region. This essay may highlight that the study of ancient Indian archaeological landscape need not be limited only to what is currently offered as 'science' but also should take note of the historical personality of the region or area concerned.

The continuity of the Indian civilization has always drawn comments from scholars. The enormity of its truth, however, escaped attention till we realized – very recently – that the archaeological columns and the literary columns of India's civilizational development can no longer be separated. Till now we could appreciate the archaeological continuity in terms of various survivals of clearly identifiable archaeological traits such as Indus religion and innumerable details of material life. In the field of literary tradition we continue to ascribe crucial importance to the ritual behaviour with its undoubted roots in the Vedic texts. The Vedic verses and the many injunctions of various later but related texts have continued to determine the Indian life-style and ritual behaviour through the ages. However, till now it has been difficult to argue that it is in the flow of the same stream since the days of the Indus tradition that we have been bathing. The river of the Indian civilization has undoubtedly received streams from various sources but this river does not seem to have lost its own momentum and flow at any point since its inception. The Indian civilization, as we understand it now, has its roots deep in the Bronze Age; it had taken its basic shape by the time the Indus civilization had taken its shape, and now that we can logically and rightfully place this civilization in the Vedic stream, our sense of our past acquires a dimension which was not possible to acquire even a decade back when we had not got the chronological frame offered by Kunal, Bhirrana, Rakhigarhi and many other related sites spread over northern India.

This new dimension of our sense of the past should lead us to a new phase of research where close examinations will be made of both the Vedic textual data and the data derived from the Indus civilization and related sites. We have already drawn attention to Bhagwan Singh's *The Vedic Harappans* in this connection and one hopes that this publication has outlined some major aspects of research in this field. Among the more recent attempts in this direction I would point out V.N. Prabhakar's article, 'Possible convergence of historic literature and archaeology: examples of Harappan burial practices and customs', *Heritage*, 2 (2014), 152-183. This leads to a good number of other related publications, including the one on Sanauli burials and their textual parallels by D.V. Sharma in *Puratattva*. The fire-pits and/or altars excavated at various sites including Rakhigarhi also indicate various Vedic rituals being performed and I would say that there can be no better or convincing example of a Hindu ritual being performed at a Harappan site than the find of 'food-balls' comprising cereals, legumes and oilseeds, which Agnihotri et al. report from Binjor.

Finally, it may be pointed out that one of the implications of the extensive Harappan finds between the Ghaggar system in Rajasthan-Punjab-Haryana and the eastern portion of the Doab is somehow being neglected by us. It is possible that behind the Mahabharatic association of many of the sites in this extensive belt, there is a strong memory of Harappan occupations in the same belt. The 'chariots of Sanauli' may be a pointer in this direction and one hopes that soon there will be enough evidence of the transformation of the Harappans into a phase which we should understand better in the light of our epic tradition.

It seems that precisely hundred years after the first excavations at Harappa we have reached a stage when the remains of the Indus civilization have to be considered to form jointly with the literary tradition represented by the Vedic texts the main trunk of the tree of our Indian civilization. The task to read archaeological data in terms of literary traditions has never been easy even in countries and areas which can boast of a more extensive and clear literary tradition than ours. There are also not many civilizational areas where the study of the ancient past is fraught with more divisive politics than ours. However, as long as we follow the ground rules of research in our field and listen carefully to the murmurs of various regional streams merging in the main flow of our civilization, we shall have a much better idea of how ancient India had come to acquire the form it had.

Index